★★★★★ THE ★★★★★
TRANSITIONED
VETERAN

Success Beyond Service

Sandy Lawrence, PfMP, PgMP, PMP

THE TRANSITIONING MILITARY SERIES

Each individual interviewee has verified that permission has been granted to publish the information included in each interview and interviewees accept responsibility for all content.

GR8TRANSITIONS4U, INC

Published by GR8TRANSITIONS4U

GR8TRANSITIONS4U (USA) Inc.
PO Box 2
Valrico, FL 33595

USA
Copyright © 2020, Sandra Hoath Lawrence

Lawrence, Sandy Hoath
THE TRANSITIONED VETERAN
SUCCESS BEYOND SERVICE

ISBN 978-1-7343933-9-2

Printed in the United States of America
Book design by Tamara Parsons
GR8Transitions4U.com

Dedicated to the Soldiers,
Sailors, Airmen, and Marines
of the United States Military

Foreword

Whether you are leaving active duty after your first enlistment/commission or a 20+ year career, you will benefit from this book.

One of the biggest challenges to overcome when you transition is to figure out how you fit into the private sector. For many of us, our military occupational specialties do not easily translate to a point that can be understood by someone who has never served in the military.

I know from first-hand experience how difficult transitioning from the military can be. Even for a retired general officer, there are hurdles to overcome. Do not get discouraged; I probably sent out 50 resumes before I received a reply that went something along the lines of "Thanks but no thanks."

As for advice, some of the best advice I received was to rely on my network; "The strongest network you have are your Marine buddies." In my case, the second strongest network I had was the local Tampa, Florida Project Management Institute (PMI) Chapter. I went to the monthly dinners, listened to the guest speakers, networked with the participants, and eventually found someone willing to listen to my 30-second elevator speech.

That exchange led to an interview with a large electronics integration company. The 90-minute interview went well. What surprised me was the time devoted to leadership questions. That's the moment that I realized there is a huge demand for leadership in the private sector. I did not get the position, but I did gain valuable interviewing experience.

As a result of my Marine network I did eventually land a position with a local aviation simulation company. I heard about the opportunity and reached out to a retired Marine buddy who worked for the parent company. He told me a Marine helicopter pilot was the president/CEO of the company with the opening, it turns out I knew the individual in charge. I gave him a call, followed the call up with my resume and a month later I was on the payroll. All because of my network.

I encourage you to use this book as intended...learn from those who have gone before us. They have walked the walk and are showing us the way. They provide excellent examples of what worked and what did not. Add to your network by reaching out to the book's contributors on LinkedIn and ask to connect; you never know where that could lead.

The Transitioned Veteran: Success Beyond Service offers numerous examples of men and women who successfully navigated the abyss to make the transition to the private sector. Their stories are inspirational and your story could be next.

I want to thank Sandy for her work in pulling this informative book together and congratulate those veterans who were kind enough to share their stories of trials, tribulations, and success with us.

Gregg Sturdevant
Major General, USMC (Ret)
Founder/CEO Mission Critical Leadership Solutions

Preface

Everyone has a story to tell. Many of us share stories for historical purposes, for entertainment, for glory, to bask in "the spotlight", to claim our 15 minutes of fame, etc.

Heidi Krupp wrote in her foreword for Chicken Soup for the Soul 20th Anniversary Edition, "Storytelling has always been a great way to pass on advice and wisdom, but it needs to be organized and thoughtful…and deliver a usable message." My favorite storytellers are those who share their vulnerabilities and triumphs offering insight to those wanting to learn as they begin their own journeys. This book is a collection of experiences shared by that type of storyteller, and is the purpose and expectation behind the stories published in this book "The Transitioned Veteran: Success Beyond Service."

According to the GAO, many veterans experience difficulty in finding a job beyond the military. Why? Key issues include being unfamiliar with effective job search strategies, and not knowing how to translate their military experience into a commercially-viable job title.

If there was a simple cookbook on military transition, it would be a #1 best seller! But, there isn't that I know of. What there are – and there are many, are information resources on military transition. Pieces and parts of solving the transition puzzle are available through social media, programs, websites, services, books, software apps and organizations out there dedicated to helping ease this life-changing event.

Simply put, if you want to "get something right the first time", most rely on their network to gain insight and understanding to tasks about to be undertaken. This book offers the reader a new network, *a new and extended network* of transitioned veterans who have 'walked the walk." In this book, fifty-three brave veterans have collaborated with me to share their journey of transition from the military to the corporate world.

The stories in this book are framed around 12 questions gathered from years of insight gained while helping serve those who have served in the books I've co-authored for military transition at GR8Transitions4U. Air Force, Army, Marines, Navy; Officers and Enlisted; men and women – 53 journeys are shared in one book.

I love each and every story, and wish I could sit with each veteran to hear all their stories! What each Veteran shares offers insight to tactics and steps that proved sometimes frustrating, but ultimately, gave them an effective roadmap to find their next best career. I've found every story truly inspirational, and hope that all readers who seek to learn and evolve from others' determination and commitment will also find their ideal job after service.

It is with humility and respect that I present these stories from the men and women of our military who have not only bravely served our country, but have also bravely transitioned into successful careers beyond their service.

Acknowledgments

Creating and publishing a book based on my passions to share knowledge and help Veterans has been an amazing journey. I would like to express my gratitude to the many outstanding people I had the good fortune to work with on this book. First and foremost, I want to thank my husband Jeff, a retired USAF Veteran for his insight, inspiration, editing, and endless encouragement and support. Second, thanks to my book writing partner, Jay Hicks, for his support and guidance on producing and publishing my own book. I am also very humbled and thankful to Major General Gregg Sturdevant (USMC, Ret) for his support and willingness to share his own story through the Foreword of this book.

My biggest thank you goes out to the 53 Veterans who did not hesitate to rally behind and support this book project. They took time out of their busy schedules to respond to each and every request associated with their story submission. Each Veteran served our Country, and for that I am eternally grateful. Now, they serve again, serving those in transition. Each story is unique and offers everyone who reads them insight to learn from, inspiration to guide from, and motivation to keep moving forward in their transition to achieve their own next best career. Thank you for your service, support, inspiration and guidance.

Thank you to all who took part in this journey alongside me and believed in my vision. As they say – "You had my six".

Table of Contents

Observations & Demographics

To get stories for this book, I relied on multiple networks to achieve my goal. I relied on my family and military network, my DoD and Combatant Command networks (USCENTCOM and USSOCOM), my PMI network, my authoring network, and the power of LinkedIn to find veterans willing to help offer insight for those who are transitioning.

Of the 53 veterans who signed up as contributors to this book, here are some interesting facts on the makeup of those answering my call to duty. Men dominated the storytelling at 79%, and 21% represented by women. As a woman, it was easy to use my network to find great female contributors. According to Wikipedia, women make up around 14% of the US Military Active duty, so I am especially appreciative of the response and support they provided for this book.

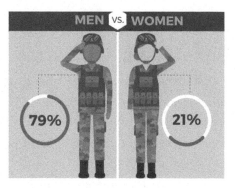

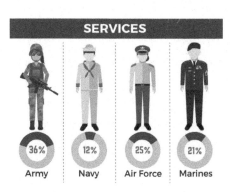

All services were well represented except for the Coast Guard. Coincidentally, the Army was the biggest stakeholder in this book, aligning itself to the fact that it is the largest U.S. Service of the big 4. Currently, nearly 1.4 million Americans, or 4% of the U.S. population is active military personnel. The US Navy, while the second largest military service of the US, ranked 4th in providing stories.

One of the questions I asked the contributors was whether or not they felt there is a stereotype attached to being a Veteran. Overwhelmingly, 3 out of 4 veterans said YES there is a stereotype! What is interesting is *how they perceived the stereotype.* While many gave specific reasons shaping a negative stereotype, there were just as many veterans saying their view of the veteran stereotype was positive. Almost all agree that there is some version of a stereotype, whether good or bad, by Veterans or by non-veterans, and that there needs to be continual improvement to understand all points of view and learn how to work within and through those views. Key takeaway → Focus on what you can control and show how you can be an asset vs. a liability.

Enlisted vs. Officers

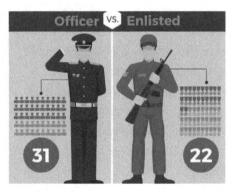

I captured a decent split among Officers and Enlisted contributors, as well as a few Warrant Officers. Enlisted members are considered the "backbone" of the military, and are trained to perform specific duties or specialties. In certain grades or ranks they have a special status. In the Army, Air Force, and Marine Corps, this status is known as Non-Commissioned Officer status, or NCO whereas the Navy uses the term Petty Officer. Warrant Officers are highly-trained specialists. Unlike commissioned officers, warrant officers remain in their primary specialty to provide specialized knowledge, instruction, and leadership to enlisted members and commissioned officers alike. A Commissioned officer's primary function is to provide overall management and leadership in their area of responsibility.

Degree and Certifications

Research indicates that military members are more highly educated than the general population. Those who enlist are required to have a high school diploma or a GED. That means that 99 percent of the military has at least a high school education. Commissioned officers must have a minimum of a four-year bachelor's degree. As they move up the ranks, if they want to get promoted, they will typically have to earn a master's degree in order to be considered for their next advancement.

An overwhelming 75% of the contributors had one or more college degrees. Of those degree owners, half had one or more certifications. I attribute that 6% of the contributors who did not have either a degree or a certification were those from a previous time in the military where the supporting resources to obtain these additional degrees and / or certifications were not readily available. Many certification owners were aligned with Enlisted contributors who were focused on capturing expertise in a particular area of technology or process.

Industries

In retrospect, using my various networks to find contributors caused somewhat of a bias.

I worked in the IT/technology side of program management; consequently, my networks primarily evolve around IT expertise, software, project and program management. My network pools included technical, programmatic, leadership and managerial references. As a result, the DoD and Defense Industry ranked highest including such positions as program and project management, consulting and analysts. Cyber Security was next, followed by those in education/training, software services (engineering) and the financial banking / investments. All of this makes a lot of sense considering the explosion of the Internet, virtual communications, online programs and other remote tasks. Some contributors were true entrepreneurial leaders on the bleeding edge of advising and coaching. Recent research showed top jobs for veterans to include positions in the healthcare field, of which I only had one contributor. Many found a real benefit in the DoD Skillbridge* program, where you can take several months of your duty time and work at a qualified civilian company. This provides you a great 'sneak-peak' opportunity to discover if you like the job, company, culture, environment, etc.

Transition Time

Most contributors started their planning early within a 12 to 18 month period prior to leaving the military, and considered it to be one of the most important life-changing projects of their life. Their ways of starting and planning the transition were varied from well planned to no planning at all. The rest spent several years or could not quantify their efforts as life

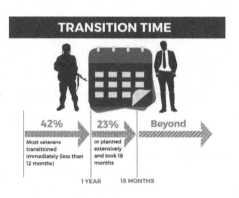

and other events interfered with their out-processing. It is important to note that most contributors felt that they should have taken advantage of every school, class, program and service offered to them as they applied for retirement or approval to leave the service. From the GI Bill, TAP, to services to help build your resume – be sure to do your research and take advantage of everything you can to best prepare you for your next job.

Veteran Support Beyond Service

If it wasn't enough that each contributor gave their time and efforts to serve in our military, many found a second calling and continue to serve by helping future veterans transition. This committed effort was represented by over 32% of our contributors making a living giving back, or volunteering to help Veterans who transition. Over the last 15 years, there has been an explosive growth in services to help veterans find a job beyond the military. Many (some large) organizations are rallying to help Veterans find great jobs by establishing in-house hiring groups dedicated to seeking out and hiring Veterans. Add to that

the global job search engines like Monster® and Indeed® who have dedicated veteran-specific job access. The internet has exploded over the last decade providing vast resources for Veterans. There are dozens, even hundreds of sites, from search engines, military organizations, networking groups – saturating the web offering insight and guidance to Veterans looking for finding their next best career. For someone new to transitioning, this saturation can be overwhelming not knowing where to start. What is really neat to see is that many of the large organizations such as Amazon, Google, Walmart, as well as many large Federal contractors have specific hiring events and HR groups dedicated to hiring Veterans. Many contributors mentioned services they used below, to include, but not limited to:

• DoD Skillbridge	• Veterati
• Candorful	• Onward to opportunities
• Hire our heroes	• Merivis
• Salesforce Military	• Transition Masters
• Project Transition USA	• American Corporate Partners
• Veterans' Employment and Training Service (VETS)	• National Veteran Small Business Coalition (NVSBC)
• Women in Defense	• GR8Transitions4U
• Sandlers Sales Course	• Federal resume writing class
• Hire Heroes (USA)	• Wheels of Success
• Recruit Military	• AMVETS

Top Issues and Lessons Learned

The details of each contributors' transition journey were revealed around 12 questions. After reading all the stories, the following is what I feel is a good summary of the top lessons and issues for anyone transitioning:

1. **Focus on your transition.** You are your own CEO of this mission! It is non-negotiable and direct all your energy towards it. This includes focus towards family – they are in this with you!

2. **Be prepared and plan well.** Many spent time finding a financial advisor and establishing a 'nest egg' for rainy days ahead. Be as debt-free as you can be. Being organized is key.

3. **Be patient with yourself** – transition is not always easy, but planning helps reduce anxiety and fear. Some felt a bit lost losing the uniform and felt a loss of family. Some incorporated planned time off with family to self-regulate.

4. **Take advantage** of every certification, degree, and support program out there in the military before you leave.

5. **Utilize every resource available** on the web and social media to make the best impression of yourself. Resume writers and interview coaches are worth it. Hundreds of military-friendly organizations, programs, associations, societies, and books are ready for your absorption.

6. **Know your self-worth** and **who you are**; have the **confidence** to go out there and get what you want.

7. **Set aside your pride** and receive / review feedback to adjust and succeed.

8. **Ask!** Learn to be curious and proactively seek out answers to questions. Go the extra mile and take on challenging roles to increase your exposure to new opportunities

9. **Establish your red flags.** Understand what you are not willing to compromise on.

10. **Translate your skills well.** Be prepared to adapt to the job and to your new community. Drop the jargon. Get out there and share with others who you are!

11. Learn to **tell your story** and express yourself in a way that new listeners will be engaged. Many reflected that it was hard to learn to 'sell' and promote themselves (the "I") instead of the "Team", which is not the military way. Create and fine-tune your "elevator pitch."

12. **Don't overuse the "Veteran" angle**; there is plenty of entitlement with being in the military, but when looking for a job, you need to sell them on how you will help them succeed.

13. **Be realistic with your goals** – you are transitioning and will be leaving your military 'family' and finding a new one. Realize that there are barriers to specific industry experience and knowledge; it can be learned.

14. **Be vigilant in your research** on companies that you are interested in working for to make it the right fit for you AND the company. For instance, if you are getting into government acquisitions, learn more about it! Also, make sure you are very familiar with the job expectations and the new role you will be taking on .... prepare questions for interviews!

15. **Be smart with applications.** Make it count. Shot-gunning resumes everywhere can become tiresome and often presents depressing results.

Last, and Most importantly.....

16. **Network! Network! Network!** The most important lesson mentioned throughout all these stories was to utilize as many networks as you have to transition. Use your networks: military, certification, educational, church, family, LinkedIn, coaches, mentors...the list goes on. Many found that as they were pursuing a certain industry / job, they would join and volunteer with local volunteer organizations supporting networking; this allowed a direct feed into the life in the day of that particular job lifestyle, as well as an introduction to companies in the local area that were hiring. *Consider this book an expansion of your military network* and utilize it to seek out and find more answers to your transition questions.

THE TRANSITIONED VETERAN

SUCCESS BEYOND SERVICE

Delilah Anderson

Service Rank: Chief Warrant Officer 4, USA

Position: Operations Manager

Industry: E-commerce

Biography

My name is Delilah Anderson, I am from Brooklyn, NY and I joined the military in April 1992. I originally joined the Army with the idea I would only do 4 years and get out, 27 years later I retired. My time in the military was an adventure full of joy, hardship, sacrifices, and pride. Serving my country and protecting our freedom has been one of my biggest passion. I travel the world, served in 8 deployments, met the bravest and incredible people, and honored those that serve before me. I served with the 82ND ABN, 1ID, 25TH Transportation Battalion, 101st ABN, 7th Transportation School, Surface Deployment Distribution Command, and 21st Theater Sustainment Command. Some of my awards include: Afghanistan Campaign, Medal Army Achievement Medal Army Commendation Medal (x8), Army Good Conduct Medal, Bronze Star Medal Defense Meritorious Service Medal, Global War on Terrorism Expeditionary Medal, Global War on Terrorism Service Medal Iraq Campaign Medal, Joint Service Commendation Medal, Korea Defense Service Medal Legion of Merit Meritorious Service Medal (x3), and National Defense Service Medal.

I retired in January 2019 and currently work as a Military Pathway Operations Manager in Amazon. Making the decision to leave the military did not come easy but it is true that when its time you will know its time.

Questions & Answers

1. Describe your journey from the service to your first job?

I started planning my transition a year out but wish I had started sooner. There are so many services and programs for veterans that I felt I did not have time to take advantage of all of them. I was very fortunate, I had a job with Amazon before I even retired. I started with Amazon while on terminal leave. The key to finding the job of my dreams was networking and building relationships. As soon as I decide to retire I started going to seminars and transition meetings.

2. How did you find your first job? Describe the process.

I found my dream job on a job fair hosted by Hiring Our Heroes.

3. When did you start planning your transition? What actions/activities did you take?

I started planning my transition a year from my retirement date. I started by taking a seminar that would help me determine what I wanted to do after-life in the military and what were my best skills and how to maximize them. Once I had that done I started writing my resume. Transition services did an excellent job helping me write a resume that highlighted my skills and was appealing to the corporate world. After I was on a networking mission. I attended every class and seminar offered by transition services.

4. Did you pursue any advanced degrees and/or certifications? Did they help?

Do you believe these helped getting a job? If so, how? I did not, I already had a BA in Transportation Logistics. I am however, currently pursuing another degree.

5. Why did you choose the work/career you are in?

Because I am a logistician at heart and no other company does logistics better than Amazon.

6. Have you encountered any obstacles in advancing your career?

It was difficult to transition at the beginning. The corporate world it's very similar, but at the same time very different than the military. I had to change my way of thinking and approaching a task. Each organization is different and each business model is different, recommend to always go with an open mind and be kind to yourself. Remember in a new organization you don't know anything.

7. What were the 2 hardest efforts about transitioning?

Not wearing the uniform and feeling my purpose was lost. My mission is very different now and it was a struggle to make peace with that.

8. What do you think are the top issues for Veterans transitioning into a career?

I believe that not doing the proper research on the company that they are seeking employment to ensure their values match. We have to ensure that number one we are seeking the right jobs that fit our values and number two what are our red lines? What are the things we are not willing to compromise no matter the pay? Once we can do that we will find the perfect job for us.

Not building a network that would help them get into these careers. You have to showcase yourself, have a professional social media presence, and ensure the hiring managers are the ones looking at you.

9. Do you believe there is a stereotype attached to being a Veteran in pursuit of a job?

Not in my experience. I do believe we get hired for our leadership skills and the expectations of our performance are higher.

10. What question(s) would you have liked to have known before taking your first job?

How my job would affect my life work balance. It is very important you understand what balance you want to have before saying yes to a job.

Some of the questions that I asked myself before accepting the offer with Amazon:

1. Is the work environment somewhere I can be productive?
2. Will I feel satisfy professionally?
3. Is this a company I will be proud to work at?

11. What are the most important lessons you can share on making a successful job transition from the military?

1. Be patient with yourself and be sure to know what it is that you want to do.
2. Take advantage of every services and programs offered to transitioning members
3. Ensure your LinkedIn is up to date and it is showcasing who you are as a professional and what you are looking for. Recruiters are always looking.

12. If you could do it again, what would be the one thing you would do (better) or not do to help in your transition?

I would have started planning 2 years from my desired retirement date. Again, there are so many programs and services for transitioning members that I feel I did not take advantage of all of them. Understand what balance you want to have before saying yes to a job.

Rob Arndt

Service Rank: Gunnery Sergeant, USMC

Position: Head of Partnerships

Industry: Staffing and Recruitment

Biography

Rob Arndt is Head of Partnerships at Shift.org where he and the team help Veterans navigate successful career changes and redefine the way that organizations connect to non-traditional, military-experienced talent.

Rob is a 14-year veteran of the United States Marine Corps, who had served in military campaigns in Kuwait and Iraq before reporting to a duty assignment in Marine Corps Recruitment & Retention that paved the road for where he is today. Rob provides a vast wealth of knowledge regarding the full military lifecycle from entering the military, serving in it, recruiting for it, exiting the service, and now providing resources to those who served in their quest for post-military success. Rob and the Shift Team have leveraged decades of insider connections, partnerships with military bases, and expansive online communities to build a diverse and talented pool of military veterans who want to find their next mission in companies just like yours.

Questions & Answers

1. Describe your journey from the service to your first job?

■ I was on Marine Recruiting Duty and in the process of re-enlisting for a 3rd term, but one day woke up and realized that it was my time to move on. I took the weekend to draft up what I thought was a great resume and began my hunt for sales management positions across every job board I could find, subsequently applying to dozens of open positions in the process and hearing NOTHING back. This rinse and repeat model had continued for about 3 months, taking me closer and closer to my end of service date, until I finally heard back from a local supply and logistics company that was interested. I only had 2 weeks left on my enlistment contract, so let us just say I was "shopping hungry" and in turn accepted a position with them although the position was far from my dream job.

2. How did you find your first job? Describe the process.

■ I took my job search and transition into my own hands, utilizing various job boards, applying to what felt like 500 jobs and never heard a peep outside of the automated "we have your application and will reach out if there is a fit" emails, until someone finally reached out.

3. When did you start planning your transition? What actions/ activities did you take?

I saw all the buzz and lip service surrounding veteran hiring and bought into the hype myself. I was under the impression that companies had this burning desire to hire vets and understood what we brought to the civilian workforce and were chomping at the bit to hire people like me. Plus, I had a background in sales and recruitment management that was a directly transferable skillset to almost any company out there and a resume to prove it. What could possibly go wrong?

4. Did you pursue any advanced degrees and/or certifications? Did they help?

When I was stationed at Camp Lejeune, I enrolled in college, majoring in Business Management, taking classes during my lunch breaks, evenings, and on weekends in pursuit of a bachelor's degree. A year into my program the attacks on 9/11 happened and shortly after my unit was slated for deployment and the initial invasion of Iraq. I then had to withdraw from school and deploy. After that, I never really had a chance to return to school since life and operational tempo took priority over my studies. I am currently a senior executive with no degree and take great pride in the fact that I had made it this far without a formal education.

5. Why did you choose the work/career you are in?
■ I love the art and science of sales and am a true student of the game. I also love working with and helping people, especially my fellow veterans. I simply chose something that I am passionate about and made it my mission, and failure is not an option with missions.

6. Have you encountered any obstacles in advancing your career?
■ I come from very humble beginnings and learned early on that obstacles are a part of life, but there are always ways to go around, under, over or worst case scenario through them.

7. What were the 2 hardest efforts about transitioning?
■ I had an unrealistic expectation of what type of positions would be waiting for me when I got out. The Marines flat out told me they would not promise me a rose garden, but the civilian world sort of did with all the noise in the military employment arena. The second hardest part of my transition was that I was not going back to my home of record and did not have a network built up in the area where I was getting out. A lot of people have jobs because of who they know, and I knew virtually no one.

8. What do you think are the top issues for Veterans transitioning into a career?
Job translation is the single biggest issue in veterans transitioning to civilian careers. Simply put, military folk do not speak civilian and civilians do not speak military very well. Not to mention there is a broken narrative where veterans are portrayed as heroes by some and victims by others making it very confusing on both sides.

9. Do you believe there is a stereotype attached to being a Veteran in pursuit of a job?

Yes! There are dozens of stereotypes of veteran job seekers and you never really know which one people buy into. The bottom line is that veterans are people and no two of us are exactly the same.

10. What question(s) would you have liked to have known before taking your first job?

I would have loved to have known my personal value to an organization and how to properly portray that on my resume or in an interview. As service members, we are taught to never talk about ourselves and that "there is no I in Team," yet civilian companies don't care what your unit did as they want to see personal accolades, accomplishments, and concrete individual work experience.

11. What are the most important lessons you can share on making a successful job transition from the military?

In the military, we have "Missions" and missions are non-negotiable. We may not always have the tools, supplies, or personnel required to get the job done but come hell or high water the mission will be accomplished. We apply this logic to our time in service, yet we somehow lose grasp of this in our own lives and career path. I recommend that veterans have a moment of truth with themselves and find out what their ideal career path is and make it their "mission" and direct all their firepower towards accomplishing it. Goals can fail and fall short... missions cannot.

12. If you could do it again, what would be the one thing you would do (better) or not do to help in your transition?

I would leverage more of the transition resources that are out there and do a better job researching the civilian job market to not hit the snags that I did early on.

Josh Atkinson

Service Rank: Captain, USMC

Position: Project Manager, Training Consultant

Industry: Training

Biography

I am a US Marine who served 11 years' active duty and 2 years in the Reserves. I now work as a logistics SME and consultant for Whitney Bradley and Brown and as a Business Development Director for PM-Pro-Learn (a veteran founded project management training company). I was born in California in 1983 and attended the United States Naval Academy graduating in 2005 with a BS in Political Science. Upon graduation, I was commissioned as a pilot in the USMC. I completed flight training and earned my wings in Jet Aviation before being selected to fly AV-8B Harriers out of Cherry Point. After finishing training at VMAT-203 I joined VMA-231 as an assistant operations officer in 2010. . I deployed with NATO in 2011 as an Air Logistics officer and transitioned to the Logistics field upon return in 2012. From 2012 until I separated from Active Duty in 2016 I served as a Battalion Logistics officer with 1st Battalion 9th Marines, Headquarters Battalion 2D MARDIV, and a Division G4 Future Operations officer. I was also deployed as a Human Intelligence Task Force Deputy Director in 2014 with SOCCENT. After leaving Active duty I worked as a Heavy Rigging Project Manager supporting the Oil Refining, and Power Generation industry. In 2017 I helped launch PM-ProLearn. In 2018 I started working with Whitney Bradley and Brown (WBB), as a Logistics consultant supporting life cycle acquisitions and analysis. I am hugely passionate about helping veterans in transition and

9

helping others navigate the emotional journey to civilian life. I am a certified lean six green belt, a project management professional (PMP), and a Prosci Certified Change Management Practitioner.

Questions & Answers

1. Describe your journey from the service to your first job?

For my transition, I started looking about 1.5 years out. I talked with mentors who said that I should get my PMP and lean six certifications. I already had my lean six green belt so I pursued PMP. In all, it took about a year to prepare for my first job. As I used a headhunter, I had a different journey to finding my first job.

2. How did you find your first job? Describe the process.

I first attended the Service Academy Career Conference (SACC) about 18 months from separation.

This was a great first start to identify companies and types of jobs I was interested in. I started talking with Orion and Bradley Morris as well. The process was straight forward enough, but I didn't really know my value or how to articulate it. I eventually connected with Alliance Careers and chose to work with them about 8 months out. They were exclusive in that they prohibited me from using or talking with any other job placement companies. They have updated this policy since. I thought this meant they were "better" but it was a means for them to ensure a better hold on their product.

Knowing what I know now I would have networked and done much more but I had a lot on my plate at the time and thought this was the best way. The training they provided in understanding various types of jobs like sales, operations, project management, etc. was great. They had us do a Strengths-finder 2.0 and DISC profile assessments; both of which were great to help me articulate my value. As for the job placement process, it was "speed dating to marriage in a weekend" as I would have called it. We interviewed with 10 companies in 2 days, but we didn't learn who they were or where the job locations would be until 2 days before the interview. At the end of the day, I had one job I was interested in and one company interested in me.

The process resulted in me getting a job, though I was making 40% less than I did on active duty. I was blessed and learned a lot but I left all "control" in the hands of the headhunter.

3. When did you start planning your transition? What actions/activities did you take?

I started planning my transition about 18 months out when I got my first "pass" at Major. I started talking with individuals and pursuing certifications through IVMF. I later learned about using unit training funding and was able to get my PMP funded by my unit which was much better training than using self-paced training provided by IVMF.

4. Did you pursue any advanced degrees and/or certifications? Did they help?

As previously mentioned, I pursed certifications. I was very interested in project management and saw that the jobs I wanted were calling for PMP. I wanted to improve my marketability. I know that being PMP certified didn't help me with my job as the company was looking to hire veterans using a headhunter. They hired another veteran with less military experience and no certification at the same time and we both got paid the same as project managers. In the first few months of being a project manager, however, I learned that my value was much higher than I was making. The customers I supported cared that I had my PMP and would prefer to talk with me about project activities. I learned as well that if I was working as a PM for my customer, I could make 70% more than I was currently making and almost double my salary. This was eye-opening for me.

5. Why did you choose the work/career you are in?

I think project management is a great field for veterans as all military operations are focused on project-based work. (a temporary endeavor that creates a unique product, service or result). The ability to build a plan and team to support a mission and then oversee the execution was great. It was a very comfortable field and allowed me to feel a sense of accomplishment when you finish a project with a satisfied customer. The issues I ran into had more to do with corporate culture and pay than the field.

I still love project management and have helped create a training company www. pm-prolearn.com with a focus to help active duty get PMP and ACP certified.

6. Have you encountered any obstacles in advancing your career?

■ Not really in the traditional sense. I learned a lot about networking and was able to connect with a friend from The Basic School (TBS) who was able to get me an informal interview with his company WBB. I learned that my value was higher and that I could do more. The only barrier I have found since is that I struggle on various government contracts to fill senior labor categories (LCATs) as I didn't retire at 20 years. I have the technical capability but don't have the years of experience on paper to get "hired" on the contract.

7. What were the 2 hardest efforts about transitioning?

■ For me, the most difficult piece was psychological and emotional.

Everyone has a different reason for leaving the military which also leads to the "emotion" of transition. For me, I got non-selected to Major and was forced out. I never wanted to leave. I felt unwanted, rejected, and betrayed in a lot of ways. This led to a lot of uncertainty about the "next" job and a desire to be valued, appreciated, and supported. There are means to find work and get hired but finding a place that would "adopt" me is what I wanted. What I have learned is that this doesn't exist.

Companies will never "adopt" you in the sense that the military did. There is no guarantee of employment, growth, training, pay increases, etc. Its capitalism and companies exist to run a business and make a profit. They can't guarantee anything like the military can. I have coined the phrase "becoming a foreign orphan" to describe this feeling for veterans. This is also why I am a huge advocate of the reserves. It's a "family reunion" once a month to go home and be around your family.

8. What do you think are the top issues for Veterans transitioning into a career?

For veterans transitioning into project management careers, the biggest barrier is specific industry experience. Construction vs IT vs government projects are all a little different. Veterans have the skills to manage and run projects but lack specific industry knowledge. I think certifications are a huge leap to understand industry terminology and processes though. Industry knowledge can be gained. Building a technical foundation of the trade is key.

9. Do you believe there is a stereotype attached to being a Veteran in pursuit of a job?

Absolutely. It is company-dependent on how much the stereotype helps or hinders a veteran but there are always assumptions to fill in the unknown. This is why it is key to network, talking with other veterans who work inside companies and learn as much as possible before applying or accepting an offer.

10. What question(s) would you have liked to have known before taking your first job?

Some internal questions I needed to answer: What industry do I want to work for? Why? Where do I want to be in 5 years? What culture do I want to have inside a company? What am I worth? How do I communicate my value to a company?

For the company: What is the employee growth plan? What does it take to get a raise? What do I need to do to achieve my own goals within this company? What is my goal for growth within the company?

11. What are the most important lessons you can share on making a successful job transition from the military?

1. Understand your job requirements before identifying your job title. The attributes of work have little to do with the title. After you identify the attributes then you can identify the solutions (job title, industry, location, etc.) Identify your skill gaps while active duty and use resources to fill them in.

2. Certifications can often be funded by your unit or there are programs like ARMY CA/Army Ignited that cover the costs.

3. NETWORK: LinkedIn allows you to identify employees inside companies who are fellow veterans. Talk with them. You can ask honest questions about the culture, work-life balance, pay, benefits, growth, etc. so that if you get an interview you already know what you want and how much you can expect to make. These insiders can potentially get you a conversation with the hiring manager who will decide to hire you or not.

12. If you could do it again, what would be the one thing you would do (better) or not do to help in your transition?

I would have started earlier and pursued more certifications. I would have networked using LinkedIn and found mentors to help. In working to grow a startup company I have learned how powerful LinkedIn is as a tool. It connects you with decision-makers at companies and opens so many doors. I have learned about veterati.com as a resource, and I have talked with so many people who have placement and access to jobs. I do not doubt that if I were to need a job I could easily find one now based on the relationships I have built, and the tools I have unlocked and learned about. All of these tools are accessible to veterans now. I'd love to help anyone I can.

Eric Aull

Service Rank: Captain, USN

Position: Director, Business Development

Industry: Defense Contracting

Biography

A retired Military Intelligence professional with 30 years' experience as a Program Manager, Project Manager and Director in the U.S. Navy. Planned, led and executed global intelligence operations with recent, wartime experience leading large, high-level, joint, coalition, Inter-Agency staffs, and command forces. Specific skills include:

- Intelligence Operations
- Information Technology Management
- Managing Change
- Business Acumen
- Training Management
- Building Coalitions

Questions & Answers

1. Describe your journey from the service to your first job?

■ I joined the Navy via the delayed entry program in my junior year of college because I was craving adventure, loved being outdoors and physical, and was not ready for car sales or insurance which was about the extent of job opportunities in my home town.

I also wanted to travel and learn about the world. Additionally, all the men in my family had served in the military and I always remember seeing their pictures and listening to their stories about military life. I considered other branches, but the Navy always felt right so I shipped out September 1987. Every few years I would explore outside opportunities, but nothing seemed to offer the education opportunities, traveling, and leading that I had in the military. I did not start planning my transition until about 1 year before retirement. It took the full year and I recommend now that everyone should be planning for transition the day, they enter the military. The problem with preparation like anything else, if you know where you want to go the more successful you will be. Also, knowing how to prepare is key, and most military personnel don't know how to prepare for the transition, so we don't make a resume and/or make networking, or additional training a priority early enough in our military career.

I found my first job a few weeks after my final out by identifying where I wanted to work, and networking and continuously following up with the people that could get me a job.

Those people included Contracting Officers, Program Managers, and Government Civilian senior personnel.

2. How did you find your first job? Describe the process.

■ I found my first job by getting the word out that I was available for employment and networking. Patience is key, continue to contact those personnel who can do the hiring, and follow-up with them routinely. Eventually, they will have openings. I learned more about the transition through trial and error than any course I took or coach I consulted. You go to interviews and find out what companies are looking for and what you need to do to make yourself more competitive. Talk to people in positions you would like to be in and listen to their advice. Always know that the good jobs will come to you through your network.

3. When did you start planning your transition? What actions/ ■ activities did you take?

I started planning my transition about 1 year before retirement. I networked, attended job fairs, and hired a career coach. A career coach can help you to build confidence particularly if you are looking to go outside your comfort zone and into an area where you do not have an established network or significant experience.

4. Did you pursue any advanced degrees and/or certifications? ■ Did they help?

I started working on my PMP certification during my transition and I did it because of advice I was given from a Small Business owner who was also hiring. I do think the PMP and other certifications can help to set yourself apart from others. Particularly for very competitive jobs where you need to separate yourself from the pack. Also, remember that you represent your organization/company and how you do that is important to your company. Certifications can help to convey a level of professionalism that represents you and your company very well. Certifications also help you build confidence in your abilities as well as confidence in you from your employers.

5. Why did you choose the work/career you are in?
■ Unfortunately, I never had a grand plan to get me to where I am. My approach was to choose a path and see where it takes me. I do not recommend this approach if you can avoid it.

In the end, I migrated to Business Development because I enjoy the strategy and planning that goes into growing a business. Knowing what I know now I should have used those same skills (strategy and planning) in my career planning and I may be further along than I am now.

6. Have you encountered any obstacles in advancing your career?
■ In the military, you become part of a team/family and you spend your entire military career with this family. In a corporate job, you may outgrow your position and when you are successful and upward mobility is not available you will probably have to move to a new company/ies to get increased responsibility, higher pay, and learn new skills. This runs counter to our team mentality in the military where you feel an obligation to serve your organization.

7. What were the 2 hardest efforts about transitioning?

■ The structure in the military, while sometimes rigid is very helpful in understanding relationships, roles, and responsibilities. In the civilian workplace, roles and responsibilities can be very different and not nearly as clearly defined. This can be refreshing to some but also challenging as you attempt to maneuver in this environment.

8. What do you think are the top issues for Veterans transitioning into a career?

The top issues for Veterans transitioning to corporate leadership careers are understanding you are starting over; you are no longer the expert in your field, and you are not the expert in business management or the culture of the business.

9. Do you believe there is a stereotype attached to being a Veteran in pursuit of a job?

Sometimes military personnel is stereotyped as rigid, and not open-minded to new and/or innovative ways of doing business. Many of your military skills (from writing, speaking, leading) transfer very well to the corporate world and make you very effective and efficient in business.

10. What question(s) would you have liked to have known before taking your first job?

I would like to have known more about all aspects of the government acquisition process as well as business and marketing. My master's degree is in Public Administration so that, with my military career kept me focused on the public vice private sector. Knowing what I know now I would have pursued an MBA vice an MPA for my masters.

11. What are the most important lessons you can share on making a successful job transition from the military?

Be patient, have your resume professionally done, and stay focused on what you want to do but don't be afraid to explore new and unfamiliar opportunities.

12. If you could do it again, what would be the one thing you would do (better) or not do to help in your transition?

Start preparing for transition early in your military career and make better choices for assignments and training with a post-military career in mind. Also, approach every meeting or event as though you may be interviewing for your next job.

Taylor Beattie

Service Rank: Lieutenant Colonel, USA

Position: Trainer, Author

Industry: Education

Biography

LTC Beattie is a trainer, educator, advisor, and published author with over 30 years of experience as a retired US Army Special Forces Officer, civilian leadership training and education consultant, and most recently a deckhand on a marine construction "spud barge." Through the course of his 22-year military career, he served in three specialties (Infantry, Military Intelligence, Special Forces) and a variety of assignments around the world including Central and South America, Europe, Lebanon, Algeria, South Korea, Bosnia Herzegovina, Iraq, and Equatorial Africa. In December of 1995, he led the first NATO Special Operations Force into Tuzla, Bosnia, Herzegovina, as part of the NATO Peace Enforcement effort, "Operation JOINT ENDEAVOR". In April of 1996, he was the security force commander for a Joint Special Operations element (including Army Special Forces, USN SEALS, USAF Combat Controllers, and US Army Paratroopers) in the Non-Combatant Evacuation Operation (NEO) "Operation ASSURED REPONSE" in Monrovia, Liberia, resulting in the rescue of 2100 civilians from the besieged embassy and hostile streets of Monrovia. In November 1996, Mr. Beattie was the first Special Operations Officer ever to receive the Veterans of the Office of Strategic Services (OSS) Award for "exceptional leadership, devotion to duty, and professionalism during a special forces operational mission." Following retirement from the U.S Army Taylor worked

DOD Contractor (Project Manager), Independent Contracting (LLC Project Lead) in training/education and marine construction (Deck Hand).

Taylor has a BA in Anthropology from the University of Delaware and an MA in Education from the University of Saint Mary. He is married to a career language arts teacher (and his editor), has two grown daughters, a grandson, three good dogs, and an indifferent cat. The Beattie's reside on Biscay pond in Bristol Maine.

Questions & Answers

1. Describe your journey from the service to your first job?

I was commissioned (through ROTC) in 1983 as a US Army Infantry 2LT. I aimed to do a conventional infantry tour as a rifle platoon leader with the 193rd Infantry Brigade in the Republic of Panama and then apply for Special Forces (SF) training. Once I had my Green Beret I would hang around in the Army until it wasn't fun anymore. The Army had other plans and IAW service needs I was (involuntarily) re-branched to Military Intelligence (MI). Following training in tactical and counterintelligence, I applied for and was accepted to attend the Special Forces Qualification Officers Course (SFQC) at Fort Bragg NC. Following graduation, for SFQC I reported to 1st Special Forces Group (A) at Fort Lewis Washington. I was an MI officer slotted to take an MI job the Group Commander decided to assign me as a commander of a Special Forces Operational A Detachment, an "A" team as he was short of SF qualified officers. While assigned to 1st Group I attempted to re-branch from MI to SF and was rejected 8 times due to the needs of the Army.

In 1992 I was reassigned to a conventional MI assignment with the Joint Readiness Training Center at Fort Chaffee, Arkansas. This was a miserable assignment where I served as the night watch officer. I made another attempt to branch transfer to SF was turned down and began to plan my exit strategy from the Army. I purchased the book "What Color is My Parachute" to explore potential career options. I was miserable in my current role and got cross-threaded with the 2 Star Commander who demanded I be removed from his command. Turns out his demand was "without cause" for a personality conflict festering for months. I called my assignments officer and informed him that I was "tapping out" of active duty. A mercurial general officer's opinion notwithstanding, I had performed well at JRTC and the Army wanted to retain me, so I was offered a MI position in a Special Operations unit in Germany. I had a wife and two young daughters and we agreed that a tour in Germany was just too good to pass up so I took the assignment.

Fast forward to 2003. I made my 20 years and the door had closed on my "action guy" time, I had made LTC and for my sins, was off the command track. My future held a series of staff officer positions trolling for IEDs in combat zones so I filled out my retirement paperwork as a stop-loss order was issued for SF officers. I had a buddy as an assignment officer who offered and assignment as the Special Operations Chair at the Joint Forces Staff College (JFSC) in Nor-folk VA. I loved My job at JFSC and as my tour came to an end I submitted my retirement as the Hampton Roads VA area offered a great deal of opportunity to former military folks. So how long did it take me to prepare and find my first job? I would say 22 years passing through 53 countries on 5 continents. When you leave the military, you are the sum total of that experience. Now your challenge is to translate that experience to civilian job opportunities.

2. How did you find your first job? Describe the process.

My first job following retirement was as a Senior Military Analyst with Camber Corporation a mid-sized, employee-owned, defense contractor. I was recruited by (3) instructor colleagues that had retired some months earlier. Camber was not my first choice, rather it was my fall back/safety choice in the event that other options did not pan out.

My dream retirement job was a leadership role in secondary education, pref-erably in a private school. A few years earlier in anticipation of retirement and a post-retirement career in education, I pursued a Master of Arts in Education. Once settled on my final PCS in Norfolk VA I conducted tons of research into Independent Private School Educational leadership positions, I conducted office calls with every private school headmaster within a one hour drive. The office calls went very well and I received tons of great advice. Still, months out from retirement I applied for several positions within the Hampton Roads region, while I continued to keep an eye out for emergent opportunities. During this time, I had another line of effort aimed at a defense contracting in the unlikely event that private education did not pan out...I still had a mortgage, college tuition, and other bills...

In my pursuit of a defense contracting gig, I scanned the "career opportunities" section of corporate web sites and on occasion, cold-called human resource points of contact (POCs.) On one occasion, I attended a job fair specifically for those with active security clearances, which are valued in the defense contracting world. The job fair was a complete waste of time. At each booth, you were compelled to stand in line, resume in hand, elevator speech ready.

Recruiters would instruct potential hires donned in ill-fitted, inappropriate, versions of business attire to visit the corporate website for current opportunities.

For the most part, I enjoyed the hours of research and analysis of the hunt. The enjoyment diminished as the letters of rejection piled in from the "educational" line of effort...that is when I got a response to my application at all. While I had a masters and 6 years of platform time in the military these did not translate to private secondary educational need. I was offered one teaching position but the basic entry teacher's salary would not pay the bills. The rejection from my primary line of effort was painful.

With retirement looming I went with Camber Corporation where I would be working (not serving...big distinction) with former JFSC colleagues who had been recruited before and after me. It was the right decision.

3. When did you start planning your transition? What actions/activities did you take?

I started planning my transition about four years out from projected retirement. In anticipation of a follow-on career in educational leadership, I pursued an MA Education from a local University using VA benefits. Before submitting my retirement packet, I worked on my resume seeking advice from local HR folks. I learned that I needed multiple resumes crafted for each position of interest. More importantly, I learned how to write cover letters or letters of interest tailored to each opportunity. I did a good deal of networking

Taylor Beattie

within secondary education circles and within Defense contracting working through folks that I knew using the same to develop leads. I did make some cold calls but none of these ever panned out.

4. Did you pursue any advanced degrees and/or certifications? Did they help?

While I was a small group instructor at the Command and General Staff College at Fort Leavenworth KS and decided it was important for me to get an MA Education. An MA combined with my military instructor experience might make me an attractive candidate. After a long day of teaching, I attended night school with local civilian teachers hoping to up their salary with an advanced degree. It took me 18 months to complete but was well worth the effort. While my aim to score a position in education did not work out my advanced degree in education translated to "master trainer/educator" in the defense contracting world and gave me a leg up on other candidates without an advanced degree.

This held true in the 10 contracting and independent contracting jobs that I held in the 12 years until my final retirement in 2017.

5. Why did you choose the work/career you are in?

From the time that I retired from active duty in 2005, it seems like most of the jobs that I had found me. As a civilian defense contractor, I have worked as a senior analyst, a trainer/educator, a task lead doctrine writer, a lesson-learned analyst, multiple jobs as a project manager, a capture manager, a hiring manager, a business development manager, a military advisor for 6 defense contractors and as an independent contractor in my own LLC. Some of these jobs were incredibly rewarding others were horrific cubicle-bound tenures endured through lucrative compensation. The best Jobs were outside work, planning, and conducting training and advising missions. This included a stint as a military advisor to the producer/actor Ricky Schroder for the reality TV recruiting show "Starting Strong." I left the defense contracting world in 2017 and have helped local businesses' in painting and other work. In 2020 at the age of 62, I am currently working as a deckhand on a marine construction "spud" gaining a whole new skill set.

6. Have you encountered any obstacles in advancing your career?

■ The contracting world is finicky and contracts come and go, are awarded, and lost. In the contracting world, salaries are paid through hours billed. When the contract ends or is lost the billable hours go with it. Whenever I interviewed for a new job I always asked about the contract "period of performance" (POP) indicating when the contract ends or is up for re-compete. It is not unusual for folks to start "jumping ship" within 90 days of the projected end of the contract so replacements are hired and laid off within that 90-day period.

My longest contract went for five years. I was promoted from analyst through to project/program manager and offered a director job. I turned the job down and took an analyst job with another company as I had the sense that the directorate was going to be cut away within the year. As Director, I would be conducting the layoffs until I was shown the door. Once I understood the lifecycle of a contract I could position myself to slide over to another contract or start searching for my next job. One key lesson learned is that it is always easier to find a job when you have a job because recruiters sense desperation when you are unemployed and looking for work. In short, the only obstacles that I encountered were self-inflicted from a lack of understanding of the contracting world.

7. What were the 2 hardest efforts about transitioning?

■ The two hardest efforts for me were:

1. Understanding my value to potential employers…What am I worth? or more importantly what is my time worth? While in the military you are on the 24 hours 365 days a year clock. In the civilian world time is money. When I started my first contracting job I understood the concept of billable hours, that I could only bill 8 hours a day 40 hours a week. I routinely came in early, stayed late, and worked weekends for free to stay ahead of the work or to anticipate potential friction points. The contract performed well I worked those hours for free and will never get that time back…

2. Loyalty...I remember being told "you can love the Army all you want but the Army will not love you back..." this is particularly true in the civilian world. Years ago, you took a job, stayed with the company for 30 years collected a gold watch and retired. Today people jump from job to job. It ain't right, it ain't wrong it just is what it is...

8. What do you think are the top issues for Veterans transitioning into a career?

Physical health is your most important asset transitioning into the civilian world.

Make sure you get a VA physical. I was in great shape. I spent 22 years in combat arms, special operations, as a paratrooper and saw no need for a physical. A buddy talked me into going. Good thing - I received a 40% disability. Evidently, I broke my back (spinal compression fracture) at some point on active duty and was showing signs of degenerative disc disease and arthritis in all major joints. In short, a 40% disability means a little extra money in my monthly retirement check and I get a preference when applying for government jobs. Additionally, in my state (Maine) as a disabled veteran, I will soon be able to apply to have a portion of my property taxes forgiven.

9. Do you believe there is a stereotype attached to being a Veteran in pursuit of a job?

I think the stereotype attached to a veteran in pursuit of a job is generally good. That stereotype includes loyalty, dependability, and discipline. I came out of full retirement to take a job in marine construction because the small business owner could not find dependable help.

I would love to get a veteran on the team but none are settling in the area (mid-coast Maine).

10. What question(s) would you have liked to have known before taking your first job?

My first job was with a midsized defense contractor conducting Joint Training and Education programs similar to what I had been doing in my last military job. Later I was appointed as a project manager of a failing project.

The learning curve was steep. I was all over the leadership portion, pushed more resources at the problem, and got the project out of the hole. From a military perspective, it was a great success. From a "for-profit" business perspective it was a failure. The company lost money, we got more work but lost money. I learned the hard way. I would have liked to understand "for-profit" project management.

11. What are the most important lessons you can share on making a successful job transition from the military?

The three most important lessons learned for my transitions are:

1. The notion that "time is money." The military is a 24/7/365-day commitment. In the civilian world time is money, every hour you put toward a project has a cost finically and physically. As the hours' slide by you have the choice between cost overruns or volunteering your time which adds to stress directly affecting your health.

   In the middle of a challenging project, my stress levels brought on a case of shingles. The stress, having weakened my immune system, allowed the virus to come out of dormancy...not fun.

2. It is important to understand (in the contracting space) that contracts are finite. Contracts are won and lost over the period of performance (POP). Sometimes contracts are cancelled mid POP due to the convenience of the Government. Always keep your resume up to date and keep an eye on the horizon for the next opportunity. I recall working for a big defense contracting firm. One day we were called to the break room to see out Program Manager receive a reward for completing 15 years with the company. The celebratory cake was excellent. A month later the program manager's multimillion-dollar contract was cancelled for the "convenience of the Government" putting hundreds (including me) on the street. I wonder if that Program Manager kept his 15-year plaque.

3. It is critical to understand the concept of Earned Value Management and other civilian project management concepts. In the military, you are

rewarded for spending all allocated funds for a project. In the civilian world, you seek to keep costs down as that is where the profit is hiding.

12. If you could do it again, what would be the one thing you would do (better) or not do to help in your transition?

If I could do it again I would learn to relax. In the military, everything is life and death. It is important to find a balance between work and personal/family time. I remember working as a task lead for a defense contractor. The money was good but the job was a soul-crushing cubicle, PowerPoint, sweatshop, located deep within a secure facility. One particular Monday we were informed that one of our colleagues stayed late the preceding on a Friday and was discovered dead in his cubicle Saturday morning. "I wish I had spent more time at work," said no one from their deathbed.

George Bernloehr

Service Rank: Lieutenant, USN

Position: Lead Associate, Military Affairs

Industry: Talent Acquisition & Corporate Affairs

Biography

George Bernloehr is a member of Booz Allen's Military and Veteran Affairs team. In this role, he contributes to Booz Allen's efforts to be known as the preeminent military employer, the most innovative partner, and a recognized leader and member of the military community. Prior to his current position, he developed and led the military hiring initiative at Booz Allen and served as the lead recruiter for the Southeast and Mid-Atlantic region. He previously served as a Senior Military Talent Acquisition Consultant for Eaton and a Recruiter and Regional Operations Manager at Bradley-Morris, Inc. where he led the development of an online military job board, a military transition newspaper, and military-only job fairs.

George launched his professional career serving in the US Navy as an avionics technician, was promoted to Chief Petty Officer and later was commissioned as a Naval Aerospace Maintenance Officer. He holds a BS in Electrical Engineering Technology from Excelsior College in Albany, NY. He lives in Cumming, Georgia.

Questions & Answers

1. Describe your journey from the service to your first job?

■ Deciding to change careers, depart from the U.S. Navy, even when considering I will have served 20 years in the Navy, was not an easy one for me. I was not quite halfway through (what I considered) my second career in the U.S. Navy; I served a little over the first half enlisted and the later as an officer.

However, after giving it significant thought, discussing the transition with my wife, and with mentors that supported me in the Navy, when I had about 18 months remaining to the 20-year mark, I made the decision I would move on from the Navy once I hit 20 years. I started my preparation right away.

2. How did you find your first job? Describe the process.

■ I decided to not just make a transition from the Navy, but to take advantage of the transition to launch a new career outside of aerospace. I was eager to learn something new and hopefully find a new career path that would excite me, and as I was planning my transition, I wasn't exactly sure what that new career that would be. I found my new career through a combination of networking and job fairs. Because I was open to pursuing something totally new to me, I found job fairs an excellent way to meet company recruiters and hiring managers, plus an efficient way to learn about a variety of career opportunities these companies were recruiting for. At a high-tech job fair in Atlanta, one of the companies suggested I investigate a recruiting opportunity they had open. Even though I had no recruiting experience, based on our conversation at the job fair as well as some competencies they assessed from my resume, they said I fit the mold of what they look for in a recruiter. I went home and began to research the industry; the more I learned, the more intrigued I became with recruiting as a potential new career.

I knew some companies focused on helping transitioning military professionals find exciting career opportunities and I determined a career in recruiting helping military-connected talent would be more rewarding for me, which I shared within my network.

I interviewed with a few military placement companies I found through my research, but networking led to interviews with the top two military placement firms. One of these companies offered me a role as a military placement specialist.

3. When did you start planning your transition? What actions/ activities did you take?

I started building my transition plan when I had 18 months left to serve. I reached out to friends and associates I worked with that had made the transition before me. Mostly I asked for their advice, what worked, what wasted time and any lessons learned they were willing to share. I Learned about the Transition Assistance Program (TAP) and signed up to participate.

I used the guidance from TAP, a book titled, "Ask the Headhunter," another book provided from TAP, "From Navy Blue to Corporate Grey," and guidance from my network, particularly those that had already made a successful transition. I found, "Ask the Headhunter," to be very valuable in setting up my transition plan—the book was written by an executive headhunter who wrote the book to show the layperson how an executive recruiter networks their way into businesses as well as how the recruiter prepares their candidates to win the job when given the opportunity. Concerning my resume, I used the books as well as examples provided through my network to fine-tune my resume.

4. Did you pursue any advanced degrees and/or certifications? Did they help?

At the time I did not pursue an advanced degree or certifications. Once I had determined the career path I wanted to pursue, there were no resources like this that would have impacted my search or results.

5. Why did you choose the work/career you are in?

As stated earlier, I was very open to considering multiple career fields. All I knew (initially as I started making my transition plans) is that I wanted a change from aerospace, and I was hoping to find a career where my rewards were proportional to my productivity. I had considered technical management opportunities, B2B sales, industrial training, and more. Once thwe recommendation had been made to me to consider recruiting, as stated earlier, the more I learned, the more intrigued I became. When doing my research in talent acquisition, one interesting nugget I came across concerning recruiting is that many people are attracted to the career field because of the money that can be made in the field, but more people fail than succeed in recruiting. That nugget grabbed my interest and was a motivator for me—my logic was if I can succeed in a field where most people fail, maybe it would prove to be a field where the rewards would be proportional to my productivity.

6. Have you encountered any obstacles in advancing your career?

■ Frankly, the only obstacle I have encountered when it came to advancing my career is me. One thing I have enjoyed is that promotions I have received were tied to my productivity, results, and demonstrated leadership, vs a rigid timeline as we experience in the military. I am confident I would be in a more senior position now if I had not moved from one employer to another. I was recruited away from employers to launch new recruiting-related opportunities that were appealing to me at the time, and it cost me advancement opportunities had I not moved from one company to another.

7. What were the 2 hardest efforts about transitioning?

■ An area I initially struggled with was trying not to be defensive about feedback concerning my resume. I remember doing my research and planning for my resume. I then put forth an effort to write the perfect resume that reflected my contributions, demonstrated my past successes as well as my potential. When friends took a red pen to it, initially it bothered me—this was my story and I was resistant to making changes to it.

However, I was relying on folks who had gone through this process before me and I realized they were sharing lessons learned that aided them in a successful transition and they wanted to help.

So, I learned to set aside my pride, review their feedback, and adjusted to succeed. The second part was learning to effectively network—not to be shy about announcing my transition and asking for help. Asking people to open doors for me, introduce me to the movers and shakers that held the keys to new career opportunities, and taking full advantage of opportunities like job fairs and visiting every single company participating in a job fair (vs just visiting the companies where I recognized their name) to learn about their organization and available careers.

8. What do you think are the top issues for Veterans transitioning into a career?

The top issue for most veterans is demonstrating you have the skills, or more importantly, the transferable skills to be successful in the role you are pursuing. When companies look at the military talent pool, often, the leadership skills of the military talent are what many companies are attracted to. However, because of the environment most military service members work and grow in, our learning agility is one of the top attributes military talent can bring to an organization. Veterans need to demonstrate their learning agility and ability to learn a role, a process, a system, etc quickly and make a timely positive impact if given the opportunity.

9. Do you believe there is a stereotype attached to being a Veteran in pursuit of a job?

There are stereotypes attached to being a veteran; some earned, some not. A stereotype, that is not true, but that I have heard multiple human resource professionals and hiring manager repeat is, "a veteran needs a structured environment to thrive, and our company just isn't like that. We're too relaxed and it just wouldn't be a good fit."

10. What question(s) would you have liked to have known before taking your first job?

Who has succeeded in a similar role I'm being considered for and what made them a success? Would it be possible to spend an hour with this person as part of the interview process?

11. What are the most important lessons you can share on making a successful job transition from the military?

1. Continue to make the job you're performing in the military your primary focus, until the day you leave the military.

However, once you decide you are going to make a transition from the military, make time, and start your planning and preparation right away. You cannot start too soon and if you delay your preparation, odds are you will struggle to make a successful transition.

2. Take advantage of TAP as soon as you're able and take it again if allowed. There is so much information provided during TAP, you'll pick up helpful guidance you may have missed the first time through it if allowed to attend it more than once.

3. Network, network, network. Learn what it means to effectively network and put it into practice. With resources like LinkedIn and other social media tools, your ability to network is now greatly expanded as compared to what it was just a few years ago. "No networking means not working."

12. If you could do it again, what would be the one thing you would do (better) or not do to help in your transition?

I'm sure there are many things I could have done better.

In fact, after most evolutions concerning the transition and job search process, I would go back and review my performance and ask the same questions; what went right, where can I make adjustments and improve, and what went wrong? I particularly used this process when I networked, when I talked to people about my transition plans, and when I interviewed. As a result, there is not one major thing that jumps out at me as the one thing I would have done better, or not do at all, but there were many very minor adjustments I made along the way—fine-tuning my elevator pitch, providing a better answer if asked that question again, try not to ramble but provide concise answers to questions, and look for opportunities to ask my own thought-provoking questions based on the interview or conversation, vs asking a rehearsed or planned question—be engaging and be genuine.

Charlie Black

Service Rank: Lieutenant Colonel, USMC

Position: Managing Partner

Industry: Advisory Services

Biography

Charlie is an engaging storyteller who artfully distills relevant insights to lead the audience to "see the world differently." He is a retired Marine Corps Officer with diverse experiences that span over three decades of service on four continents. Post military service his endeavors include the board room, C-Suite, educator and advising start-ups. His mission-focused leadership consistently enabled success in the most demanding and uncertain environments by building resilient and adaptive teams.

He often speaks on the disruptive, turbulent and unpredictable nature of our world and what is required to successfully navigate the fog of uncertainty, especially those in leadership positions. He is the Co-Founder and a Managing Partner at Xundis Global, LLC, which specializes in helping clients navigate complexity through creative application of design, strategy and planning to realize favorable futures. Additionally, he is a Non-Resident Fellow at the Joint Special Operations University co-leading applied research activities to meet emergent 21st century challenges.

Questions & Answers

1. **Describe your journey from the service to your first job?**

As I approached the end of active service my family and I began to explore what might be of interest after retirement to include where to live, life style, and type of future work. We really spent a good amount of time identifying what this really means to include salary, paid time off and other benefits. In the end, we framed key criteria from which we would later judge future employment opportunities. Concurrently I reached out to a large network of cop-workers and friends I had developed across industries. In particular, I had made close connections to private research companies that worked in the national security sector. This was of interest to me because I am a life-long learner, enjoy research as well as contributing in some way to the security of our country. We didn't have to take too many trips since my wife and I were familiar with the Mid-Atlantic. I think its critically important to appreciate the community within which you will live.

2. **How did you find your first job? Describe the process.**

The search for my first civilian position was found through my personal network. I found that the few job fairs that I did attend did not represent my interests. I was not simply looking for a job or replacement for income. I wanted to continue to explore and grow in areas of interest that would also provide income and opportunities for advancement. Therefore, I began to solicit those who knew me best, my friends and colleges, about unannounced opportunities that would be of interest and for which I was qualified. Moreover, those I trusted most and knew me best were in a position to sense how I might fit in various industry or positions. My friends would connect me with accomplished individuals to learn their unvarnished perspective so I could ask questions and gain deeper insights. This was most beneficial to rule out certain jobs so I could focus my search.

3. **When did you start planning your transition? What actions/ activities did you take?**

I began formally planning my transition a year from the date I expected to begin terminal leave. As an experienced planner, I approached my transition with the same rigor as I would a campaign plan. The first six months were used to survey the external market for opportunities that aligned with my goals. Additionally, I began to create a master resume that would be used to tell the story of my accomplishments, skills and value. I participated in several transition workshops and found them lacking a focus on those reaching retirement. They were more aligned with the younger service members transitioning after only a few years of service. Again, I used my external connections to give me insight into resume building and what was different in each industry. I also began to apply for positions I knew I was not fully qualified so I could participate in actual interviews and gain feedback on my resume and ability to interview. I found this to be extremely useful in both confidence and ability to communicate to hiring personnel.

4. Did you pursue any advanced degrees and/or certifications? Did they help?

I had completed two different graduate programs of study while on active duty. I found that an advanced degree was an key discriminator for many positions that I was considering after my retirement. Given that I desired to work in the National Security sector it increased my credibility and in most instances, was a requirement. Dependent upon the industry the advanced degree requirements were very different. If entering the general business sector most mid-level, and certainly those on track for senior positions had acquired an MBA. It was a barrier for entry to many management programs. However, in many start-ups and technology companies I found that tangible skills and experience far outweighed an advanced degree. This would usually include various types of certifications to demonstrate mastery of specific skill sets be that coding, IT and networking etc.

5. Why did you choose the work/career you are in?

I chose to remain associated with the National Security Sector because I felt I could continue to contribute to our nation's security through a different path. I had almost three decades of diverse experience combined with advanced education that aligned well with this area. I also chose my first position based on organizational values and culture. Beyond monetary benefits I wanted to work with people I shared a common perspective, and that I liked. Your transition is one time where you can decide on a path that shapes the type of people you will spend your day working.

6. Have you encountered any obstacles in advancing your career?

■ The civilian work environment is very different than I experienced in the military. First and foremost, there are significant biases and assumptions about military. One bias is that we are rigid, lack creative skills and are under educated. In fact, I found that most of my civilian peers were single faceted and did not enjoy the depth and breadth of experience and skills as my fellow veterans. We in the military are more generalists with skills that cross over various functional areas. Comparatively, many in the civilian sector especially larger corporations (except in small companies) have created siloes such an HR, Operations, or Supply Chain. Beyond fast tracking executives, few individuals have had much expose to or understand the unique requirements beyond there specified positions or role. As a military commander, I was responsibility for my people, their training, there day to day performance. What is bifurcated in many civilian organizations is the opposite in the military. I also found that veterans are more practical and direct- a bias for action. This can be misinterpreted, and in some instances viewed as an undesired attribute in a world where political correctness is often favored. This cognitive blinder can be overcome once a veteran becomes aware that their direct problem solving approach can be perceived as threatening.

7. What were the 2 hardest efforts about transitioning?

■ The most difficult point of my transition to civilian sector was the pace of work. While in uniform you are seldom afforded a 40-hour week and always accountable for the mission and your people. We are taught and practice that the mission has priority. In the larger world, this same work ethic can exist but within constraints of labor law related to salary, overtime, paid time off etc. It is important that your new co-workers did not take an oath and you should have no expectation for the commitment level required of a service member. They are simply different.

8. What do you think are the top issues for Veterans transitioning into a career?

I think the biggest challenge is for a veteran to "drop their tools" and over-riding identity as a service member. Take the hard-earned soft and hard skills, as well as experiences and translate them to the new industry and profession. Too often veterans have expectations based on their prior rank or position. Beyond being thankful for your willingness to serve, don't expect nor should you expect anyone to understand what you have lived. Build upon your strengths and skills, but also recognize you are in a new place with many things to learn. Assimilate into your new community and work place. Don't separate yourself, join the new team and adopt their perspective while never forgetting the past.

9. Do you believe there is a stereotype attached to being a Veteran in pursuit of a job?

The biggest stereo type is that we veterans are rigid thinkers and require pre-scriptive directions. I think this is due in large measure due to the decreasing number of Americans that have served or personally know someone that has served. Their ideas of the military come from film or books. My transition experience tells me this is quickly overcome when we veterans show initiative on a daily basis when we see problems – big or small.

10. What question(s) would you have liked to have known before taking your first job?

I think I would like to have known more clearly how my future boss intended me to fit into his larger plan for the organization. It took me months to dis-cover and learn which limited my ability to show initiative in the first year.

11. What are the most important lessons you can share on making a successful job transition from the military?

My three lessons are simple and follow the theme of my answers.

1. Do something you like and interests you.
2. Plan for and have balance in your life (you no longer serve selflessly).

3. Retain your sense of honesty, ethics and doing the right thing always.

12. If you could do it again, what would be the one thing you would do (better) or not do to help in your transition?

If I were given a "re-do," I would, from day one, start my own company founded on my values, oriented on an industry I enjoyed, and working with people I liked and trusted. I am there today, but it took my first three years in this journey to reach my goal. Take the risk and follow your passion.

Pete Blum

Service Rank: USN 87-91, PR3

Service Rank: USMC 91-98, Staff Sergeant

Position: Operations Manager

Industry: Healthcare

Biography

I am a Business Continuity and Information Technology Professional. A trainer, a mentor, a Certified Scrum Master, and a Scrum Product Owner. Aside from helping others understand and protect what is most important to them, I have a passion for enabling U.S. transitioning military, Veterans, and their families to be successful after the military.

I continuously promote Veteran outreach for multiple organizations as I believe in educating Veterans on the resources available, getting involved with the community, and growing their support network. I also educate companies on what it takes to hire and retain Veterans.

I train Veterans on LinkedIn, networking, career readiness, job searching, and starting a business. I also provide resume reviews, coaching/mentoring, and meaningful introductions. If you are transitioning or already separated from the US military and need assistance, just connect with me and ask.

Questions & Answers

1. Describe your journey from the service to your first job?

I think so many of us getting out of the military believe it is going to be easy. I know I did. After being deployed to different places in the world I knew one thing, I wanted to live by a beach. All the favorite places I have been stationed were warm and they had beaches. I think my favorite two were the Philippines and Australia. So probably a year before I decided to get out my biggest decision was choosing either Florida or California. In doing research I quickly found out the cost of living was higher in California which was not good, and that Florida did not have a state tax, which was great. I started planning a couple of months before I got out, I had decided not to reenlist and to pursue my desire to work in information technology (IT). So, I picked the city I wanted to live in, Tampa, I researched apartment and prices, picked a few in an area that looked great, and then I rented a U-Haul and drove from Virginia to Florida to start a life after the military in a state I had never even been to before. I knew where I was going and I knew what I wanted to do, and I had 30 days' terminal leave (out of the military while still getting paid for vacation time) to find a job.

2. How did you find your first job? Describe the process.

After getting settled into an apartment in a new state and city I jumped on the internet and started looking for a job in IT based on the area I had moved into. I used Google and searched for positions which brought me to websites like Monster or Indeed. I looked up sample resumes and used them to create one for myself. I applied to probably a dozen places. Some I never heard back from, a few others I went to an interview. I did land one of them within a couple of weeks, it was more of a low level, entry type of position.

3. When did you start planning your transition? What actions/ activities did you take?

I honestly thought it was going to be easy and did the worse thing possible which was to not prepare at all. I relied on my confidence and the fact that I had 30 days' terminal leave to get it done. I could relax, have fun, and explore the new city while looking for work. I did work on a resume during the 30 days, but it was not good. I did not know then about master resumes and tailored resumes, or even the best format. Do your research!

4. Did you pursue any advanced degrees and/or certifications? Did they help?

This was probably the one thing I did, almost right. I know I was eventually going to get out of the military and start a career in IT, and I knew I had to know more than just how to work on websites so while still in the military I signed up with Strayer University on the IT path and started by taking classes for Novell so that I could be certified in that as a Certified Novell Engineer (CNE). It was the dominant form of personal computer networking at the time so I knew having those skills would give me an edge in getting hired.

Later after getting out of the military when I realized Novell was not the dominant form of personal computer networking in the industry I used my GI Bill and went back to school at Phoenix University and started by taking classes for Microsoft so that I could be certified in that as a Microsoft Certified Solutions Expert (MCSE).

Both times I took these courses, the knowledge helped me to get into a position at a new company. One important thing to note is that some companies require a degree or a certification for the position and others do not, so if that was split 50/50 then with the degree you qualify for 100 of the jobs, without the degree you only qualify for 50% of the jobs.

5. Why did you choose the work/career you are in?

I have always loved information technology. As most of us can now see technology is the future and you can see it grow every day. While I was still in the Marines, I wanted to switch my job from logistics to information technology but that was not going to happen. It is not easy to change jobs within the military unless they determine there is a need. And I was told everyone wanted to get into IT so there were no positions available. So, after hours I worked at an internet coffee shop in Quantico Virginia called General Javas doing IT work. I worked on websites as well, that was back in the days of needing to know HTML.

6. Have you encountered any obstacles in advancing your career?

■ My biggest obstacles have always been not having a degree or certification. When I took IT classes for Certified Novell Engineer (CNE) and then later Microsoft Certified Solutions Expert (MCSE), both times I took the knowledge and got a job but did not follow through with getting a degree OR getting the associated certification that goes with the classes I took. That knowledge gets you so far but that's it. Also, knowledge is soon outdated which means new classes need to be taken. So, when that job ends it's like starting over and goes right back to needing a degree or certification to better my chances.

7. What were the 2 hardest efforts about transitioning?

■ **One is getting past the applicant tracking system.** Most people take the approach of applying online and blasting their resume out there to better their chances. It does not work. It leads to a loss of confidence and even depression. What happens is that it goes into a computer system and stays there, no one ever sees the resume at all. Your resume only gets pulled out of the black hole if a recruiter happens to do a search and ALL the keywords they use are on your resume.

The other is not knowing the right people. Many of us getting out of the military only know military people, besides our families back home. Networking is what gets you connected to people outside of the military. Connect daily with new people! My personal experience is LinkedIn is the best way. I believe in it so much that I teach that to transition veterans and spouses with Nancy Laine and Project Transition USA. Connect with people in the industry and companies that you are interested in. See who they are connected to and ask for introductions to others and then connect with them as well. The better your network, the better your chances of meeting the person who is going to hire you. Networking is what will get you hired!

8. What do you think are the top issues for Veterans transitioning into a career?

- **Outsourcing,** many companies outsource labor to other countries to save money. Many companies will do this with technical support or customer service, and even development.

- **Going to the cloud,** many companies go to the cloud to reduce their physical footprint. This saves the company the money on needing, managing, and updating servers, they need less square footage and can have a smaller building, they spend less on electricity and need fewer employees to manage and maintain IT.

- **Saturation vs need,** the IT industry is always changing and growing so research is needed to determine the best road to take when choosing what to do in IT. For instance, recently cybersecurity has been one of the most critical areas, needing the greatest influx of personnel, and that means higher pay. However, with everyone going for cybersecurity certifications, that means hundreds and hundreds of applications for the same positions. To beat this, you have to either research to find the next up and coming most needed skills, like in robotics or AI or, have other skills certifications to go along with what you are pursuing to make you stand out when going up against the competition.

- **Technology is always changing,** the best way to succeed in IT is to be a lifelong learner who believes in continued education. Stay up to date on current technology, research new technology trends. Learn about data analysis so you can better understand the future of IT.

9. Do you believe there is a stereotype attached to being a Veteran in pursuit of a job?

No. I have on occasion heard people say there is a stereotype of veterans being messed up, damaged, crazy, and aggressive. I have never in my life personally seen this with any company. Everyone I have talked to thinks that veterans are the best people to hire due to work ethics, leadership, they show up on time, and they get the job done. Companies also get a tax credit for hiring veterans, so all around I have heard, seen, and experienced a positive result around hiring veterans.

10. What question(s) would you have liked to have known before taking your first job?

What was the culture of the company and did that align with my own goals in life? There are two aspects to that. One is coming out of the military we are used to working in a team, so a great cultural fit would be a company that has that same mentality and a team environment where you can thrive.

The other aspect of the culture of the company has to do with its mission and the beliefs of the people that work there. Are they a culture of people trying to solve a world problem or just trying to sell a product? Is that culture something you see as a fit for yourself, where you can be happy? If not, you won't be there long.

Another question is about advancement and personal growth. Can you move up to another position after a certain amount of time or are you stuck where you started? When it comes to personal growth will the company send you to any training so you can increase your skills?

11. What are the most important lessons you can share on making a successful job transition from the military?

1. Have a degree or certification! In practically every circumstance where I applied for a position, even if I knew someone that worked there, and I didn't get the job, it was due to not having a degree or certification. It boils down to this, the competition is tough out there, many others are applying for the same job (sometimes hundreds, honestly). If the rest of the competition has a degree or certification and you do not, you lose. They will choose the one who has it. This especially goes for the higher level, higher-paid positions.

2. Network! The absolute best opportunities will come through networking! Sometimes jobs are never even posted but you can find them by networking. Networking can find you that person to give you insight into a company and potentially walk your resume to the recruiter or hiring manager and say this is the one you want. Networking can get you that introduction to the person that might hire you. When networking, ask those you know for introductions to others. Ask for infor-

mational interviews to learn about companies (do not ask for a job during them).

3. Ask! The number one thing I have found out is that you get nothing if you're not asking and people don't know and cannot guess your needs. When interviewing, ask questions about the company so that you can decide if it's a fit for you.

12. If you could do it again, what would be the one thing you would do (better) or not do to help in your transition?

When I got out this was not available, but I think it is the greatest opportunity possible that a veteran could take advantage of and that is the DOD Skill-Bridge program. When transitioning, with approval from your command, you can leave the military up to three months early and get a job at a qualified civilian company. This is a huge win/win situation. You are still getting paid by the military for that period and get to work for a company that you're interested in which lets you discover if you like that culture, that environment, that industry, basically getting your feet wet. And it is a benefit for the company as they do not have t pay you since the military is paying you, so they are motivated to bring you on board. The best part is if you and the company both feel it is a great match for you to work there after the time is up the transition is seamless as you are already established there. If you feel it is not a fit, you can start looking for something that is a fit before those three months are up while still gaining industry knowledge and connections.

You can apply for this program yourself and do all the work but there are organizations out there now that make it easy. They help you with the paperwork and they know the companies that are already part of this program. I suggest reaching out to Hiring Our Heroes if interested. They do a fantastic job. There are also programs out there for spouses and caregivers.

Diane Boettcher

Service Rank: Captain, USN

Position: Architect Manager

Industry: Software

Biography

Diane Boettcher is a strategic leader who takes organizations through change into high performance. An expert in IT, change management, and leadership, as well as military operations, Diane is an executive at Microsoft, leading a team of architects who support customers' digital transformations.

She is known for constantly raising the bar of performance and consistently adapting her organization to meet current and future needs. Diane has previously led various large network operations programs for U.S. Special Operations, the Joint Staff, working in the United States, Africa and Europe. She has assisted the Defense Information Systems Agency and the Navy with Knowledge Management and online collaborative decision-support software. While at Microsoft she has supported National security customers as well as being based in Singapore, supporting customers across several countries.

Retired from the US Navy after 30 years, Diane commanded five times and served a short tour in Kabul, Afghanistan. While on active duty, Diane served in Washington, DC, Spain, and Hawaii. She flew as a Naval Flight Officer with Fleet Reconnaissance Squadron One (VQ-1) in Guam, and is a qualified Information Warfare Officer.

Diane attended Marquette University, graduating with a BS in Economics. Her Master's degree in Information Assurance is from Norwich University. She holds the SANS GSLC certification, PMI's PMP certification, and the ITIL Foundations certification, and is a trained Lean Six Sigma Green Belt. She is a member of the Jesuit Honor Society, Alpha Sigma Nu.

Diane enjoys camping with her children's Scout groups. Diane's favorite and best mentor is her husband, a retired Marine and full-time, stay-at-home dad. They enjoy their East Coast home, and often travel and scuba dive with their three children.

Questions & Answers

1. Describe your journey from the service to your first job?

■ My preparation started a few years before I left the service, exploring the various professions available, and thinking about what I enjoyed doing most. At least two years prior to my transition, I volunteered for extra duties that would allow me to explore these professions and build the experiences and skills necessary to be successful.

As my transition date approached, I started attending job fairs and applying online.

2. How did you find your first job? Describe the process.

■ My first job was through a job fair. It was surprisingly easy in retrospect. I met with someone at the job fair, interviewed, and then was offered the position. At the same time, I must have gone on at least a dozen interviews, even for jobs that I knew weren't particularly good for me, just for the practice.

3. When did you start planning your transition? What actions/ activities did you take?

My preparation was mainly working on my resume and networking.

4. Did you pursue any advanced degrees and/or certifications? Did they help?

During my first transition, I didn't pursue any degrees or certifications. In hindsight, these would have been helpful.

5. Why did you choose the work/career you are in?

My current career field is in Information Technology, leading teams. As someone who grew up with technology, who loves to mentor and coach others, the role both takes advantage of my abilities and allows me to pursue my purpose.

6. Have you encountered any obstacles in advancing your career?

Oh, boy, have I encountered obstacles! My first boss lied to me – which I didn't even realize that people might do. Other bosses I've struggled to find the right cadence with.

7. What were the 2 hardest efforts about transitioning?

First, it's figuring out what I enjoy doing. For so many years, I had simply gone where I was told to go and did the job that was assigned to me. The first time my manager asked me if I was happy at work, I was genuinely confused. Nobody ever cared about whether I was happy at work before!

Second, it's recognizing how other people on the team are motivated and incentivized. In the military, we generally can agree to focus on the mission. In the civilian world, people often have a variety of equities and concerns that they are thinking about.

8. What do you think are the top issues for Veterans transitioning into a career?

Veterans need to understand how compensation packages work. Benefits like bonus eligibility, stock options, 401K matching, vacation, etc., are all part of the package. Many times, people get focused on the number that represents their base salary. Comp is much, much more than that.

9. Do you believe there is a stereotype attached to being a Veteran in pursuit of a job?

A bit. When I think of a Veteran, I usually think of someone who is so unsure of what they want to do, they're casting about, willing to do almost anything, without a clear sense of the value that they can create for an organization.

10. What question(s) would you have liked to have known before taking your first job?

I wish I would have known that culture and value alignment was more important than money. I assumed that the people at my first employer would share my values, and never even considered that they had a culture that was not well-suited for me.

11. What are the most important lessons you can share on making a successful job transition from the military?

1. Know what you're worth. Research and understand compensation packages. Your salary will only be a portion of what your compensation package will look like. Learn about stock options, equity, bonus eligibility. Know what the market is for people of your experience, education in your preferred location.

2. Know that you're interviewing the companies as much as they are interviewing you. Finding the right cultural fit the first time will save you from having to look again soon.

12. If you could do it again, what would be the one thing you would do (better) or not do to help in your transition?

I would care more about the culture than the money. I would know my worth. I would exit active duty debt-free.

Karen Bosco

Service Rank: Colonel, USAF

Position: Financial Consultant

Industry: Small Business Organizations

Biography

Karen was born and raised in Southern California. She graduated from the U.S. Air Force Academy and entered active duty in 1990. After assignments in Oklahoma, Italy, and California, she left active duty and joined the AF Reserves in 1999. She then deployed three times, twice for Operation Enduring Freedom, and once for Operation Iraqi Freedom. She forward deployed as the senior communicator onsite at the 2002 NATO Summit for Operation Combat Air Patrol (CAP) where she was responsible for direct lines of communication between the SECDEF and the onsite air component commander for NATO's Allied Forces North (AIRNORTH). At her second deployment, she was the senior U.S. communicator for the Kuwait City International Airport. Her last deployment supported the busiest and most complex airfield in the DOD at that time, leading the communication team responsible for the bed-down of the first Reaper UAV squadron in Iraq. Her Reserve assignments included 7 years as a commander and 3 years as the senior reservist for HQ Special Operations Command's Chief Information Officer and senior communicator.

Karen started her small business financial consulting in 2000 with clients primarily in construction, architecture, and landscaping. From 2006 to 2018, one of her clients hired her to run not only the finances but HR and client relations side of his construction business, which was her primary job. In 2018, she returned to full-time small business consulting. In addition to this work, she owns multiple properties and actively manages them. She currently resides in the San Francisco Bay Area with her dog Winston, a certified therapy dog who does VA Hospital visits.

Questions & Answers

1. Describe your journey from the service to your first job?

I've had two transitions, the first upon leaving active duty and joining the AF Reserve, and more recently after retiring from the AF Reserve. For my active duty transition, I had a short 120 days from my decision to getting out (I turned down an assignment). Although that sounded like a lot of time, it would have been great to have more time. Trying to turn over my current job, plan and then move, decide on a new career and with no future income, my situation was intimidating. I think a year or more would be ideal. It was a good two years before I had a solid monthly income that I could live off of without randomly having to dig into savings.

2. How did you find your first job? Describe the process.

I knew that I did not want to continue in my military career field (IT) so I was open to any idea. I initially went down the teaching route, taking the required test to start substitute teaching to see if I would like it.

Then an opportunity landed in my lap.

I was asked to help out a friend who was struggling with her business and dealing with the financial challenges as a small business owner. I ended up working with her for a few years, first for free than as a paid consultant.

I realized I enjoyed helping these types of owners and grew my business from that one opportunity. 20 years later and I'm still consulting. Starting my own new business, in a new town, with no connections took time, and thankfully I had a nice savings account to get me through the growth period. Being self-employed and coming from a set pay scale military environment, I struggled with determining how much to charge to my clients. When I researched the type of work I was doing, the pay range was very wide and I had no formal training so it was more difficult to justify to myself the higher range. I found for what I do, experience, and personal skills (especially getting along well with others) were far more important than the degrees I had or any I could have obtained for what I do.

3. When did you start planning your transition? What actions/activities did you take?

I took the required "separating the AF" classes but not as seriously as I should have. I do remember taking a personality test that identified what career fields would be a good fit. I found that very useful since it matched me with military and financial related jobs. There were some surprises which I found useful to consider as well. I don't remember a resume or interview class but I think those are now part of the training. For those who have done very few interviews, this is a must. I still struggle with the interview process to this day.

4. Did you pursue any advanced degrees and/or certifications? Did they help?

For most jobs, I think degrees and certifications are important but for what I ended up doing, I find my clients aren't interested in any paperwork, they want to see what I bring to the table. Although I am now considering getting certified on a piece of financial software.

Since I use the software with all my clients, I will benefit from the additional training as well as the networking/advertising that comes with the developer.

5. Why did you choose the work/career you are in?

My first goal in trying to find my future job was finding something I would enjoy, having a consistent income, and finally having quality free time. I knew early on that a corporate environment was not for me although I did not expect to be self-employed. I've also always enjoyed numbers and finance so combining these elements into a profession has been amazing. I find observing, coaching, and teaching business owners solid financial skills has been so rewarding. The added benefit is the flexibility of my work hours. I can work a larger number of hours one week or two then enjoy lots of quality time to go on small or larger trips. There are concrete examples of how my assistance has paid off.

I have one client who I started consulting within her kitchen with her 3-month-old next to us. Now she is running a multimillion-dollar environmental consulting company with employees and subcontractors, operating and traveling worldwide.

6. Have you encountered any obstacles in advancing your career?

■ Being told by others that I could make so much more money being in the corporate world and that I was worth more than I was charging. By choosing my new career, I was choosing quality free time versus working crazy hours for some huge corporation. I knew my choices meant that I would never make the income I could, but I had the flexibility and freedom to choose which was a higher priority and has remained that way.

Staying in the AF Reserves after active duty was a challenge for advancing my civilian career as well.

Since my clients tended to not have previous contact with the military, let alone hiring someone, there was a steep learning curve when I was activated and deployed a few times over the years. I realized after the first time that I needed a solid back up plan for my clients and a team of people who do what I do who were willing to take over for me. Growing that network of peers was key to future deployments and to keeping my consulting business strong and not having to rebuild each time.

7. What were the 2 hardest efforts about transitioning?

■ Self-motivation! I thought it would be great to work at home initially. What I realized is that I needed to work in person with my clients. I was more engaged and they got my undivided attention.

Having to go out and look for work was constantly a concern for the first few years.

Inconsistent income was a huge downside. I had definite seasons and once I realized I was super busy during certain months, I made sure to budget for the slower times.

8. What do you think are the top issues for Veterans transitioning into a career?

How to value yourself as an employee or contract worker? We were previously told our financial value by the set payscale based on rank. Turning a veteran's experience into a quantifiable amount is not as easy as I thought it would be. As I gained experience in my new field and my calendar filled up, learning to say no was easier to do. The first time I turned down a potential job was empowering. After meeting with the client, I knew that it would not be a good match for me. Having the confidence that other job opportunities would be just around the corner, was a turning point for me and the success of my business. I also found that potential clients who didn't question my rates were now valuing my time and effort in the same way I was valuing it.

9. Do you believe there is a stereotype attached to being a Veteran in pursuit of a job?

The assumption was that I already had my healthcare covered as a veteran and that I was receiving a retirement check so what I was paid could factor those financial benefits in.

Both of these are not pertinent to any discussion on what my pay should be. Living in an area with a very small military presence, most of who I interviewed did not understand what they would be gaining by hiring a veteran (experience, leadership, unusual skills, flexibility).

10. What question(s) would you have liked to have known before taking your first job?

How long would the transition period take?

Since I remained in the Reserves until retiring this year, I feel like my transition from active duty to civilian life occurred very slowly and there was never that day when I said to myself "I'm out". I think I'm adjusting more now that

I've retired to the idea that I won't be putting a uniform back on than I did back leaving active duty.

11. What are the most important lessons you can share on making a successful job transition from the military?

1. Organize everything early. You will have a lot to do in transitioning, so get things done as early as you can.

2. Don't assume you need to start your job right away. This might be the first time you have had a break from normal life. Take this time to breathe and relax before jumping into your next career.

3. Finances. Have a solid savings account. Your expenses in the first few months/year will be more than you budgeted for.

12. If you could do it again, what would be the one thing you would do (better) or not do to help in your transition?

I should have taken advantage of the training opportunities provided by the military before getting out and also taken some of the VA provided training. When I took the separation briefings, I just looked at it as a mandatory class to checkmark off instead of an opportunity to prepare.

Mike Callahan

Service Rank: Staff Sergeant, USAF

Position(s): HR Director, Director/ Adjunct Faculty

Industry: Information Technology, Higher Education

Biography

Mike Callahan was a Staff Sergeant in the USAF from 1967 to 1973. He supported the Bomb/Nav systems for the B-52 G and H aircraft and was stationed in Guam during the increased bombing runs toward the end of the Vietnam War. When he separated from the Air Force, he went to work for Electronic Data Systems and was trained to be a Systems Engineer. Ross Perot was hiring a lot of veterans during this period, and Mike was able to take advantage of that opportunity. He had recently earned his MBA while in the military and was well-positioned to launch his career upon graduation. He worked for EDS for 24 years at several locations in the US and Brazil.

Most recently, he was Director for the College of Business' Internship and Career Management Center at The University of Michigan – Dearborn for over 14 years. In that role, he worked with employers to develop challenging internship and job placement opportunities for Graduate and Undergraduate students in the College of Business and then worked with the students to help them develop the Skills and Knowledge, Track Record, and Relationship skills necessary to help them launch viable careers. Mike retired from this position in January 2020.

He currently is a Managing Partner with Callahan & Rose Consulting providing Career Planning and Change Management support to individuals and companies. He has recently completed a consulting engagement with the global business fraternity, AKPsi, helping them develop and implement leadership and career development processes for their members.

He has also written two books on Career Planning and Development. They are: I Inc., Career Planning and Personal Entrepreneurship and Tiger in the Office, How to Capitalize on Opportunity and Launch your Career.

Questions & Answers

1. Describe your journey from the service to your first job?

■ I served for two, 4-year enlistments. When I was originally discharged, I had done no preparation and struggled both in finding a job and a place in society. I wound up re-enlisting for four more years.

The second time was better but still not as good as it could have been. I secured a position with EDS before I was discharged, but I still was not completely prepared for civilian life. I actually considered re-enlisting one more time, but it was at the end of the Vietnam War and there were very few opportunities in the Air Force. I wound up staying with EDS for close to 25 years, but I have to admit that the first couple of years were pretty rough due to a strong desire to get back into my comfort zone in the military.

2. How did you find your first job? Describe the process.

■ I was going to college while on active duty under a program called Operation Bootstrap. I sent out approximately 100 applications, all hand-typed, and had gotten two favorable responses. One was with EDS and I wound up going with them. I had a phone interview and then they flew me to San Francisco for the final interview, where I was hired.

3. When did you start planning your transition? What actions/activities did you take?

My main plan was earning a bachelor's and master's degree while still in the service. I had no idea where they would take me, but I had the blind belief that I would do better with more formal education.

Other than securing the degrees, I did not do much more planning. I can remember thinking about being a manager, but not having any real idea of what a manager did. The only manager I had known was the manager of the local grocery store. I was only focusing on earning the degree and I guess I thought I would figure out what came next after I left the Air Force.

4. Did you pursue any advanced degrees and/or certifications? ▪ Did they help?

Yes. I did pursue my MBA while I was in the service. However, the main reason I did so was that there was a program whereby I could go to school, live in military housing, and not have to work for a year. It was such a great opportunity, that I could not pass it up. It was a program to recruit officers from enlisted ranks, but by the time I graduated, the need for more officers had diminished and so I was not moved into that role. Instead, I was able to separate based on my original timeline.

The irony is that I was well educated but there was no plan or strategy; nothing more than the blind belief that education would serve me in one way or the other.

5. Why did you choose the work/career you are in?
▪ While I was in the service, I was working to help set up a new computer system and wrote my master's thesis on that topic. When the opportunity came to work for EDS and be in the field of computer systems development, it seemed to make sense to continue in that kind of career field.

In hindsight, I realize that I fell into the opportunity more than actually choosing to do it.

They were hiring, and I needed a job and so I joined the company.

6. Have you encountered any obstacles in advancing your career?
▪ It has been close to 44 years since I separated from the Air Force and I have had three careers during that time. I worked for EDS for close to 25 years and lived in several locations in the US and Brazil. I had a very good career with them, but as the company grew, I did not expand my skill set, and hence

my value to the company diminished, and so I became obsolete and wound up leaving.

My second career was in Education where I worked for the University of Michigan – Dearborn as the Director of the Career Center for the College of Business. During this time, I wrote two books on Career Planning, developed a course on the subject, and counseled several students with their career aspirations. In hindsight, the time with EDS gave me great insight into how to do things correctly and what things to avoid regarding your career. That knowledge helped me in my second career very much.

In January of 2020, I retired from U of M – Dearborn and am now a full-time consultant helping people and companies be more empowered in the pursuit of their aspirations. The time in EDS and UM – Dearborn has prepared me to be more effective in the current role.

Overall, there have been many obstacles but as I take the time to look back on them, I have gained some valuable insight into how I can pursue a more viable career strategy as well as help others in their personal quests.

7. What were the 2 hardest efforts about transitioning?
- For me, the two hardest things I ran up against were:
  1. Letting go of the current way of doing things and
  2. Realizing that I am in control of my life.

It even took me a long time to realize those concepts when I left EDS.

I have found that I get tend to get into a role, become comfortable in it, and then choose to remain, even when things become difficult. I have only learned in the past 5-10 years how dis-empowering that idea is and the more I can let go when the time is right, try new things, and embrace change, the more I can realize what I am truly capable of creating.

8. What do you think are the top issues for Veterans transitioning into a career?
First, the challenge would be to know about the opportunities especially in

project management and information technology. Even though I worked in the IT field in the Air Force, seeing how I could make the transition was not always obvious.

The second challenge is what we all face. Namely, is a given opportunity a good match for my personal interests, and value that I can bring to the job market? It has to be more than just finding a job. It is all about finding a career, or even a calling, and military personnel is just not introduced to these concepts while they are still on active duty.

9. Do you believe there is a stereotype attached to being a Veteran in pursuit of a job?

I never thought much about this question. I always felt accepted in my first job but it probably was due to the fact that many of the people around me, including many of the senior leaders, were all vets. I had one manager tell me that working for EDS was just like the military. You just did not wear your rank on your arm or have a name tag, but even the idea of a uniform was consistent. We all wore suits with white shirts. Not much variation in the clothing area.

10. What question(s) would you have liked to have known before taking your first job?

It would have been to know that I can fail and it will not be the end of the world. It is such a new experience and the fear of failure is very powerful. I came to grips with that idea after I had been with them for about a year, but earlier on might have made things a little less stressful.

11. What are the most important lessons you can share on making a successful job transition from the military?

1. Take some time to truly know yourself. Look at how you deal with change. Think about how empowered you feel. Have a strategy to continue to grow and improve your mental attitude.

2. Take control and instead of looking for someone to hire you, pull together your own idea of a perfect job description, and then look for opportunities where that job description would be valued.

3. Learn to tell a compelling story about who you are, the value you bring to a given opportunity, and what you can do to help someone else with their problems. Don't make it about you. Make it about how you can help someone else.

12. If you could do it again, what would be the one thing you would do (better) or not do to help in your transition?

It sounds pretty simple but I would have tried to cut back on the number of changes going on in my life.

We were pregnant with our second child and we would not have wanted that to change and the job I went into was fine.

However, with all of this change, we also moved to a new city (San Francisco) which is a great place to visit but it is hard to live where you have a 2-hour commute one way.

I think it was a combination of factors and if I had attempted to live closer to my home or in an area more consistent with my prior experiences, things might have gone better.

Everyone is different, but I would strive to reduce the number of stressors in one's life while they are going through this change.

Aldo (Al) R. Calvi

Service rank: Colonel, USA

Position: Project Manager / Senior Engineer

Industry: Department of Defense
(DoD) Contractor

Biography

Mr. Al Calvi is currently serving the PMI (Project Management Institute) volunteer role as the Region 14 Mentor supporting 24 PMI Chapters in Alabama, Florida, Georgia, South Carolina, Tennessee, Jamaica, and Southern Caribbean. He is also the PMI North American Military Liaison Program Champion working with various PMI Chapters promoting military to civilian project management career transition efforts.

Prior to his 2016 retirement, Mr. Al Calvi was the site lead engineer and project manager for the CACI Inc. INSCOM (Intelligence and Security Command) Genesis contract. He has over forty years of project management, engineering, military, and industrial experience in support of US Army active duty, reserves, National Guard, civil affairs, military intelligence, inspector general, and mission-critical IT equipment.

Before joining CACI in early 2005, Mr. Calvi was serving in an active duty assignment in Ft. McPherson, GA as a US Army Reserves Colonel with Army Central Command C9 Civil Military Operations.

Mr. Calvi US Army assignments included; 352nd Civil Affairs Command Chief of staff Task Force Commander during Operation Iraqi Freedom combat operations, 401st Civil Affairs Battalion Commander, 98th Division

Assistant Inspector General, certified military instructor, and 82nd Airborne Division Combat Engineer & Maintenance Officer.

Concurrent with his US Army Reserves career and before joining CACI Inc., Mr. Calvi held key project management and senior mechanical engineering positions at Eastman Kodak Company during his twenty-four-year tenure with the Fortune 500 Company. Mr. Calvi was the senior facilities management group executive with the Heidelberg and Kodak joint venture Heidelberg Digital LLC supporting the new $250 million digital color print equipment manufacturing market.

Mr. Calvi is a graduate of the University of Virginia with a bachelor's degree in Mechanical Engineering, a graduate of Rochester Institute of Technology with a master's degree in Manufacturing Management and Leadership, and a graduate of Colorado Technical University with a master's degree in Information Systems Security. Mr. Calvi is a certified Project Management Professional (PMP), and a registered professional engineer (PE) in the state of Georgia.

Questions & Answers

1. Describe your journey from the service to your first job?

■ I started planning my military to civilian transition approximately seven months prior to my release from active duty from the US Army Reserves being part of Operation Iraqi Freedom. After my interview with the VA counselors as part of my out-processing, I went to a professional resume writer and career guidance counselor. I also networked with a few professional organizations, the American Society of Heating & Refrigeration Engineers (ASHRAE) and the American Society for Quality (ASQ) for potential career transition. I estimate it took almost 12 months to prepare, plan, and execute my military to civilian career transition. Even with the 12-month planning efforts, I was still unemployed for nearly six months before finally finding a civilian career.

2. How did you find your first job? Describe the process.

■ After attending around a dozen job fairs and networking events, it took me about six months of unemployment to finally find a job, but it was my willingness to relocate from Atlanta to Augusta, GA at Fort Gordon to finally land the career of my choice.

3. When did you start planning your transition? What actions/ activities did you take?

My situation may be a bit different from other regularly retiring active duty career service members who are transitioning into the civilian workforce. I was a US Army Reservist who was activated in December 2002 in support of Operation Iraqi Freedom. At the time, I was ending a 24-year career with the Eastman Kodak Company through an early retirement program. Therefore, I knew that at the end of my activation in early 2004, I would be coming off active duty and facing a mandatory retirement date (MRD) of thirty years' military service in the US Army. At the time of my redeployment to the states, I was able to finish my military career by working as a liaison officer with Army Central Command at Ft. McPherson, GA until my MRD in July 2004.

So, the answer to the question is I started planning my transition from the military and retired Kodak career around six months until my MRD. Even then I was four months until I was able to secure a cleared TS/SCI position with CACI in Ft. Gordon, GA. It was my networking with other military veterans that helped me secure the position with CACI.

4. Did you pursue any advanced degrees and/or certifications? Did they help?

After finally getting my job at Ft. Gordon as a DoD Contractor with CACI, I used the CACI tuition reimbursement program to get a Master's Degree in Information Systems Security. It was my military experience, TS/SCI clearance, and civilian engineering degree that finally helped me find the career I wanted. Also, joining CACI was beneficial as an extremely Veteran Friendly company with many prior service employees and managers.

5. Why did you choose the work/career you are in?

■ I chose the IT/Project Management/Cybersecurity career field since much of my professional experience and educational background in that particular skill set. It was also very beneficial to my future employer's goals and objectives.

6. Have you encountered any obstacles in advancing your career?

■ Some obstacles I have faced in my career was moving from various job locations and establishing my professional and personal connections. As a DoD contractor, many career advancements had to involve either relocation to another geographical location with the same company or switch companies to maintain the same location but advanced career opportunity.

7. What were the 2 hardest efforts about transitioning?

■ The hardest two efforts about transitioning I found was finding a reliable network in the location I was trying to secure employment in the Atlanta area. The US army did their best to prepare me for my transition back to the workforce after my deployment, but finding employment in a new city with few professional contacts was very difficult. I found that many of the good jobs available were already filled with experienced professionals with contacts in the area.

The other effort I quickly realized that it was all up to me to find employment on my own. The effort of looking for a job turned out to be a job in itself with hours of preparation, calling individuals, and set hours of employment for my job search. I was very fortunate to find a career with CACI that perfectly matched my professional engineering and military experiences.

8. What do you think are the top issues for Veterans transitioning into a career?

One of the main issues for transitioning military veterans is to understand the various career paths and connections needed to move forward in their careers. In the military, career planning, education, job assignments, and rank achievement are very clear cut. In a civilian career, paths, job assignments, and duties are not as straightforward as they are in the military.

9. Do you believe there is a stereotype attached to being a Veteran in pursuit of a job?

I think there are certain higher expectations and ethical standards associated with being a veteran. However, there can be an underlying "bias" with those without a military background and a certain sense of "professional jealousy" in the civilian workforce.

10. What question(s) would you have liked to have known before taking your first job?

I wish I had known about the value of networking and getting to know professionals in the PM/IT/Cyber field. I also wished I could have started my job search and networking opportunities earlier from my military release date from active duty. I thought with an advanced degree, a military background, and an engineering credentials, I would have no problems finding a job. That did NOT turn out to be the case!

11. What are the most important lessons you can share on making a successful job transition from the military?

1. No one cares about your rank, so drop the military jargon, examples, and war stories.

2. It's not about you, it's about the business!

3. Military values and goals are very different from civilian business goals. But, many of the tools techniques are the same, just called different names.

12. If you could do it again, what would be the one thing you would do (better) or not do to help in your transition?

If I had to do it all over again, I would employ more online searches and networking opportunities such as: Job postings, Indeed, Linked In, others. I also would "drop the ego", listen more, and try to match my talents to the company's needs. Replace "I need a job" with "this is how I can help achieve your business goals"!

Stephen P. Corcoran

Service rank: Colonel, USMC

Position: Chief of Cyber Strategy

Industry: Cyber Software

Biography

Colonel Steve Corcoran retired from the United States Marine Corps in 2012. During his 28 years of active service, he commanded from the Platoon to Regimental level, contributed significantly to numerous wars and operations, and was recognized for distinguished service in combat and peacetime. Additionally, Steve served numerous tours at sea with Marine Expeditionary Units (Special Operations Capable), with Marine Air Ground Task Forces in Panama, the Balkans, Somalia, and Iraq. He served in positions of National significance with United States Central Command and with Joint Special Operations Task Forces in Iraq, Afghanistan, Pakistan and Horn of Africa. He attended every level of service school attaining academic honors, two advanced degrees, and was an instructor at the Expeditionary Warfare School.

Since retiring in 2012, Steve has been the Chief of Cyber Strategy for the Telos Corporation. In this role, he assists the Special Operations Community and the Intelligence Community with special mission applications and support. He is listed as a co-inventor for two proprietary software applications owned by the Telos Corporation.

Questions & Answers

1. Describe your journey from the service to your first job?

I was very fortunate to attend the USMC senior officer transition seminar about 18 months from retirement. The key points that I took away from the seminar were:

- Understand the VA programs and process
- Prepare your resume.
- Prepare your professional clothing
- Prepare your finances and prepare for a different tax situation.

I took about 4 months after retirement to research and learn about the industry that I was targeting (It/Cyber).

To best prepare for my transition, I did the following analysis and research:

- Find trusted individuals in small, medium, and large companies in the areas that you are interested in. Ask all the questions you can. In the beginning phases, I always told people that "I am not looking for a job from you I am looking to learn about the business and get your views on your experiences in company X" If you have the opportunity, talk to the CEO to the janitor.

- Regarding work-life balance, there were non-negotiable things to me. As an example; I wanted control over my schedule from the daily to the weekly to the travel when and where. That was number one for me and prioritized the money question for me.

- Value - I looked at it this way - I don't know *&$t about business but I know a lot about X and Y. I deeply respect professional businessman and I had no illusions that leaving the USMC with multiple commands, handling lots of money, people and things qualified me to be a business peer. "Lt Blatz" is not my equal because he joined the team. It was important for me to find an organization that respected what I did and what I know and one that I could readily reciprocate that respect. Finance is the lifeblood of business and I have no desire to crack my head against the wall to master it. If you think of yourself as a functional attachment to an organization, that might help you find a fit. I say this because I have watched guys get out and get very frustrated that they were not asked to run the company the second day. There are exceptional leaders in business and I am blessed with a great chain of command with solid and self-confident leaders.

- Salary - Location matters. Companies that are in Tampa with a large presence pretty much have a defined range. Companies with no presence in Tampa operate a little differently. In Tampa, big companies have a set range and they are pretty comparable. Medium-size companies tend to be more flexible and they will work with you depending on how you break out your priorities in. Small companies are a crapshoot and they come with more downsides than up unless a; you receive an equity position upfront or it is based upon performance.

2. How did you find your first job? Describe the process.
■ I was very fortunate to have had a vast network of resources and the time to carefully look at opportunities. I found the process to be educational and relaxed.

3. When did you start planning your transition? What actions/activities did you take?
1. 3 Months out - Clear Medical/process VA medical documents.
2. Retire
3. 1 Month completely off
4. 2nd-month draft resume
5. 3rd-month network and research
6. 4th-month interview/refine resume

4. Did you pursue any advanced degrees and/or certifications? Did they help?
I was very fortunate to have the experience, two advanced degrees, certifications, and training that fully qualified me for the position that I was interested in (Senior Executive).

5. Why did you choose the work/career you are in?
■ I found in my research that many industries and companies were actively seeking my skills and experience.

6. Have you encountered any obstacles in advancing your career?
■ No. I prepared well.

7. What were the 2 hardest efforts about transitioning?
■

1. Consensus-based leadership vice direct non- consensus leadership. The transitioning veteran would be very well served working hard to develop the skills to work in a collaborative environment where consensus is more important than expediency.

2. The pace.........it slows considerably.

8. What do you think are the top issues for Veterans transitioning into a career?

• Certifications and experience trump education. Everyone does not need a degree unless they want to manage (People/Money/Projects).

• Failure to assimilate. Every company has a culture and it is not going to change for the veteran community.

9. Do you believe there is a stereotype attached to being a Veteran in pursuit of a job?
My experience has been veterans are actively sought for many positions within a company. I would say there is a positive stereotype in the industry in regards to the veteran community.

10. What question(s) would you have liked to have known before taking your first job?
By talking to a lot of people as I transitioned, I came up with some simple rules:

• No companies owned by venture capital. They will mortgage tomorrow to make numbers today.

• No Rolodex companies. Those companies with a habit of pressing you for your contacts and pressing you for access.

- Believe in what they do and how they do it.

- Stable financials (these are all available online)

- Stable and positive leadership structure.

- Low turnover rate from the top to the bottom.

- Knowing someone in the company

- Understanding that all things are negotiable and figuring out my strategy ahead of time.

- Understanding the JAG/Ethics requirements for post-retirement employment.

- Went to ground and took the time to research the area that I wanted to work in (Cyber) I established a new rule the day I walked away from command; what I say and think should not be followed without solid and defensible rationale. Everything I propose or suggest is academically/operationally defensible and I can align it and produce it on demand. I am not knowledgeable only because I am an experienced Colonel, I am also knowledgeable because I have studied, researched, and produced the synthesis and rationale. Having the opportunity to do one thing well and understand it at the DNA level has been refreshing. That was huge when I was interviewing and it got the attention of a few people. I still follow it and it has helped me establish credibility on another plane.

11. What are the most important lessons you can share on making a successful job transition from the military?

1. Talk to an accountant and had a plan for taxes. It will be a frozen mullet smacked across your face if you are not prepared. It's not SBP as a big decision, it is taxes as your big decision. This factor goes into compensation #5 below.

2. Cleared medical both active and VA before leaving active duty.

3. Took a break for a couple of months (coached swimming and helped the boys with school) to let the dust settle and figure some stuff out. Don't overdrive the timeline and try to have all your ducks lined up in

a neat row. Corporations work on a totally different time/space concept and it takes some getting used to. Their fast is our slow or glacial.

4. Gave myself the time to evaluate options and opportunities.

5. Learned about compensation and how to structure my own package. I prioritized what was most important and what was negotiable and what was not negotiable. For example; I figured my base salary at a high number and a low number. My strategy was to only work in that range and if in it, to trade money for time, equity, 401 K higher percentage or other things as the situations came up. This was huge and it paid off big for me. This goes hand in hand with the points about value determination. Lead with the high number and work from there.

12. If you could do it again, what would be the one thing you would do (better) or not do to help in your transition?

- Organize your constellation of experts - No one person or book has the answer. Search for stars and plug them into your own constellation. Every time I talked to someone I learned a little bit more. I still don't have the complete picture and continue to learn.

- Figure out the big questions:

- Ratio of work to life - You can drive this but it is caveated with the following:

- How much money you need to earn and where do you want to live? Also, consider how much money you want. Now figure out your value.

- Value is in the eye of two beholders; you and the organization you seek to get the package you want. Simply put, it is lining up the front and rear sight on the target you want. No front sight alignment and you get nowhere. The following was Pablum most people ask what will the market bear and what should I ask? To follow.

- What type of work won't you consider - If you are like me, you more than likely know more about what you don't want to do rather than what you want at the point where you are now.

Claire Cuccio

Service rank: Colonel, USA

Position: President & CEO

Industry: IT Services

Biography

Claire has over 29 years of military expertise and experience in Cyber, Network Operations, IT R&D, and as a Congressional Liaison while serving as a US Army Officer (Colonel, ret). She has deployments to Southwest Asia as the Director of the Southwest Asia Regional Cyber Center, Camp Arifjan, Kuwait, and Director for Congressional Affairs for Headquarters, Resolute Support, Kabul, Afghanistan.

She also held several executive-level cyber and information technology jobs in the Department of Defense which include Chief of Staff and Assistant Chief of Staff, G3 for the 311th Theater Signal Command, Fort Shafter, HI, and Deputy Director for Cyber at Office of the Undersecretary of Defense for Acquisition, Technology, and Logistics (OUSD AT&L).

Claire earned a B.S. in Computer Science from Siena College, six Masters Degrees, and a Ph.D. in Science and Technology Studies from Virginia Tech. She is an Adjunct Professor at the University of Maryland Global Campus for the Master's Degree in Cybersecurity, was a big proponent of Sisters in Arms, and serves on the Girl Scouts Nation's Capital Advisory Board.

Questions & Answers

1. Describe your journey from the service to your first job?

I thought I was going to transition in 2014. I was tired of moving and thought I would settle down in DC and do something else. I owned a townhouse, had a nice circle of friends and as a Colonel, I was satisfied that I had gone as far as I was going to go in the military. I went through TAP (Transition Assistance Program), started a resume, and looked into the painful process of buying civilian clothes. After 25 years in uniform, I was not looking forward to choosing clothes and styling my hair. Then, I unexpectedly got remarried and my husband PCSed to JBLM in Washington State. My choice was to PCS or retire. I could not find a position within my MOS at JBLM, so I took one for the team and moved to Hawaii and worked to move my husband there with the help of a mentor. After four years in paradise (with one spent in Afghanistan), I retired out of Hawaii on the USS Missouri and PCSed back to DC with my husband who is now stationed at the Pentagon. I went through TAP again in Hawaii and almost finished my resume. Overnight, I went from Army Colonel to Army Wife.

2. How did you find your first job? Describe the process.

Four months before my retirement ceremony, I sent my draft resume for review to three people from my first unit in the Army, 73rd Signal Battalion (Pirmasens, Germany) who were already retired and successful in the government contracting world in DC. Two sent me back input on my resume and one said, "Pretty impressive resume. If you want to be a CEO, give me a call." I was supposed to be TDY in DC the next month so made an arrangement to meet and talk about it. It was easy to commit to since I have known my business partner for 30 years and he is one of the nicest, most honest, intelligent people I know. I knew he would help me with my transition and teach me what I needed to know about the business. That being said, I had no idea what I was getting into and what the life of a government contractor would be like. It was a whole new culture and I felt like a 2LT again. I never did finish that resume.

3. When did you start planning your transition? What actions activities did you take?

To prepare for my transition, I went to TAP twice and I talked to people who had already transitioned that were working in my unit in Hawaii. I asked people, "What is the one thing you wish you knew before your transition?" I probably asked 30 people that question and each person had a different answer. I learned a lot from that drill of the pitfalls and areas to concentrate on so I would not make the same mistakes. I also read a book by a retired USAF Colonel, Curt Weldon called *Well and Faithfully Discharged, Financial TTP for Military Veterans*. I still reread that book every six months and each time I learn something new. I highly recommend it.

4. Did you pursue any advanced degrees and/or certifications? Did they help?

Before I retired, I earned a Ph.D. from Virginia Tech. The new GI Bill came out which is an incredible benefit, and I did not have any children to pass it to. I did not want to leave money on the table and I wanted to allow my parents to call someone in the family doctor...In doing that, I gave up the opportunity to earn certifications while on active duty. I wish I had taken the time to get a PMP and a CISSP, but after the Ph.D., I was tired and done with school. As an IT business owner, I would encourage people to get their certifications before or during transition, especially if they are in the IT/Cybersecurity sector. They are a barrier to entry for the senior positions and a "must-have" if you want to work for the government.

5. Why did you choose the work/career you are in?

I chose Computer Science as an area of study in college back in the mid-'80s. As a 17-year-old, I had no idea what I wanted to major in and my Dad told me, "Computers are the wave of the future. If you are not there, you are missing out." So, I signed up for Computer Science. I wanted to quit a million times because I wanted to socialize in college and not spend 40 hours/week working on computer programs. I had an ROTC scholarship and my military instructor told me I had to stick it out in Computer Science. So, I did and I am thankful to him for forcing me to do it.

6.

Have you encountered any obstacles in advancing your career?

■ I think in the 80's and early '90s, the Army was very focused on Divisions and tactical units. I was sent to a fixed station Signal Unit as my first unit and without a lot of field experience, was not looked at as someone with value to add, especially when later reporting to Fort Bragg. Somewhere in the late '90s, it became fashionable to know TCP/IP and know-how to put together networks, and all of a sudden, the computer nerd was part of the cool crowd. I also had some great mentors along the way who ensured I was at least given opportunities and a chance to prove myself.

7.

What were the 2 hardest efforts about transitioning?

■ The two hardest efforts about transitioning to civilian work was (1) learning a new culture and (2) learning how to sell. The government consulting culture is very similar to the military, where there are leaders that have been around a while and successful, there are definite cliques, and it is hard to break in when people have already formed relationships. You have to understand the culture, find some champions, and find yourself a niche within the available work. The second is that all business development is selling. You are selling yourself, you are selling your company, and you are selling your ability to be a good partner. In the military, our customers are built-in. There were plenty of people who want to use the network and they have to abide by the rules set by those who run the network. I hear many transitioning veterans say, "I do not want to sell anything." It seems to me unless you become a government civilian, it is all selling, even if you are working in an operations position- you have to believe in your company (and yourself), you have to be able to keep your customer happy and sell your company.

8.

What do you think are the top issues for Veterans transitioning into a career?

I think the biggest issue for a veteran is the hierarchical structure that exists in the military is not quite the model of the civilian world. In the military, promotions are not only based on merit but on time served and promotion boards and standards are predictable. In the civilian world, a niche skill, the ability to get along with the boss, or being in the right place at the right time can get you ahead. So, can hustling. In the military, besides as a 2LT, many times your boss is older and wiser than you. Not so in the civilian world and as a 50-year-old retiree, you may be working for a 30-year-old client and have to be OK with that.

9. Do you believe there is a stereotype attached to being a Veteran in pursuit of a job?

As a business owner, I actively seek veteran employees. I got my company involved with Hiring Our Heroes, Military Friendly Employers, and Virginia Values Veterans. 50% of my current employees are veterans. I know and appreciate the value and work ethic a veteran possesses. However, I have some business acquaintances who think veterans rest on their past accomplishments, are too aggressive and/or pushy, and tell too many war stories about how the way they performed a job in the military was far superior to the way their company approaches the work. They think veterans are arrogant and always one-upping whatever story they are telling with tales of jumping out of planes, driving tanks, serving in third world countries, and saving the world. Which are all probably true, but you have to tone it down when you work with civilians who have not done all the fun stuff we have.

10. What question(s) would you have liked to have known before taking your first job?

What I wished I understood before taking this job was what the difference between working for a small company vs a mid-size or large company. I wish I had talked to people in all three of these situations a truly understood what I was getting myself into. It probably would not have changed what I did, but I would have gone into with eyes wide open.

11. What are the most important lessons you can share on making a successful job transition from the military?

1. Talk to as many veterans in your field as you can and ask them if they are happy with their transition decisions.

2. Focus on your family first. Retirement is a second chance at being a better parent or spouse, and work will survive without you on special occasions.

3. Learn how to negotiate your benefits – it's all negotiable and you are worth more than you think. Talk to a trusted advisor (that you will not work for) in your field and figure out your going rate. Check it on glassdoor and other job sites. Remember, the highest paying job, may not be the most rewarding, figure out what is also important – i.e. time off, 401K matching, health care, work from home, etc.

12. If you could do it again, what would be the one thing you would do (better) or not do to help in your transition?

I squandered the opportunity to get my PMP from the Syracuse Onward to Opportunity program. I started it before I left Hawaii and thought I would have time to finish it while I was PCSing, buying a new house, moving in, and starting a new job. I wish I had waited until I was stable in my living and job situation and then could put the time in to get the certification. I ran out of time and was removed from the program. I overestimated my ability to focus during the transition and left money on the table.

Dr. Wanda Curlee

Service rank: Lieutenant Commander, USN

Position: Program Director & Consultant

Industry: Academia/Consulting

Biography

D r. Wanda Curlee is the Program Director of Business Administration, at American Public University. Her business career spans over thirty years in several industries, including IT, Government, Insurance, Telecommunications, and Consulting. Dr. Curlee is active with the Project Management Institute's certification and standards teams and serves on the Ethics Review Committee. She served on the Requirements Practice Guide and Program Management Standard (4th edition) core teams and was part of the team that developed the Portfolio Management Professional (PfMP) certification. Dr. Curlee has published three books; two delve into complexity theory and one is about virtual PMOs. She has earned four PMI credentials: PfMP, PgMP, PMP and PMI-RMP.

She is proud to be the mother of three children who have served or currently serve for the U.S. Military. She met her husband, Steve, while both were serving in the U.S. Navy.

Questions & Answers

1. Describe your journey from the service to your first job?

When I was in the Navy, there was no formalized transition process.

My husband and I decided that when we exited the Navy (we were to separate within a couple of months of each other), whoever found the best paying job, that would be the path we would follow. So, I guess we started the transition planning about five months before leaving the Navy. The time we allowed was much too short, but what did we know as there was no one to guide us through the process.

My husband found a better paying position, and we were grateful because we separated during a rather big recession. Trying to find a job once I had separated was futile. I decided to go back to school and study to be a nurse. During that time, we did not have the GI Bill. My education came out of our pocket.

While I was in nursing school, I did stay in the Naval Reserve. As I was starting my last year of nursing school, my husband was transferred. Do not feel sorry. It was great, as you will see later in this story. We moved from upstate New York to North Carolina. It took me about two years to find my first job.

2. How did you find your first job? Describe the process.

■ Finding my first job was painful and a long road. I was in nursing school and had to give that up when we went to North Carolina. I was heartbroken but knew I had to do it. Remember, I said I was in the Naval Reserves. I was an Intelligence Officer, and my clearances were still active. I had no idea that they were valuable. My husband's company was looking for individuals with clearances for a new contract that it had won. I did not have any other skills that the company was looking for at the time, but clearances were valuable, and I learned that the leadership in the company was willing to train me.

This job trained me to become a project manager. The training was excellent, and I could not have asked for a better career for me. I have been a project manager with more in-depth responsibility as time went on. I ended up volunteering many hours with the Project Management Institute, which led to other job offers and friendships that have lasted over 20 years.

I also continued my studies, which ultimately led to a doctorate and a parallel career in academia.

3. When did you start planning your transition? What actions/activities did you take?

I naively started my transition about five months before I exited the Navy. In those days, you had to mail (US Snail Mail) a resume with a cover letter to companies. I am sure I sent over a thousand resumes. There were no career fairs or a place you could go to find job openings, except to go to the company itself. That was a lot of driving or just sending your resume to the Human Resources department and hoping and praying. If you were lucky, you might have a buddy that worked at the company who could give you names to send your resume to for a more personal response.

In those days, most junior employees would not forward, or hand carry a resume to their boss or the human resources department. Things were just different in the early '80s. I even used some of my dad's contacts, and I would hear back from them, but it was usually we have nothing, or you will hear from my human resource department if there are any openings.

The only replies I received back from companies were rejection letters. However, I did hear from several three-letter government agencies that were interested in my clearances and the fact that I am fluent in Spanish. Unfortunately, I did not make the connection that my clearances were valuable.

4. Did you pursue any advanced degrees and/or certifications? Did they help?

When I first transitioned to civilian life, I was unable to find a job. I decided to go to Nursing school, and I also studied to become an EMT. Because of a move, I did not finish nursing school, but I did become a volunteer EMT. After our family's move, I was able to find a position with AT&T. There I had the opportunity to advance my education. Because of the work I did, I decided to pursue an MBA in technology management.

Following my MBA, I decided I wanted to pursue a doctorate. I decided to do so because I wanted a backup to my corporate job. I started teaching online. With a terminal degree, the teaching opportunities would be greater. During future recessions, I always had some employment because I was teaching as an adjunct.

I would highly recommend at least a master's degree in an area like your career. Doing this demonstrates your commitment to your discipline and shows initiative to your employer.

As a project manager, it was important to become certified. Early in my career as a project manager, I was certified through the Project Management Institute as a Project Management Professional (PMP). Throughout my career, I have continued to pursue advanced certifications in project management. Demonstrating your expertise through certifications in your field helps to distinguish yourself from others who may be applying for the same opportunity.

5. Why did you choose the work/career you are in?

It was not a choice. I am what is called an accidental project manager. Unbeknownst to me, project management is what junior officers and senior enlisted do in their daily lives. Project management was familiar to me. When I started studying project management and what it entailed, a light bulb went off in my mind. Being a project manager comes naturally to me, and I had an enthusiasm for it. I decided to continue in the career path but always keeping my parallel career, academia, up to date as well.

Today, I still consult in project management, but my primary career is now in academia. I oversee an MBA program. At this point in my life, giving back to those pursuing their educational pursuits is most fulfilling and rewarding.

6. Have you encountered any obstacles in advancing your career?

Yes. As I have mentioned before, finding a job was difficult. At one point, I was going to nursing school. That was stopped because of a move. In hindsight, the move was a great opportunity. I was able to find a job that provided me a career.

During my career, I was downsized four times. Downsizing became a way of life in corporate America. When being downsized, it can be challenging because I took it personally. However, if I had truly watched the politics and the dynamics going on, I should have been able to read the tea leaves. Had I been astute enough, I should have started looking before the downsizing occurred.

While I can play the politics game, I prefer not to. Whether you do or not, I learned that it is vital for your career to build a network and ask the right questions. My network can help you to understand what is happening with leadership and where the company is headed. Keeping in tune with politics helped with my career and being in control. At my last downsizing, although no one told me I was going to be downsized, I knew it was coming. I decided to accept the package because it was generous. I also started looking for a new opportunity. Within a week after I was downsized, I found a job that I loved. I now had a job and the perks of the downsizing package.

7. What were the 2 hardest efforts about transitioning?

■ I was downtrodden because I could not find a job. I went from being a part of a team with a focused mission. I no longer had a purpose or a vision for what would happen next. It took me several months to refocus my goal. Becoming an EMT and going to nursing school. I was a volunteer EMT for over 30 years, so that was an integral part of my life.

In the Navy, you are a team working toward a common goal and mission. Once I was employed, corporate America is not the same. There are hidden agendas; you need to be aware of who might be against your goals; you need to be mindful of politics; you must understand how to work in this type of environment. This is not to say that politics did not happen in the Navy; it did; however, everyone still drove to the mission and goal.

8. What do you think are the top issues for Veterans transitioning into a career?

Veterans need to understand civilian terminology for the type of position you are pursuing. Translating what you do in the military to civilian language is critical when presenting oneself for an opportunity.

Networking is also tricky for transitioning vets. It is essential to stay in touch with those that have transitioned to civilian life and jobs. These individuals can help with your resume, how to set up social media, where to look for jobs on social media, and, most importantly, to give you contacts. These new contacts extend your network. Networking is essential to find a civilian job.

As I found out way too late after I transitioned, when contacting someone that was referred to you, you do not know if they are ready to hire someone. Never call to ask for a job. Call to understand what would make you more valuable to a hiring manager. I was doing this one time, and lo and behold, I was offered an interview and later was hired. You just never know what will happen in an expanded network.

9. Do you believe there is a stereotype attached to being a Veteran in pursuit of a job?

Yes, there is. Some are good and some are bad. Veterans are known as hard workers and focused on getting the job done. They are relentless, no matter what the obstacles are. They know how to work on teams. They are trained for leadership. These are all great qualities, but, at times, civilian employers do not see these as benefits. The employer may have a preconceived notion that veterans are inflexible; they do not adapt well. Employers also fear veterans showing leadership when the veteran is not in a leadership position. Unfortunately, some employers do not understand the qualities that vets will bring to their organization. It is fear of the unknown.

10. What question(s) would you have liked to have known before taking your first job?

I learned through trial and error on the questions I needed to ask during an interview. The questions I would ask are as follows:

- What is the culture of the company?
- What is the culture of your organization?
- What is your leadership style?
- What training, if any, will I receive for the position?
- What other training will I receive?
- In your mind, how does an employee succeed in this position?
- Is this a new position, or is it replacing someone?
- If it is a replacement, why?
- Finally, ask questions about the company, including strategy, how it has changed, etc.

Many of these questions may be answered during the interview process. I found that being too direct with questions may turn off the hiring manager. Be vigilant for opportunities to finesse the questions. However, I also found that understanding the organization and leadership style, being direct, may be alright. Doing homework before an interview is essential. Know the hiring manager and as much as you can about the company.

11. What are the most important lessons you can share on making a successful job transition from the military?

1. Network, Network, Network. Had I maintained my network of all those that I knew from Intelligence School and those that left the Navy before I did, it would have helped in many ways. I would have contacts in corporate America; I would have had individuals to help me format and translate my resume to Civilian speak. These same individuals could have expanded my professional network as well.

2. Research different careers in the civilian world. I did not do this. I had no idea where even to start. Had I decided what path I wanted to take, I could have joined societies or associations affiliated with that career, which goes back to networking. Joining the societies and associations would have increased my network and provided information on potential jobs and how the terminology used in the field.

3. I also would have asked what training I could do to make me a more valuable potential employee.

12. If you could do it again, what would be the one thing you would do (better) or not do to help in your transition?

I would maintain my network. Networking was essential back in the '80s as it is today. Not keeping my network made finding a job extremely hard. It also took a long time to build a new one.

John DiPiero

Service rank: Colonel, USAF

Position: Commandant, Military Affairs Senior Program Manager

Industry: Military School, Financial Services

Biography

John is a 29-year veteran of the Air Force and Texas resident for many years. During his Air Force career, he spent most of his time in the training and education business. He was a pilot and amassed over 3,500 hours in both helicopter and fixed wing jet aircraft, and retired in the rank of colonel. Immediately upon retirement, he spent two years as Commandant of Cadets at Randolph Macon Academy, Front Royal, Virginia. John began his career at USAA in military marketing. He then moved to military recruiting focused on veteran and spouse hiring for USAA. John then moved to Military Affairs as part of the Military Advocacy Group where he was focused on influencer engagement and advocacy in the veteran and spouse transition space. John received his undergraduate degree from Southwest Texas State University (now Texas State) and his masters from the University of Oklahoma. He also attended numerous military schools, including Squadron Officer School, Air Command and Staff College, Air War College and numerous flying training programs in a number of aircraft.

John is now fully retired and resides in Texas.

Questions & Answers

1. Describe your journey from the service to your first job?

I didn't have much time to plan as I made my decision to retire rather abruptly. It was in 2000, and transition programs were not very well developed. I was pretty much on my own. I was in San Antonio, and wanted to stay there but didn't know how to begin so I connected with some friends looking for help and also connected with a headhunter group. Nothing was panning out. Then one day a letter crossed my desk addressed to the vice commander of an Air Force major command. At the time, I was the Director of Staff, so I saw all correspondence going to the generals. The letter was from a retired general officer who was now the president of a military high school. He was looking for a new commandant and was asking for the vice commander's help. I knew the retired general well as I had worked for him in the past and we had a very good relationship. With the vice commander's permission, I reached out to the retired general. Long story short, I got the job. Staying in San Antonio didn't pan out as the school was in Virginia. I attribute my success on what I like to call the four pillars of success in transitioning: luck, timing, competence and who you know. One could also call it divine intervention – either way, it worked for me.

2. How did you find your first job? Describe the process.

Finding my first job was luck and timing. The letter couldn't have crossed my desk at a better time. The retired general knew my skills and personality and it was almost too easy. I knew I would be a good fit after a conversation with the retired general. I still had to interview so I asked him what type of resume he needed, as I didn't even have one yet. Now this is even easier – he said to just send him my top ten officer efficiency reports and that would be fine. Really? This is too easy! I actually interviewed with friends who I thought would beat me out, but in the end, my relationship mattered.

3. When did you start planning your transition? What actions/activities did you take?

I didn't have a lot of time to plan since my retirement decision was abrupt.

Transition programs were virtually non-existent, so I was on my own. I did reach out to some retired friends for advice and to a headhunter. If I had more time, these efforts might have been helpful, but I was on a fast-moving train.

4. Did you pursue any advanced degrees and/or certifications? Did they help?

I did not pursue advanced degrees or certifications. I already had a master's degree. At the time, I was not knowledgeable about certifications such as a PMP. Again, with more time, I might have taken advantage of these opportunities.

5. Why did you choose the work/career you are in?

I accepted the commandant role since I needed to work, I knew my boss well and liked him, and I had training, education and command experience. I knew it would be a comfortable niche and I wouldn't need a lot of time to prepare for the role.

6. Have you encountered any obstacles in advancing your career?

I was only in the commandant role for two years and had to move back to San Antonio for family reasons. I stumbled upon an opportunity at USAA that looked like a good fit so timing and networking played significant roles in my successfully getting hired. I was at USAA for 16 years in a number of different roles. I attribute my successes to knowing my role, helping others, taking advantage of opportunities out of the norm, and not being too proud to ask for help. One minor obstacle was understanding the corporate culture and language. It took a little while to become comfortable with a more civilianized communication style.

7. What were the 2 hardest efforts about transitioning?

For me, it was patience and being unsure of how my skillsets fit. Being patient for me was difficult as I like to get things done quickly, so I struggled. Aligning roles with skillsets can be challenging if you are trying to get a role that's not a good fit. You may take one role that fits you and then take time to develop for the next opportunity. That requires patience to develop.

8. What do you think are the top issues for Veterans transitioning into a career?

Being able to convince a hiring authority a veteran is a good fit is always a challenge. Resume writing and interview skills play a major role. Overcoming these obstacles is not always easy, but perseverance and good networking play significant roles.

9. Do you believe there is a stereotype attached to being a Veteran in pursuit of a job?

I believe stereotypes still exist, but not as much as in the past. Many organizations now have veteran specific hiring programs and reach out. Other veteran transition programs help in the journey and help not only the veteran but organizations better understand needs and skillsets.

10. What question(s) would you have liked to have known before taking your first job?

I would've liked to have more practice for an interview and more help with a resume. While that didn't hurt me for my first role, it would have shown me to be more professional in my search.

11. What are the most important lessons you can share on making a successful job transition from the military?

1. Know yourself. What do you want to do and where do you want to do it. That being said, maintain some flexibility.

2. Don't be afraid to take a risk. One "imperfect" opportunity can lead to what you really want.

3. Ensure you know and understand your skills, both hard and soft, and how they support the organization.

12. If you could do it again, what would be the one thing you would do (better) or not do to help in your transition?

Time. Start planning early if you can – like two years out. Doing that will get you closer to your goals.

Danielle Dodge

Position: Captain, USA

Position: TBD/PM

Industry: TBD

Biography

My name is Danielle Dodge and I am a mother, wife, and Army veteran. I spent eight years as an active duty service member immediately following my commission from Western New England University in 2010. My first duty station was Fort Stewart, Georgia with the 3rd Infantry Division Sustainment Brigade where I was fortunate to be assigned a variety of leadership positions to include Platoon Leader, Executive Officer, and Support Operations Mobility Officer. It was within this unit that I had the opportunity to deploy to Bagram, Afghanistan, and Arifjan, Kuwait. Immediately following my return from Kuwait, I was promoted to the rank of Captain and scheduled to attend the Logistics Captains Career Course in Fort Lee, Virginia.

Upon completion of the career course in 2015, I was selected to be a Company Commander for an Ordnance Advanced Individual Training (AIT) company for 18 months. A final change of command and a year as Brigade Assistant Operations Officer later, I completed my transition from the Army in November 2018. This was followed by the successful completion of my Master of Business Administration (MBA) with an emphasis in Project Management in June 2020. I am currently a stay-at-home mother and am pursuing my Project Management Professional Certification with support from Syracuse University. I volunteer within my local project management chapter, and with a local non-profit organization helping provide information technology (IT) solutions to other non-profit organizations. My goal is to someday become a project manager within the supply chain, logistics, or transportation industry when the opportunity presents itself.

Questions & Answers

1. Describe your journey from the service to your first job?

I currently don't know when I will be able to obtain my first job. With my husband working full time on active duty, my oldest son in virtual elementary school, and a toddler at home, I don't have the ability to work full time. I plan on capitalizing on every moment of free time I have by networking and researching to make the transition from stay-at-home to a full-time job as smooth as possible, something someone who is in the midst of transitioning from the military should be doing in their free time as well.

2. How did you find your first job? Describe the process.

N/A. I haven't found a job yet. However, lessons learned in the job search I did conduct is that networking and significant individual effort is key. Pair these efforts with research and utilization of resources available to veterans and the job pursuit will become more rewarding than blindly submitting resumes to a list of online job applications with little to no follow up.

3. When did you start planning your transition? What actions/ activities did you take?

I was always someone who assumed the Army would be my career until at least 20 years, so I poured myself into every aspect of every job I held without a single thought to transitioning out of the military. My perspectives changed after the birth of my son and upon returning to work as a Brigade Assistant Operations Officer. I was dual military with a step-son and a baby, the hours seemed longer, and it became difficult to find the necessary work-home balance. I started planning my transition after three months of returning to work post-maternity leave. I immediately dove into potential advanced education degrees and applied to Norwich University in pursuit of my MBA in Project Management. My transition timeline started ticking 6 months before my end of term date; I rushed my exit from the military.

4. Did you pursue any advanced degrees and/or certifications? Did they help?

I began my online Master of Business Administration (MBA) with an emphasis in Project Management the same month I completed my final day in the military. I didn't want there to be a gap between my transition and the start of school to enable a stronger resume upon completion of graduate school. I chose an MBA degree paired with project management, because I wanted to learn about the commercial sector to make myself as marketable as possible and because I had a genuine interest in project management theories and frameworks. I graduated from Norwich University in June of 2020.

I am currently seeking my Project Management Professional (PMP) Certification with assistance from the Onward to Opportunity program through Syracuse University with a goal to obtain my certification before the end of 2020. I believe having an advanced degree paired with a PMP certification will assist in the pursuit of a job relevant to the degree/certification, but I am not planning on relying on this alone.

5. Why did you choose the work/career you are in?

I chose project management because it is a career that I believe I can find similar fulfillment as I did during my time in the Army. I thoroughly enjoy learning something new each day and being challenged in a diverse environment where I can capture knowledge and manage it to drive success. Every business implements projects, and I wanted to be a part of something that could help contribute to something important, as I did in the military.

6. Have you encountered any obstacles in advancing your career?

I graduated with my MBA in Project Management in June of 2020 and initially expected that I was marketable enough on paper, pairing my experience with my newly obtained education, that I could simply submit my resume to any job and expect a callback. I acted on impulse and sought instant gratification through the submission of my resume to a "wide net" of job openings only to find myself rejected or ghosted by not hearing anything back at all. I told myself that it was because the job market was flooded, jobs are only looking for those with an active PMP certification, and a litany of other external excuses.

Over the two months following graduate school, I not only learned to look inward at the mistakes I was making, but my personal environment changed significantly. Some initial lessons learned were my resume was broad and not tailored to the jobs I was seeking, I didn't make any attempt to network the correct way, and I didn't have a clue which industry-specific branch I wanted to pursue within project management. Due to COVID-19, my son's elementary school decided to implement a completely virtual school year. A virtual school year paired with a toddler at home, a husband on active duty, and a very limited local family support system, my job search came to a temporary end, and my strategy needed to change in order to remain in the home.

In order to continue to support my family while simultaneously pursuing advancement in my career, I have had to sacrifice the potential additional income and find creative ways to remain marketable. I have found that volunteering (when time permits) is a way to gain experience on a flexible schedule. I am also pursuing certifications that contribute to my industry field and conduct endless research on the specific jobs and companies I have an interest in pursuing when I can.

7. What were the 2 hardest efforts about transitioning?

Although I haven't transitioned into civilian work, yet, the hardest part for me thus far is transitioning from military jargon to a language that is understood by civilian employers. Translating my experience in the Army to tangible outcomes in industry terms is difficult and takes time and practice.

8. What do you think are the top issues for Veterans transitioning into a career?

I think top issues include keeping prospects too broad and not narrowing down the specific industry in which you want to conduct project management. As military officers, we are taught to be broad in our tangible skills to remain flexible and adaptive. Project managers do require a specific set of skills that can be paired successfully with the skills developed throughout a military career if the veteran takes the time to educate themselves on the necessary frameworks.

I also think the expectation when becoming a project manager is that you will have the opportunity to jump in and lead a team right away, like what you did during your service. This isn't always the case and can be hard for a veteran to take a step back from the leadership role they were once in.

9. Do you believe there is a stereotype attached to being a Veteran in pursuit of a job?

I have only heard of general stereotypes potentially associated with veterans in pursuit of a job. Some of which are negative and involve employers dismissing a veteran's experience due to a naïve perspective, or a severe lack of understanding. Other stereotypes include an automatic assumption that a veteran comes with a set of mental baggage and instability which may not be a risk an employer is willing to take. Positive feedback from other veterans who have obtained jobs is that employers they have interviewed have a real passion for veterans and the experience they bring to the table. "Soft skills" aren't necessarily taught in a disciplined manner within the civilian sector, and these skills are valuable to any organization.

10. What question(s) would you have liked to have known before taking your first job?

N/A. Still working on this.

11. What are the most important lessons you can share on making a successful job transition from the military?

I do not currently hold a full-time job in the commercial sector, which is a choice I have made to support my family in the best way that works for us. However, the three most important lessons I would like to share are as follows:

1. Network. his word was something I heard throughout my transition, and not something I personally took seriously enough. There is a "right way" to

network and learning this is essential to obtaining a job referral, learning about potential companies of interest and your potential role, and learning opportunities that you may not have known about otherwise.

2. Try not to get tunnel vision based on your reason for transitioning. I found myself disinterested in transition resources and opportunities because I was entirely focused on starting grad school. I figured since I had the next two years mapped out, that I didn't have to focus on my resume or interview techniques as much as others. However, after graduating, I spent a lot of time digging up past resources that were valuable in my job pursuit and found myself wishing I had put more time and effort into the opportunities that were presented to me during my transition.

3. Capitalize on what the military can offer you, and step away from your current job to focus on your transition. There are a lot of programs that are offered upon exit from the military, but these opportunities need to be acted on as far as a year out from your end of term. I was torn between my current duties and my need to focus on my future outside the military. In the end, you are only doing yourself a disservice if you don't think about yourself throughout your transition; it will only lead to a smoother entry into the civilian sector.

12. If you could do it again, what would be the one thing you would do (better) or not do to help in your transition?

Hindsight is 20/20, and there is no way I could have anticipated COVID-19 having such an impact on my career advancement prospects, but If there was one thing I would do better, I would have pursued more transition opportunities that were available to me at the time. Opportunities included additional resume building workshops, LinkedIn lessons, interviewing practice, and mentorship programs. Although these resources are available to Veteran's post-transition, after two years of being out of the military, my job experience was no longer as fresh in my mind, mentors have provided me with the knowledge that would have been beneficial prior to actively searching for a job, and my ability to reach back to obtain resources takes longer than if I would have taken advantage of it in the first place.

Terry Dutton

Service rank: Master Sergeant, USAF

Position: Senior Project Manager

Industry: Financial Services

Biography

Igrew up in Rochester, NY, and graduated from high school in 1985. Two weeks after graduation, I started my 23-year journey in the Air Force by departing for Basic Training. After working in the Base Supply career field for seven years, I cross-trained into the Supply Systems Analyst career field where I did database programming on mainframes and provided internal IT support for Supply squadrons. When promoted to E-6, I was given the opportunity to cross-train yet again, this time into the Communications-Computer Systems Controller (Tech Control) career field, which I did for my last eight years. Throughout this journey, I was blessed to have had ten great assignments, five stateside, and five overseas. My most memorable one was when I was assigned to the Office of Military Cooperation – Egypt, located in the US Embassy in Cairo, Egypt. This is where I was able to work side by side with military officers and enlisted members from all four military services as well as the Department of State employees and local nationals. Our mission was of significant strategic importance between the United States and Egypt and had its genesis in the historic 1979 peace treaty between Egypt and Israel. My last assignment was in Arlington, VA with the Joint Task Force-Global Network Operations (JTF-GNO), where I was able to gain a strategic perspective of the DoD's global communication/computer systems, infrastructure, and services.

Most importantly, this is when I married my wife Germaine (June 2006) and when our daughter Autumn was born (February 2008). After retiring from the military and a brief foray into the D.C. area DoD contracting sphere, we moved to Tampa in late 2008, which is where we have lived since.

Currently, I'm a Vice President in Project Management with Citi.

Questions & Answers

1. Describe your journey from the service to your first job?

■ In 2007, we were pleasantly surprised to find out that my wife was pregnant. After determining when our daughter was due and when I was to complete my Bachelor's degree in IT Management, we jointly agreed it was time for me to submit my retirement paperwork with an effective date set for a few months after I completed my degree. Looking back, I realize that while my decision was made in mid-2007 to retire in August 2008, I had been preparing for years by looking at experience/education/certification requirements in job postings then checking off those items as I progressed through my military career. While my preparation was years in the making, it was only six months from the time I started working on my resume, with the help of a professional resume writer, to when I was hired for my first post-military job.

2. How did you find your first job? Describe the process.

■ I found my first post-military job through networking. One of our previous Network Operations Watch Officers, who had retired a few months before I made my decision, reached out to me when he heard that I was retiring and asked me to provide a copy of my resume to share with his hiring managers. He had landed a position with one of the D.C. area's leading DoD contractors who I was already interested in applying to so I provided a copy of my resume and what type of position I was interested in. A few weeks later, I had my first in a series of interviews and a month later I was offered and I accepted a position that aligned with my post-military career plans. The entire process was remarkably smooth with absolutely no issues.

3. When did you start planning your transition? What actions/activities did you take?

Once I made the critical decision in mid-2007 to retire twelve months later, I started the process of collecting all of my performance reports and award citations to be used as source material for my resume then reached out to a professional resume writer for assistance. With my freshly minted resume in-hand, I updated my LinkedIn profile with my work history and started checking other online resources such as Monster.com, Indeed.com, and USA-Jobs.gov for job postings. When offered the opportunity, I attended the first available Transition Assistance Program (TAP) class where I learned some valuable lessons regarding interviews and dressing for the position you're applying for; if you want a position responsible for million-dollar budgets, then dress the part. I completed my Bachelor's degree a few months before I retired since I knew it was something potential employers were looking for. My wife and I also started the process of paying off all of our credit card debt so the only debt we had was one car payment. Accomplishing this goal allowed us to focus on the transition process itself, have funds for a down payment on a new house, and enough left to handle transition costs not covered by the military.

4. Did you pursue any advanced degrees and/or certifications? Did they help?

I did not pursue an advanced degree prior to transitioning from the military since I was still completing my Bachelor's degree up to a few months before my retirement. Almost two years after I retired, I did start working on my first Master's degree, in IT Management with a concentration in Information Security/Assurance and Digital Forensics since I recognized its potential for adding value to my marketability. I think that having that advanced degree, in addition to my experience and security clearance, placed me above others applying for the same positions. While pursuing my Master's degree, I also earned my Certified Information Systems Security Professional (CISSP) certification. After working as a DoD contractor for eight years, I decided to make a slight trajectory change in my career and earned my Master's in Business Administration (MBA) so that I would better understand the perspective of C-Level executives and learn to communicate with them using terminology they were familiar with.

In my pursuit to further improve my marketability and validate my knowledge and experience, I took the Project Management Institute's (PMI) Project Management Professional (PMP) certification exam and passed the first time.

5. Why did you choose the work/career you are in?

After 23 years of hands-on work in all aspects of information technology and short forays into project management, I decided to combined these two elements into a career in project management, with my first position as an IT Project Manager. I've always enjoyed using a structured approach to problem-solving, so using a structured approach to manage projects seemed like a natural progression.

Additionally, when I was in the military and tasked to complete a major "project", I always enjoyed identifying/gathering the needed resources and "rallying the troops" to successfully complete the "project" in ways that exceeded the Commander's expectations.

Since entering the project management career realm, I've found that it continues to be interesting as new ways to effectively organize resources and manage projects are being developed and refined.

6. Have you encountered any obstacles in advancing your career?

I've been very blessed to have had no obstacles in advancing my post-military career with each position progressively having greater responsibility and a higher salary. I think a lot of that came from the foundational work I did before retiring from the military and the advanced degrees and certifications I've earned since retirement. I continue to take advantage of educational, professional development, and expanded experience opportunities to remain as marketable as possible.

7. What were the 2 hardest efforts about transitioning?

The two hardest efforts about transitioning were adapting to the civilian work culture and changing my military verbiage to something my civilian peers/managers better understood. In reference to adapting to the civilian work culture, when I was in the military, the focus was all about accomplishing the "mission", even if that meant everyone, regardless of rank/position, working 24 hours to make it happen. The idea of personal sacrifice to "get it done" was prevalent throughout my military career and is in stark contrast to what I've experienced in the civilian sector, where the focus seems to be more on self than the organization. It took me a while to finally understand that I couldn't expect my civilian co-workers to work on an issue all night, that there were no limitations on "overtime" both from the company we worked for and from a personal perspective. The second hardest effort, changing my military verbiage to something more civilian oriented, was effectively like changing a habit I'd had for 23 years.

Habitually referring to time in a 24-hour format without using AM/PM, using acronyms as actual words, and using other terminology only used in the military was something I had to work hard on since my civilian co-workers would look confused when I used military lingo.

As with any habit, it just took persistence and forethought to change my verbiage to something more in line with what my civilian co-workers and managers understood.

8. What do you think are the top issues for Veterans transitioning into a career?

- The first issue is obtaining the requisite certifications, such as PMI's Project Management Professional (PMP). The PMP exam is a comprehensive exam that tests the candidate's knowledge and application of the Project Management Body of Knowledge's (PMBOK) ten knowledge areas, 49 processes, and five process groups. It's not an easy exam and you have to answer the questions based on what the PMBOK says, not your real-world experience. Preparing for this exam may have the transitioning military member totally disregard how they did "project management" during their military career; not an easy task.

- The second issue is translating their military experience into tangible project management experience. This ties into the first issue, taking the PMP exam, which requires you to submit your project management experience "resume" as a precursor to being allowed to schedule your exam. While we have all done some sort of project management during our military career, looking back on everything you did and determining which project phase your work was in as well as finding someone to validate your experience can be daunting. This is where maintaining your professional network throughout and after your military career is critical, as well as keeping copies of your performance reports/decoration citations since much of your project management experience can be gleaned from them.

9. Do you believe there is a stereotype attached to being a Veteran in pursuit of a job?

I don't think a veteran typically has a stereotype attached to them when pursuing a civilian job. Conversely, I think the typical veteran applies a stereotype to civilian companies; thinking a company will offer them a position with a similar title/responsibility to positions they've held in the military. This stereotyping only leads to disappointment as they are continually passed over for candidates who have actual experience in the industry.

Moving from being a program manager in the military to being one in the civilian sector may require the person to start at a lower level and work up the career ladder as they build experience in the specific civilian industry.

10. What question(s) would you have liked to have known before taking your first job?

What are the paths for internal advancement in the company? As a DoD contractor, I was hired to fill a specific position on a contract that was outside of the company's internal operations, which meant I was still, to an extent, an outsider looking in. If you're lucky to land on a multi-year contract you might be able to move up within the contract's management structure, but it's not a given. This is one of the reasons why I left the DoD contract world and entered the financial services industry with a global-level company that has multiple vertical and lateral career paths.

Since my first position was on a DoD contract, I would have asked about opportunities within the company outside of the contract. Many companies that hire people to fill positions on a DoD contract don't have paths within the company for employees to take if the contract is not renewed. This can create significant stress on the employee during the contract renewal process or if the contract just ends leaving them desperate to find a new position or try to get hired by the new contract awardee. This is one of the reasons I left the DoD contract world so that I would be a "permanent" hire vice a contractor who is vulnerable to the ebb and flow of the contract.

11. What are the most important lessons you can share on making a successful job transition from the military?

1. Be prepared to pay out of pocket for everything. The military provides a very structured lifestyle with a built-in safety net that you won't have in the civilian sector. Where the military provides tax-free money for food and housing above your base pay, a civilian company will only provide your salary and if you're lucky, locale pay.

2. If possible, pay off all of your revolving debt such as credit cards before exiting the military. It'll be one less thing you have to focus on when you're transitioning from the military where you had a guaranteed payday twice a month. Before my wife and I decided that it was time for me to retire from the military, we had already started paying off our credit cards and vehicle loans so that we only had one monthly car payment when I retired. This helped us to easily qualify for a loan for our first post-military house; a low debt-to-income ratio increases your credit score.

3. Know your worth! Realistically assess your military experience from a civilian perspective along with your education and certifications then find civilian positions you would qualify for. With this in-hand, use an online source such as Glassdoor.com to determine what the typical salary for that position is in the area you decide to settle in. When negotiating a salary with your potential new employer, use your research to provide a realistic salary range expectation.

12. If you could do it again, what would be the one thing you would do (better) or not do to help in your transition?

Looking back on my transition from the military to the civilian sector, the only thing I would have changed is to have completed my Bachelor's degree earlier in my career so I could have obtained an advanced degree and more certifications prior to retirement such as the Certified Information Systems Security Professional (CISSP) and Project Management Professional (PMP) certifications.

I think that would have made me considerably more marketable and opened up more opportunities.

Jay Garcia

Service rank: Master Sergeant, USMC

Position: Program Manager

Industry: Cybersecurity

Biography

Jay Garcia brings over 15 years of human resources, program management, leadership, diversity & inclusion, and personal & corporate branding to Fortinet. Prior to Fortinet, Jay supported recruiting, onboarding, curriculum development, equal opportunity, corporate and personal branding, training and development, and sales support operations at the Department of Defense. He also held sales and quality control leadership roles and was a key player in the creation of California Marine Families, a non-profit organization that provides support to service members and their families in Northern California.

Jay has excelled in the cyber-security industry by capitalizing on a flexible blend of human resources, marketing, sales, training, technical and business development skills, and by applying the intangible traits acquired in his 20-year military career. Leveraging this experience and the passion for helping Veterans, Jay focuses on developing best-practice based Veteran recruiting initiatives amongst partners in the cyber-security industry. For his efforts, Jay was awarded the Young AFCEA's 40 Under 40 Award in 2018, and Fortinet was honored with Military Times Best for Vets Employer Award in 2019 and 2020.

Jay leads Fortinet's Global Veterans Program and sits on the Board of Directors for VetCTAP (501c3). He has presented at numerous companies and military bases around the United States, Canada, and all major cyber commands. He is a Fortinet Network Security Expert-3.

Questions & Answers

1. Describe your journey from the service to your first job?

■ I always knew that I was only going to serve 20 years in my beloved Marine Corps. I started planning for my transition when I reenlisted for the last time at the 16th year mark. I took ownership of my transition. Since the day I started applying for jobs until I found my first job, it took about 3 months.

2. How did you find your first job? Describe the process.

■ One could say that I'm the prime example of a perfect transition. I found my job through a series of events. It started with applying for a job on LinkedIn (easy apply), I interviewed for that role but since I was still active I didn't get the job. However, I stayed connected with that employer and they referred me to another organization, where I found my dream job. It was a mixture of online applications, attending job fairs, and networking.

3. When did you start planning your transition? What actions/ activities did you take?

I started my transition in late 2012. First, my focus was to obtain a college degree. I went from no college education to obtaining my Bachelors and a Master's degree in 5 years. During this timeframe, I leaned on non-profit organizations like O2O and VetCTAP to help me obtain certifications, and help me with my resume and interview techniques. I've always been a social butterfly. I think my time on Marine Corps recruiting duty helped me break that fear of talking to strangers, so when it came to networking events, I was all over them.

4. Did you pursue any advanced degrees and/or certifications? Did they help?

Yes, I got my BA in Social and Criminal Justice and a Masters in Psychology. I also obtain an HR certificate from Syracuse University's Onward to Opportunity Program. Obtaining these degrees and certificates definitely helped me because I believe it showed employers that I was serious about learning and bettering myself.

5. Why did you choose the work/career you are in?

I spent 15 years enlisting men and women in the United States Marine Corps so when this opportunity came about I took it. Currently, I lead the veterans' program for the number 1 cybersecurity company in the world. What better way than to be in apposition to help our veterans find meaningful employment after their service.

6. Have you encountered any obstacles in advancing your career?

I've had no obstacles so far. I have worked with an amazing team's that truly care not just about me professionally but also personally.

7. What were the 2 hardest efforts about transitioning?

I would say that one of the hardest things many service members face is fear of the unknown, the lack of information. Many don't really prepare for their transition until they are months away from exiting the military. That's definitely too late and many often take roles only to find themselves leaving those jobs months after, not good. The majority of transitioning service members leave their first job within a year, sometimes even months. That should be the exception, not the norm.

8. What do you think are the top issues for Veterans transitioning into a career?

Lack of corporate experience and not developing a strong network. The network is their net worth, many fail to see this.

9. Do you believe there is a stereotype attached to being a Veteran in pursuit of a job?

I still think that many employers see veterans as damaged goods. I mean how many employers have programs that target veterans? They have recruiters that target college/university candidates right, why not have recruiters that target veterans and military spouses. If they were to target this pool they would get candidates that are educated, experienced, and with a proven track record to get the job done under the most stressful conditions.

10. What question(s) would you have liked to have known before taking your first job?

I really can't think of any, I was prepared and have all mine answered.

11. What are the most important lessons you can share on making a successful job transition from the military?

1. Start early.
2. Lean on mentors.
3. Be humble. Just because you were an officer or a senior enlisted person it doesn't mean you're going to start in a C-level role.

12. If you could do it again, what would be the one thing you would do (better) or not do to help in your transition?

I would get my degrees in Computer Science or Cybersecurity, that's a field that's constantly growing, and with a zero percent unemployment rate, it definitely offers a sense of job security.

Nathan George

Service rank: Lance Corporal, USMC

Position: CEO

Industry: Software Value Added
Reseller

Biography

My name is Nathan George and I was in the USMC from 1978 until 1981. I was discharged from the Marine Corps with the rank of Lance Corporal (E-3).

Although I have been in the hospitality sector, the services sector, and the financial sector since leaving the military I am currently in the Information Technology sector. I got into this industry about 25 years ago and am the CEO of a software reseller where we resell commercially available software packages and provide implementation services for those software packages.

Questions & Answers

1. Describe your journey from the service to your first job?

When I was discharged from the military, times were different than they are now. It was not too far removed from the Vietnam era and there was not an appreciation for the military and veterans that there is today. When I was discharged, I was returned from Okinawa to CONUS where I spent three days at Camp Pendleton, going through the discharge process. We did not have the type of support system that is available today to help the transition process. Once discharged, I made my way back home (Texas). I knew I wanted to go to college but knew I would need money to make that happen. I walked some and rode a bicycle other times over the first three days I was home and walked into every business I came to ask if they had an opening for a job.

Frankly, I did not care what job it was, just one that I could make a living with. I got a job driving a wrecker and used that first job to get an apartment and a vehicle so I could start preparing for college. So, for me, it took two days to find my first job.

2. How did you find your first job? Describe the process.

I found my first job after the military by going into every business I came to until I found someone who would hire me as outlined in the previous question/answer. I do realize that this would be obsolete in this day and time since the internet and digital age exists and did not back then. In 1981, however, this was a common way to find a job.

3. When did you start planning your transition? What actions/ activities did you take?

I did none of the above. I went back to my home (a suburb of Dallas, TX) found a friend who let me sleep on their couch for a couple of weeks, found a job, a place to live, and bought a vehicle. I had a dream and knew I had better things ahead but had to do whatever I could at the time to get on my feet.

4. Did you pursue any advanced degrees and/or certifications? Did they help?

I did pursue a college degree and along the way got an associate degree and a bachelor's degree. I managed to get both degrees in 4 years along with having a job. My degree was in Political Science and although I have never used that degree in and of itself in any field I have been in, the fact that I had a college degree shows prospective employers that I had what it took to stick with something and gave me the added confidence that I had achieved something. For those reasons, I would say that having those degrees helped not only in getting certain jobs but in my professional career overall.

5. Why did you choose the work/career you are in?

■ I did not choose my career as much as life brought me into it. Approximately twenty-five years ago I had just gotten divorced and sold my hospitality business and was at a crossroads in life trying to figure out where to go from there. I met a man who worked at IBM and after listening to him decided that the IT field would be attractive. I signed up for some continuing education (non-credit) classes at the local community colleges about different aspects of computers, computer programming, etc. About six months later I took a job doing desktop support at a local hospital and when that contract ended my contracting company placed me with a software company.

From that my career was launched.

6. Have you encountered any obstacles in advancing your career?

■ Absolutely. The business world is very competitive and if you do not encounter obstacles you have a job and not a profession. I have learned the hard way not to predicate my success on another person's or organization's direction. If you do, you are always just one management change away from being out of business.

The more you achieve and attempt to achieve the more obstacles you can expect to encounter. The true measure of an individual is not the obstacles you encounter but whether you have what it takes to face those obstacles head-on and persevere even when it seems impossible.

7. What were the 2 hardest efforts about transitioning?

■ The military is very regimented and when you discharge you go from having someone telling you where to be and when to be there to have only yourself to answer to. If you are not extremely self-motivated that will be the number one top challenge. The second hardest challenge is transitioning into "civilian speak" from "military speak."

Some of the things that are important to you in the military are not necessarily material in the civilian world and there is an adjustment of getting comfortable being a civilian and resetting daily priorities.

8. What do you think are the top issues for Veterans transitioning into a career?

As stated above, just getting comfortable being a civilian and learning what is important in the civilian world and the civilian job. The military tends to tolerate mediocrity much more than the civilian world does from a career perspective. While the military does reward achievement, it is done in a very methodical fashion, whereas in the civilian world, you can rise – and fall – very quickly, and being in the right place at the right time and outworking your competition is extremely important to achieve success.

9. Do you believe there is a stereotype attached to being a Veteran in pursuit of a job?

I do think there is a stereotype attached to being a veteran in pursuit of a job. It is typically a good stereotype that will open doors for you to get an interview. Once the door is opened for you, however, simply being a veteran is not necessarily enough to get you the job. You must get the job on your own merits, but the stereotype will generally create opportunities. It is up to you to take advantage of those opportunities.

10. What question(s) would you have liked to have known before taking your first job?

In my rush to get a job – any job – I probably set myself back slightly from achieving my goals by not getting a job that aligned with those goals. If you have the luxury of taking some time before getting a job the question you need to ask is "what job would most help me get to where I want to be?"

11. What are the most important lessons you can share on making a successful job transition from the military?

1. Do not embellish and exaggerate what you did in the service. There is always someone around who will know when you are exaggerating about it, and even if they do not say anything, it will damage your credibility. What you did go through is impressive enough. You do not need to embellish it to impress anyone.

2. Do not overuse the "Veteran" angle. Craigslist and other apps are full of people promoting their "Veteran owned businesses." Although I prefer to hire veterans if they are qualified, if they lead with their veteran status, I typically walk away. And I personally will not use a business using the veteran status to try and get business. I think it is great that our country has an appreciation for our military, but it is offensive to me to see people trying to monetize that. Those veterans who quietly go about their business and use their experiences from the military to get ahead are the ones I seek out, not the self-promoters.

3. Do believe in yourself. The fact that you made it through the military experience will give you an added advantage that you may not appreciate initially. You have been yelled at, demeaned, and treated harshly and you are still going strong! Most people's military experience makes them strong and resilient even if they do not know it right away. Your military experiences have laid down a foundation that will carry you to great success if you will never give up.

12. If you could do it again, what would be the one thing you would do (better) or not do to help in your transition?

It was a different day and time when I got out than it was today. My experience was commonplace for that era. Because of that, I do not know that I would do anything differently. It has been a great ride and I would not change anything about it.

David Gonzalez

Service rank: Sergeant, USA

Position: Director, Web Applications

Industry: Government

Biography

David Gonzalez was born and raised in southern New Jersey. He graduated high school in June 1992 and join the military shortly thereafter. David spent 8 years in the Army from November 1992 to May 2000. David was a 54B2P, Nuclear Biological, and Chemical Operations Specialist who served in both US and overseas locations. Upon leaving the military, David moved to Southern California and attained a number of Information Technology certifications followed by a Bachelor's of Science degree in Information Technology from the University of Phoenix and a Master's Degree in Business Administration with an emphasis in Business Information Systems from Walden University. David has held many roles throughout the nation in both the private and public sectors and currently resides in Michigan.

Questions & Answers

1. Describe your journey from the service to your first job?

My journey was not how I planned it. MY original plan was to join the military after high school and serve my country until I was no longer physically able to serve. Unfortunately, it occurred sooner than expected. I was medically retired in 2000 due to injuries sustained while on duty. Like the preverbal professional athlete who is too injured to continue playing the sport s/he loves, I had to reinvent myself and chart a new course. Unlike the afore-mentioned athlete, I didn't have a chain of restaurants to fall back on for a new career and a steady income so I had to pivot quickly to get my life back on track. I always had an interest in computers and thought I could give that a shot. In 1998, when I was placed on the Temporary Duty Retirement List, TDRL, I used my GI Bill to attend a computer education technical school in Southern California. Within a few months, I graduated from the school with a Microsoft Certified Systems Engineer certification, CompTIA A+ certifica-tion, and several other vendor-specific certifications as well. I applied for and landed my first IT job and first job since leaving The Service prior to leaving the school.

From the time I left the service preparing for and securing my first job took a total of 8 months. This time included attending a technical school, building a resume, interviewing for and landing my first job. Before leaving The Ser-vice, I began preparing for my transition by attended the required transition training which helped me navigate the GI Bill process, unemployment, and start school.

2. How did you find your first job? Describe the process.

I found my first job via online research. It was relatively easy as I had help with my resume and taught me how to conduct a job search online through my technical school.

3. When did you start planning your transition? What actions/ activities did you take?

As answered above, I began my transition while I was still in the Service. I attended the required transition classes which covered basic resume writing and interviewing skills. The real preparation began when I was in my tech school and was given more help with my resume and how to conduct online job searches. Lastly, having the opportunity to acquire certifications and build a new skill set greatly improved my ability to secure a new role and ultimately a new career.

4. Did you pursue any advanced degrees and/or certifications? Did they help?

Answered above...

5. Why did you choose the work/career you are in?
■ Answered above...

6. Have you encountered any obstacles in advancing your career?
■ I have encountered obstacles in my career. The transition to civilian life was hard...like really hard. There are a lot of unmotivated and undisciplined individuals who are not willing to put in the work and effort that many veterans do. For the transitioning soldier, it's "do or die," meaning this is our second career and necessary for the soldier to provide a living for themselves and their family. The warrior ethos and mindset will serve the soldier well but will also make it hard to work with some coworkers who do not share the same mindset. Once I was able to understand and accept that we are all in the same race, but in different heats, working with others became easier. The transitioning soldier must learn to tailor their response to the environment and work at the pace appropriate for the role. In hindsight, I wish I would have taken some sort of support or class to help with that transition to help set the expectation.

7. What were the 2 hardest efforts about transitioning?
■ The two hardest efforts to transition to civilian work were knowing where to begin and when to begin. The when is easier to answer...as soon as possible. The more time one has to prepare, the better prepared they will be. Where to begin is a little tougher and an individual choice. I knew what I liked and was able to turn that passion into a career. That was a leap of faith as I didn't know if I could make it in my new career field, but I took a lot of time to decide what I wanted to do and how I wanted to do it.

8. What do you think are the top issues for Veterans transitioning into a career?

For the IT field certifications, education and experience are all needed to "break into the field." If the transitioning soldier has all three of these criteria, great! If not and they want to get into this line of work, I'd recommend they use their education benefits to begin as soon as possible.

9. Do you believe there is a stereotype attached to being a Veteran in pursuit of a job?

Yes, I touched on it above in…the "Hooah!" mentality, drive, and actions. Soldiers are often seen as too rigid, too strict, inflexible, or unable to make decisions without explicit orders. Although when the soldier first exits the service, some of these characteristics may be true, we can easily adapt to most circumstances and quickly assimilate into a new role while still maintaining our individuality and completing our mission.

10. What question(s) would you have liked to have known before taking your first job?

What to expect and what the challenges the transitioning soldier would face.

11. What are the most important lessons you can share on making a successful job transition from the military?

1. Be easy on yourself. Celebrate what you've accomplished and not what you didn't get done.

2. Set boundaries. I know it's your first job and your new normal, but take it one day at a time.

3. Ask for feedback and don't be afraid to ask how you're doing. Be ready for the feedback and don't take it personally…everyone knows your trying and many others have done it as well. Don't be afraid to reach out to veterans' groups, therapist, family and friends for support. You will be under a lot of pressure but in the end, you will put more pressure on yourself than your new employer will.

12. If you could do it again, what would be the one thing you would do (better) or not do to help in your transition?

Answered above in A11

Flay Goodwin

Service rank: Colonel, USMC

Position: Program Manager

Industry: Financial Software

Biography

Flay is Program Manager for Inuit, the makers of TurboTax, Quick-Books, and Mint. He manages the Virtual Expert Platform, Intuit's latest Big Bet to power prosperity around the world. Prior to joining Intuit in 2019, Flay worked for Qualcomm as a Program Manager for 3 years responsible for adapting emerging technologies to government use cases. Flay transitioned into the private sector in 2015 after 25 years in the Marine Corps and landed his first job with CGI, an IT services provider. While on active duty, Flay served as an F/A-18 pilot, Air Officer, Headquarters Marine Corps Program Manager, and Assessment Director at US Special Operations Command. Flay has an MBA from Indiana University, Kelly School of Business, MS in Systems Engineering from Penn State University, and BS in Computer Science from Indiana University of Pennsylvania. He is a certified Project Management Professional (PMP), Scrum Master (CSM), and SAFe Program Consultant (SPC).

Questions & Answers

1. Describe your journey from the service to your first job?

I had the benefit of watching 3 co-workers transition a year ahead of me. They all began the transition process about 3-4 months prior to their retirement and they all regretted waiting to the last minute. Hearing their growing concerns, I elected to attend the local transition program with one of them which put me about 14 months out from my retirement. This was the best decision I made in my transition and allowed me to take a very deliberate approach in planning my transition. Even though I started the process early, worked thru several iterations of my resume, and stepped up my networking activities, I still set unrealistic goals for myself in transition. I focused all my efforts on 5 target companies and was hoping to have offers months prior to retirement. I quickly realized, after seeking guidance in the veteran networks within the target companies, that it was not going to be an easy journey. I learned a lot in the months prior to my transition which helped shape the strategy leading to my first job. I was not willing to give up on the target companies and continued the pursuit deep into my terminal leave period. Unable to get traction at any of the 5 companies, I expanded my aperture to hopefully increase my odds. This new approach resulted in more interviews, more options, and ultimately my first role. While the transition was stressful at times, I felt like the time spent prior to transition prepared me well for the process and allowed me to take a more deliberate approach towards landing my first job.

2. How did you find your first job? Describe the process.

I found my first job by searching LinkedIn Jobs and applying for the position thru the company's career site. I went in cold, without a referral, and without knowing anybody in the company.

3. When did you start planning your transition? What actions/ activities did you take?

I started transition planning about 14 months prior and focused on networking, gaining a PMP certification, and doing a self-assessment. I put a good amount of effort into demilitarizing my resume by having friends and colleagues, with no government association, provide review it and provide feedback. I never considered using a resume writer. My networking efforts were focused in two areas; networking with other project manager thru organizations like PMI, networking with veterans in target companies, and networking with other veterans in the local community. Probably the most valuable thing I did was to conduct a self-assessment. This allowed me to set clear objectives and establish guardrails that would guide me thru the process.

4. Did you pursue any advanced degrees and/or certifications? Did they help?

I completed my MBA after about 12 years in the military when I first began to consider what I wanted to do after my time in the service. As I started the transition process and decided to pursue a career in project management, I obtained the Project Management Professional certification. My hope was that with this certification I could demonstrate my willingness to develop new skills, validate my military project management experience thru an industry recognized certification, and meet certification requirements for many of my target companies.

5. Why did you choose the work/career you are in?

Project management seemed like a logical career for somebody transitioning from the service. Most of the work we do in the service is project-based and requires the same skill sets. Most of the successful project managers I have worked with, with or without a military background, have very strong soft skills. Service members develop and refine these skills through their careers, and they translate very well into the private sector.

6. Have you encountered any obstacles in advancing your career?

Service members will have to deal with both institutional and personal bias's and stereotypes. These can manifest themselves in the way an organization handles veteran applicants or a resume that is overlooked because a hiring manager does not want to take the time to understand it. My approach has always been to acknowledge that they exist but work thru them by educating, informing, and demonstrating that they are unfounded.

7. What were the 2 hardest efforts about transitioning?

The level of uncertainty associated with the process and effectively translating how my military experience qualified me for a civilian employment were the hardest aspects of the transition.

8. What do you think are the top issues for Veterans transitioning into a career?

The lack of comprehensive transition programs and the unchecked proliferation of veteran resources with no quality control are major issues for transitioning veterans. This results in a situation where veterans are not adequately prepared for transition and when they seek to fill the gaps, they are presented with options which may not contribute to their objectives.

9. Do you believe there is a stereotype attached to being a Veteran in pursuit of a job?

Yes, there are stereotypes that veterans will need to navigate during their transition. Many are tough to recognize or prevail in unspoken assumptions that could impact hiring decisions or influence follow on career opportunities.

10. What question(s) would you have liked to have known before taking your first job?

I would have loved to better understand the hiring process and the factors that go into a hiring decision. I assumed that every application I submitted was reviewed and that every rejection meant that it was unlikely that I would be competitive for other roles in the company. As I learned more about the hiring process it became evident that every hiring decision was unique and that there were many factors that influenced that decision.

11. What are the most important lessons you can share on making a successful job transition from the military?

Unless you are going into government service, your transition should be viewed as the start of a second career and not an extension of your military career.

1. Leverage your soft skills and aggressively pursue degrees and certifications to fill the gap in hard skills.

2. Before you begin your transition, do a self-assessment and develop clear transition objectives.

3. Network to learn; not to get a job. If you truly understand what the company wants and what you can offer, you will have the connections to help you get hired and they will do more to pull you in because you are a better fit.

12. If you could do it again, what would be the one thing you would do (better) or not do to help in your transition?

I would have pursued a broader strategy in transition, focused on a target industry instead of a limited number of target companies. The variability in hiring cycles and company needs made it unlikely that I would succeed with my original strategy without waiting a while for that perfect fit. This broader approach allowed me to get my foot in the door, gain valuable industry experience, and opened other opportunities. With this approach, I have been able to land positions in two of my original target companies. Companies that I could not get traction with when I transitioned.

Dion Hart

Service rank: Captain, USA

Position: Chief of Staff Business Strategy

Industry: Financial Services

Biography

As a transitioned Army Captain and West Point graduate, Dion Hart spent the majority of his five years of service as a combat engineer operations officer for 36th Engineer Brigade in Fort Hood, Texas. During his time as an operations officer, Dion planned numerous high-visibility operations engaging senior leadership and more than 650 Soldiers. Prior to his operations role, Dion served as the route clearance platoon leader for the 3rd platoon, 510th Route Clearance Company. Dion's service also includes a brief combat tour of duty in Afghanistan. His military awards and decorations include the Army Commendation Medal, Army Achievement Medal, and Global War on Terrorism Service Medal.

While in his last few months of active duty, Dion was a participant in the Army SkillBridge Internship Program. Dion became the first Soldier in the program's history to be selected as a business intern at Phoenix Children's Hospital, a top 10 nationally ranked children's hospital in Phoenix, Arizona. As a business intern, he implemented process improvement practices he learned in the Army to assist the talent acquisition strategy execution in efforts of opening a new hospital in 2021. Prior to completing his internship, Dion connected Phoenix Children's Hospital with the SkillBridge program manager at Fort Hood to open additional internship opportunities to other transitioning Soldiers.

After his transition out of the Army, Dion was hired as a Vice President within Citigroup's Military Officer Leadership Program (MOLP) in Tampa, Florida. MOLP is a transitional leadership development program that identifies and develops high potential, post 9/11 military-experienced leaders and positions them for long term growth within Citi and the financial service industry.

As a first-generation college graduate, Dion graduated from West Point with a Bachelors in Economics. West Point's swim program recruited Dion after his high school Academic All-American senior year.

Questions & Answers

1. Describe your journey from the service to your first job?

Transitioning from the service to my first job was a lengthy, eventful journey where at times I found myself highly frustrated while also highly optimistic and excited for the unknown. I began planning for my transition well in advance of my ETS date, about a year out. For the first six months of that year, my planning consisted mostly of internal searching. Where did I see myself in the next year, two years, five years? Where did my interests lie? How much risk was I willing to take? Did I want to pursue an avenue charted by many others before me or create my own? I pursued opportunities to network with individuals that worked in the fields I believed I might have interests in. I used LinkedIn HEAVILY. I spoke with multiple transitioning headhunting firms. I spoke with alumni from West Point. The last six months of my transition consisted of building civilian work experience through the Army's SkillBridge program, utilizing transition assistance services to help with writing and revising my resume as well as interview preparation, and signing up for multiple job fair conferences.

2. How did you find your first job? Describe the process.

Finding my first job was more difficult than I initially anticipated; however, not impossible. Ignorantly, I believed my West Point degree and military accomplishments would speak for themselves. After many failed job interviews, I began to realize I needed to translate my military experience into terms civilian hiring managers understood. I was applying for sales roles yet nowhere on my resume spoke of sales experience. Typically, a soldier wouldn't be accustomed to stating they have sales experience. Yet upon reflection, I began to elaborate during my interviews that my "sales experience" consisted of briefing senior leaders on the capabilities my platoon could provide them during a combat mission. To a civilian hiring manager, I explained how I had to sell my organizations capabilities to an external stakeholder in order for my organizations services to be utilized. Admittedly this was a stretch. But it worked. And it was true. Consequently, learning to reconstruct my military experience into a language civilian hiring managers could understand, I placed myself at the hiring table of a top-tier medical technologies firm, Stryker Corporation. Unfortunately, this was also when the Covid-19 pandemic hit, resulting in a hiring freeze across multiple industries. My potential offer with Stryker was rescinded. I had just moved to Seattle Washington to accept the job and now found myself jobless. This is where my many months of networking and signing up for job fairs paid off. The same day Stryker rescinded their job offer, I received an offer from Citigroup as a Vice President in their Military Officer Leadership Program. The offer required me to relocate from Seattle, Washington to Tampa, Florida. I did so willingly, exercising my military-hardened ability to be adaptable.

3. When did you start planning your transition? What actions/activities did you take?

I began planning for my transition well in advance of my ETS date, about a year out. Over the course of that year, I networked extensively, especially on LinkedIn, with people who worked in the companies and positions I had an interest in transitioning into. I utilized LinkedIn to find the decision-makers within a company's hiring process such as recruiters and hiring managers. This tended to lead to more interviews than just solely applying to a job posting. I also revised my resume more times than I can remember, working with consulting firms like Korn Ferry. I even took job interviews that I had no interest in purely to get practice with interview questions.

4. Did you pursue any advanced degrees and/or certifications? Did they help?

Pursuing an advanced degree and/or certification is sometimes required depending on the job someone is looking to transition into, but not always. While many of my Officer peers chose to pursue an MBA immediately after their transition, I decided it was best to gain work experience first instead. This has allowed me additional time to figure out the specific field I would like to pursue my advanced degree in. Additionally, my current company provides tuition assistance and a network of colleagues with connections to institutions I otherwise would have no connection to when applying.

5. Why did you choose the work/career you are in?

■ I've always had an interest in pursuing a career in financial services largely due to my upbringing being born to a mother who was fourteen, poor, and homeless. I am always searching for a better comprehensive understanding of how money functions within an economy, how to maximize its functionality, and how financial firms fit into this system. In doing so I hope to change the financial future of not only my own family but also those families I come in contact with during my lifetime.

6. Have you encountered any obstacles in advancing your career?

■ I am still relatively fresh in my transition from the military. I have been given plenty of opportunities to continue to grow every day within my firm. Any encounter of an obstacle is usually due to my lack of experience or expertise. Both are resolved through volunteering for strategically important tasks, building relationships with key stakeholders, consistent hard work, self-development and passage of time.

7. What were the 2 hardest efforts about transitioning?

■ Two hardest efforts included:

1. Understanding that I am not always the best fit for some of the job postings that I am interested in. I may have to take a lower position in a company than initially anticipated in order to gain the appropriate experience and knowledge to succeed later on at a more senior level.

2. Reconstructing my military experience into a language civilian hiring managers could understand.

8. What do you think are the top issues for Veterans transitioning into a career?

Top Issues for veterans transitioning:

- Understanding they don't have to be confined to the status quo. Their transition journey doesn't have to look like everyone else's. Chart the Uncharted.

- Understanding they may have to take a lower position in a company than initially anticipated in order to gain the appropriate experience and knowledge to succeed later on at a more senior level.

- Reconstructing military experience into a language civilian hiring managers can understand.

9. Do you believe there is a stereotype attached to being a Veteran in pursuit of a job?

I'm sure there are both positive and negative stereotypes attached to transitioning veterans. I like to compare it to a Ranger Qualified Soldier who shows up to a new unit. Upon arrival, the soldier is presumed to be high-caliber. Sometimes they are, sometimes they aren't. The unit's initial presumption is either strengthened or completely dissipates after an extended period of time working with the Soldier. As I transitioned, I recognized some people may have certain stereotypes attached to me being a veteran. I focused on what I could control: my ability to demonstrate how I can be an asset to an organization and not a liability. Stereotypes will inevitability dissipate over time.

10. What question(s) would you have liked to have known before taking your first job?

I honestly can't think of one. I asked a lot of questions.

11. What are the most important lessons you can share on making a successful job transition from the military?

Important Lessons learned during my transition:

1. Treat every conversation like an interview. You never know where your next opportunity might come from

2. Be open-minded and take risks: You don't know what you don't know. Don't follow the status quo if the status quo is not what you truly see for yourself

3. Enjoy the process. Don't worry about the things you can't control. Control the things you can

12. If you could do it again, what would be the one thing you would do (better) or not do to help in your transition?

The one thing I would have done better is to have been more open to where I was willing to relocate. In the beginning of my transition, I was fixed on Seattle, Washington. I said no to a lot of job opportunities purely because of location. I was fortunate enough to be more open-minded at the end of my transition to accept a job offer that relocated me to a city I never even had on my radar.

Darin Hartley

Service rank: Petty Officer First Class, USN

Position: Vice President of Business Development & Solution Architecture

Industry: Software

Biography

D arin Hartley is the VP of Business Development for an HR Tech SaaS-based software company, Frontier Signal (NYC). He works remotely from his home office in Tampa, FL. Darin joined the Navy at the age of 17 and, in fact, was sworn in by his father in Jacksonville, Florida in 1981.

Darin went into the nuclear power program, including completing Nuclear Power School in 1982 and Nuclear Prototype Training in 1983. He served on the USS Arkansas, CGN-41, the USS Hunley, AS-31 (in Holy Loch, Scotland), and the USS Eisenhower, CVN-69. After over eight years in the Navy and with a new son a few months old, Darin decided to leave the Navy and pursue a civilian career.

Darin's first role out as a civilian was to do training development as an Instructional Designer for a government contractor, working at a startup nuclear waste vitrification facility in Aiken, SC. This entailed conducting job analyses, creating design documents for classroom and on-the-job training, and often conducting classroom training.

This lead to a similar for EG&G and Lockheed Martin. During these four years, Darin completed his undergrad and graduate degrees.

He parlayed the new degree into a full-time position at Dell in Round Rock, TX (where he wrote two of his four books). After five years at Dell in various learning development roles, he started working for a professional association remotely from Georgetown, TX. Two years later, he moved to the Seattle area to work for a start-up company, Intrepid Learning, and was there for over 12 years.

He started a consulting firm and managed that until he took a full-time role with a professional association (BICSI) in Tampa, FL. Darin started working for Frontier Signal in September of 2019, where he is currently employed.

Questions & Answers

1. Describe your journey from the service to your first job?

When my wife was pregnant with our first son, I was in my seventh year of enlistment. As a Navy Nuke, you don't have many options for shore duty. You basically can go work in the shipyards for refit or new construction or become a recruiter. Neither of those choices appealed to me at the time, so when I had about six months remaining, I really started weighing out my options. Should I stay in? Should I go?

I made lists of "pros" and "cons" for each decision. In the end, there were as many pros as there were cons for the decision to leave the Navy.

I believe what pushed my decision to get out was the outlook of more interminable sea duty. Being gone all the time wasn't an appealing thought for me, especially when you considered the wages being paid to enlisted personnel at the time. I was making around $18,000 a year. Also, in 1989, when I was getting out, when you went to sea, you were really gone.

There was no email or video conferencing on the internet, etc. Snail mail was still the order of the day. So, deployments were pretty grueling from that perspective.

I started researching potential employers for about a month when I was getting ready to get out.

When my last day of service arrived, I was still in active search mode for a job. About two-three weeks after I got out, I landed a job. For me, those three weeks were some of the longest of my life at the time. The uncertainty of getting out, free-falling, and scrapping to get re-employed.

The company that hired me had a special affinity for ex-Navy Nukes, so working with them (General Physics) worked out well. In fact, most of the people that worked there were all former Navy Nukes, so there was an instant comradery with my peers there.

2. How did you find your first job? Describe the process.

■ I found my job using classified ads, looking through postings on a very different internet, networking with friends, and former shipmates who were either actively employed civilians or looking for work like me. In retrospect, there were people that got out and were unemployed or under-employed for much longer than me. It was stressful but not painful. My wife worked outside the home then too, which was a great help financially.

3. When did you start planning your transition? What actions/ activities did you take?

The biggest activity I undertook was to get my resume written. I literally went into the Navy at seventeen, so my naval service was the bulk of my experience. There was a special challenge with that then, as there weren't ready ways to transfer navy nuke skills into civilian skills.

I didn't go to college until a couple of years after leaving the Navy, although I had some PACE and Dantes credits under my belt.

4. Did you pursue any advanced degrees and/or certifications? Did they help?

My degrees were completed after I was a civilian. I have a BS in Corporate Training from Idaho State University and a MS in Training Management from Idaho State University. My Navy Nuclear Power qualifications and experience was the equivalent to my entire freshman year of college. This enabled me to complete my undergrad and graduate degrees in four years. They are both very aligned with what I have done as a civilian and have helped my career development.

5. Why did you choose the work/career you are in?

■ My last year I was in the Navy, I was in the Reactor Training Division of the USS Eisenhower, CVN-69 (nuclear aircraft carrier). Our role there was primarily to onboard new nukes (baby nukes) and to run drills twice a night when we were underway. I have always liked helping people learn, so I knew I really wanted to be in a role where I could do that. That's why I ended up in the training and development world and why I pursued the degrees I did.

6. Have you encountered any obstacles in advancing your career?

■ I was always promoted in the various roles I had at the different companies I worked for. The biggest thing I discovered is if you want to do something, you have to tell your management you want to do something new or with more responsibility AND you have to do things in your current role that demonstrate you have the aptitude and capability to do something bigger and better. This is where I see many people struggle. They don't put in the extra work, they don't stretch themselves, etc. and just expect to be promoted.

As an example, Lockheed Martin had a great tuition reimbursement program. I got both my degrees paid for with that program, which meant I was working full time and going to school full time. Everyone had the same opportunity that worked with me there. Not everyone took advantage of it.

7. What were the 2 hardest efforts about transitioning?

■ The hardest transitions were dealing with ambiguity and getting used to new work cultures, etc. Especially in the nuclear navy, there are rules, guidelines, regulations, operating procedures, etc. for nearly everything you do. That takes some getting used to when you exit, especially if you went straight into the military from high school. I graduated second in my class of 475 and was expected to go to college, but was ready to get out of the house and get on my own.

8. What do you think are the top issues for Veterans transitioning into a career?

Now there is a tremendous amount of competition given the fallout from

COVID. I have seen lots of resumes from Veterans, which are laden with military lingo and acronyms. You have to make your resume map to civilian roles.

9. Do you believe there is a stereotype attached to being a Veteran in pursuit of a job?

don't think so. I didn't experience it. In fact, the stereotype, I had was Navy Nukes are super smart and we want to hire you.

10. What question(s) would you have liked to have known before taking your first job?

I didn't know enough to know what to ask.

11. What are the most important lessons you can share on making a successful job transition from the military?

1. Research the industry or company(ies) you are looking to work for,

2. Learn as much as you can every day

3. Go the extra mile; ask for the most challenging roles, and be innovative in as much as you can possibly be.

12. If you could do it again, what would be the one thing you would do (better) or not do to help in your transition?

The biggest difference now for me is the wealth of information available at everyone's fingertips now. Job boards, LinkedIn, massive social networks focused on military and Veterans. I just think it would be much easier to search more broadly and assess more opportunities than back in 1989. And for people transitioning out now, take advantage of as many of these things as you can now.

Alexsander Hernandez

Service rank: Chief Warrant Officer 4, USMC

Position: Audit Analyst

Industry: DoD

Biography

Alexsander Hernandez is a civilian DoD professional who currently specializes in audit remediation for United States Special Operations Command. An active citizen, he participates in local community redevelopment activities and advocates for all Veterans since his military retirement from the United States Marine Corps. Because of his VA employment and multiple recruiting efforts with companies he has worked with, Alex shares valuable tips for individuals seeking employment and military transition assistance through LinkedIn articles and social media channels.

He and his wife of 25 years are Tampa Bay Rays season ticket holders and currently can be found in the Twitterverse during every game encouraging their team on.

Questions & Answers

1. Describe your journey from the service to your first job?

I was fortunate in my transition as my wife and I decided that she would retire from the Marine Corps a year before me. This allowed me to journey with her, participate as an assistant to her transition, and really to help prepare me for my own. Knowing that I was going to pursue employment outside of my military career field I was extremely anxious. I can honestly say that once our retirement timeline was settled between us, it lifted one anxiety and replaced it with another.

Remembering just now of how I attended Transition Assistance Program (TAPS) 3 times throughout my last year and a half, I was extremely worried about leaving the Marine Corps. I did take full advantage of the allotted time you could take in submitted an Appendix J, retirement papers. There were other circumstances that did not assist in calming my nerves during transition. I was after a 20-year commitment, like most service members, near the pinnacle of their career field. All the hard work and dedication culminates in a position of authority and extreme dedication, making it even harder to put yourself first.

I was very proud of having reached the second-highest rank of my MOS, CWO-4, lead of my field at an elite unit, Marine Corps Special Operations Command and was a voting member of the future direction of the field via the Marine Corps' Operational Advisory Group.

I submitted my Appendix J with as much lead time as possible to give the service an opportunity to move the pieces in place to find my replacement. When that resulted in identifying a gap of coverage between myself and my replacement, I figured that I had enough time to put controls in place to minimize any requirements. I was not expecting that my request for retirement would be denied. Specifically, that the leave I had earned being the best I could be was being denied. The oddest part was that the Appendix J request does not even have a portion to deny retirement. My Reporting Supervisor hand wrote his denial on what should have been a rubber stamp application. I deserved my position but simultaneously deserved to decide my exodus. What resulted was a conversation between 3 0-6 officers deciding my fate where I wasn't even privy to attend. This uncertainty led to even more anxiety as I battled with now having to beg to attend the necessary classes, medical examinations, and taking advantage of all local job fairs. Did I mention it was a hard pill to swallow?

Again, my wife's transition had just occurred, and I saw nothing but 100% support and assistance. She was very valued at her post and our two different transitions only seemed to heighten the stress involved, for both of us. As a Marine she understood Mission Accomplishment but where was the Troop Welfare, we had both spent a lifetime promoting for others.

Things didn't change until I acknowledge that I had to put myself first, put my family first. They would be bearers of all my transition decisions, and we would be financially affected by the outcome of these decisions. So, what did I do, I rescinded my retirement application and opted to work until the very last day. I sold back 58 days of leave. That's not the end of the story.

After having changed my priorities, using for fuel the hard reality that I was a place holder to the unit, I attended every possible transition service available to me. I went to all the medical exams, transition briefings (Troops to Teacher, Boots to Business, etc.), one on one transition counseling, job fairs, VA appointments, and even attended TAPS again. I went to so many appointments that in my final week with the unit who had a history of giving away a Rudis sword, was engraved with the quote, "I have an appointment". I was bitter, but I got some satisfaction from my wife's retirement. Not pursuing my own earned ceremony is something that I still regret.

My only consolation was that I became extremely knowledgeable in the transition process to which I still assist people today with.

2. How did you find your first job? Describe the process.

■ As mentioned, I put in a lot of time to seek out events and people who could assist me. I became very comfortable with the notion of looking up companies and matching their needs against prior experience. The very first job I got was with the very people I had been spending all my time with, transition services. I spoke with, interviewed with and was hired by a company who was contracted to give the TAPS classes. It was in the position that I got some very behind the scenes access to federal laws and policies that oversee transition requirements. This was eye-opening, seeing how federal mandates were turned into service policies.

This seemed to be the answer to all my prayers as the position was not full time, it required being available 8-10 days out of the month and I would give the classes that I was so familiar with. I could not have asked for a better job as I did not want to keep the same grind I had throughout my career.

Do you know what the worse kind of hit is? The one you least expect.

There is nothing worse than going from a secured position where you are accomplished and respected and then you experience a company's "At-Will" clause. Not even 2 days into my new career, 2 weeks after being hired and studying all the material, 2 hours after assisting my first class, I receive a call that I was no longer needed.

All the preparation, all the hopes and even the turning down of another job offer, this was the last thing I ever expected. I'm writing this as I've come to some kind of acceptance. 20 plus years of dedication and being able to advance myself against some of America's finest and I was let go and worse, no reason as to why. You won't find it in my LinkedIn profile, and I think it more to do with embarrassment, but I write it now in hopes that it can help someone who reads this. You are not defined by your job!

Funny enough, I met a recruiter for a call center who offered me a temporary position during their holiday rush season. I took the job more out of curiosity and was determined to continue our family's quality of life as the retirement paycheck was incredibility short compared to pre-retirement and the holidays were upon us. I continued my job search as I worked as a recruiter for the call center and was happy to again to thrive and be recognized for my hard work. I was offered a permanent position. Because of the length of time, this position is also not on my profile, but I was really affected by others, mainly military spouses who were also on their own job search journey. I wrote an article about working at a call center that I think it more available now as it discusses communication in a telephone world, something that has grown exponentially in this pandemic world.

3. When did you start planning your transition? What actions/ activities did you take?

I won't reiterate all the classes and programs I participated in during my transition. I would like to answer this question and say that I did not take my military departure seriously until my one and only pass for promotion. I was at the 16-year mark and my wife and I was both passed for promotion. After the self-doubt, realizing that I was not the greatest thing since sliced bread, it hurt to know that eventually I would not be wanted the Corps needed any more. The problem that I had was because of the blemish of not getting promoted, I didn't venture out and seek anything to help my transition. I now knew it was important, but I doubled down on my career. So, the realization that I was entering my twilight, I fought harder to stay on top and delayed real transition planning.

4. Did you pursue any advanced degrees and/or certifications? Did they help?

I did not pursue any degrees or additional certifications. I was extremely upset to learn that I could have attained multiple degrees had I started earlier. More specifically, I was unaware of the importance of how certifications played a role in job hunting. I left the military with a "Can Do" attitude, but the legality of what a company will allow you to do is based on the proof that you have some experience, at a minimum educational experience.

5. Why did you choose the work/career you are in?

My current job now is the proverbial networking cliché. I was fortunate to know all of the same professionals as my wife and you don't hide from the conversations they are having. You fill in your experience with their discussions and you find that people like communicating with you. It is then that you hear more and more about opportunities and their good word about you helps to push you into that unknown. The work I'm in now isn't so much about the job but the people. I can honestly say that I chose this career now because I genuinely enjoy the people I work with. When an opening became available, I was asked to apply, which sold me on wanting to be part of that team.

6. Have you encountered any obstacles in advancing your career?

My biggest obstacle in advancing my career is that I had no career. No civilian career to speak of anyway. When you enter the military, you have four years and you reenlist and get promoted and it all happens to one day someone says "Hey, you have done well in your military career."

With going to be a civilian, you 100% know that you are at Day 1 of your career. You can't even call that a career. That 1st step is literally a first step in shoes other than your combat boots. That was an obstacle that I had to overcome. My military career did matter but didn't count toward my "civilian career". At least not for me. Even now I don't say that I have been associated with government auditing since 1994.

I get around that by now specifying I have worked with the U.S. military since 1994 and it helps to capture some of my experience but more importantly for me give me street cred which I subconsciously have to state since I don't have a degree.

7. What were the 2 hardest efforts about transitioning?

■ I did not have this obstacle, but having passive income helped to relieve a lot of stress. Friends of mine were not so lucky.

8. What do you think are the top issues for Veterans transitioning into a career?

Transitioning requires a lot of appointments. Because of the mentality of getting the job done, I have seen that.

9. Do you believe there is a stereotype attached to being a Veteran in pursuit of a job?

Negatively: We all have trauma.

Positively: We all work hard.

10. What question(s) would you have liked to have known before taking your first job?

None

11. What are the most important lessons you can share on making a successful job transition from the military?

1. Learn to see yourself.
2. Learn to be honest with yourself.
3. Learn to express yourself.

12. If you could do it again, what would be the one thing you would do (better) or not do to help in your transition?

I would learn the word transition in my first year. Being more aware of what I was to do after I got out would have assisted me with my military career choices. I would have changed my MOS, applied for a second one, pursued certifications, and invested in myself (specifically, I would have gotten a personal computer much sooner).

Mike Hoal

Service rank: Sergeant First Class, USA

Position: Director of Operations & Senior PM

Industry: Technology

Biography

I am an Army Veteran (10 years of active duty, Sergeant First Class, 98G/35P (Korean Cryptolinguist)). Accomplished Salesforce Professional, Project Manager, and CFO with more than 14 years of experience within large, diverse organizations. Experienced working with 100% distributed team (onshore, offshore, and contractors) with expertise in project management, process improvement, and executive communication. Skilled in managing multiple projects simultaneously and executing high-visibility strategic initiatives. A natural communicator, effectively liaising at all levels and across divisions/cultures, while guiding multifunctional teams toward a common goal. Success derived from the application of lessons learned analysis and industry best practices to identify gaps, develop solutions, resolve conflict, and thrive in high-tempo, deadline-driven environments requiring keen attention to detail, organization, and efficiency.

Questions & Answers

1. Describe your journey from the service to your first job?

I transitioned from service in Dec 2014. I started planning for my transition about 2 years from what would be my transition while I was working in the S-3/Operations shop at Brigade. I started realizing how my everyday job duties at the staff-level really broken down to Operations and more importantly, Project Management. I decided in order to transition from service successfully in my own eyes, I would need a graduate degree(MBA) and relevant industry certifications to give me the best chance at employment in the civilian sector. I completed my MBA and a handful of IT certs about 6 months prior to my transition and got serious about finding out how to do my resume again, and how to interview properly, and network professionally. I also read several recommended books, including Steve Dalton's 2-hour job search. The LAMP exercise in this book really helped me identify what I wanted to do, and what I was looking for in a civilian employer. At about the 120 days from the ETS mark, I started using the network I had built and applying for jobs, ultimately landing a Project Manager job with a local school district about 30 days from the start of my terminal leave. I didn't yet have my Project Management Professional (PMP) certification then, but I had studied the PMBOK and other terminology to be able to translate my military-related project management experience into terms that would matter to the civilian sector. I would go on to obtain my PMP within 9 months of starting my career as Project Manager and it has been well worth it.

2. How did you find your first job? Describe the process.

■ I did a combination of all of these (to be honest) as it had been 10 years since I had to look for a job and the job ecosystem had changed. I had also changed in the soft and hard skills I brought to the table, my education level, and what I was looking for employment wise. I started with research online to find recommended resources and agencies that helped transitioning Veterans with resumes, interview preparation, job leads, and more. I also went to numerous job fairs and informational interviews to build out my professional network. There are great programs out there now that didn't exist when I transitioned such as Veterati, Candorful, Onward to Opportunity, Deloitte CORE, Microsoft Software & Systems Academy, Hire-our-Heroes Corporate Fellowships, Salesforce Military, Merivis, Trade skills transition platforms, and many more who consistently continue to serve Veteran and Military Spouse populations. Overall, I think the transition period difficulty is based on the amount of effort an individual puts into it. You are the CEO of your transition, nothing will be handed to you, you have to put in the work! It's a competitive landscape, and you have the soft and hard skills to succeed, but you have to meet these employers' half-way and convince them why you are the right person for the job!

3. When did you start planning your transition? What actions/activities did you take?

Answered in first question above

4. Did you pursue any advanced degrees and/or certifications? Did they help?

Before I transitioned, I earned my MBA in Finance from Colorado State and several IT certifications (Lean Six Sigma, CompTIA, Microsoft). Since getting out of service, I have also earned my Masters of Science in Accounting (MSA) and am pursuing my CPA. Looking back on my degrees, the MBA was certainly relevant and helped me stand apart from others when networking and applying for jobs. For the IT certs, in hindsight, I wish I had done more research on earning ones that were solely relevant to the industry or industries I had interests in. Earning my PMP before getting out would have allowed for higher potential for increased salary offer and potentially more job offers as I had relevant experience and that certification would have helped prove that with a civilian-recognized professional certification. The combination of your professional experience enhanced with industry certifications that are relevant to what you bring to the table makes you an easier choice for most hiring managers.

5. Why did you choose the work/career you are in?

I have four different careers at the moment that keep me busy. I'm a Director of Operations for a Salesforce Partner, a Co-owner of a small-business accounting firm, a Business Development Consultant for a PMI-Authorized Training Provider, and a Management Consultant. Most of my career path, excluding the accounting side, has been built upon my experience towards the end of my military career, operations, and project management, though I have changed industries a few times. I like the communication skills and relationship-building side of this career path, as well as the planning, and attention-to-detail that goes into successfully managing a project. This career path also allows me to continuously learn; not only in my abilities as a project manager via different methodologies (waterfall, agile, scrum), but also by being a consultant, I get to learn about others' business and industries I wouldn't have necessarily had exposure to. Being in operations and project management also allows me to focus on overall process improvement and efficiencies. I also ensure to stay active in the Veteran community and give back through volunteering on Veterati and by serving on non-profit boards.

6. Have you encountered any obstacles in advancing your career?

■ I ran into a bit of a set-back when I changed industries to enter the Salesforce ecosystem about 2 years ago because I didn't have direct experience in the CRM sector, and I was newer to consulting as well. This gave me an opportunity to learn quite a bit and be able to use technology to help solve business problems, which I now love. The industry change came with a bit of humble pie, as I ultimately had to initially take a salary reduction, despite having held an executive position and more senior roles in project management. My best recommendation is never stop learning and seeking more education, no matter the industry you are in.

7. What were the 2 hardest efforts about transitioning?

■ In the military, it's very easy to tell what background a person has, or what they have accomplished, by the rank and/or skills/badges they wear. On the civilian side, that's not as apparent, so you have to get used to talking about yourself and your accomplishments versus the team mentality that was common in the military. The other aspect I think is difficult about transitioning into civilian work, is the culture change. For me, I knew the men and women on my left-and-right had similar skillsets to me in the military, I knew the values that were instilled in them in the military, and knew what to expect from them as far as work ethic is concerned. In the civilian sector, there are certainly hard-working, dedicated people, who go above-and-beyond in their professional careers, but that may not always be the case, and as a transitioning Veteran, you should always strive to lead within your new sector and not settle for a culture that isn't mutually beneficial.

8. What do you think are the top issues for Veterans transitioning into a career?

I think the three top issues that transitioning Veterans are up against are education, communication, and entitlement.

- Education: it should be a lifelong pursuit, be it college degrees, trade skills, career transition books, and other resources, or even your networking connections. All of these things can set you apart when you are changing careers and never stop grinding.

- Communication: learning to talk about YOU instead of WE, learning to communicate how your soft and hard skills are valuable to an employer or your clients if you start your own business, and communicating your value proposition and what it is you want in a professional culture.

- Entitlement: you served your country, and you should be proud of this, and there are plenty of Americans who appreciate your service including several corporate employers, but you still need to be able to help them understand how your skill-set fits the job requisition they are trying to fill and why they should pick you, not depend on your status as a Veteran expecting a hand-out. Once you obtain that new career outside of the military, never leave a Soldier behind (sorry, Army), reach back out to those behind you in the transition-window and fellow Veterans and help them network to get a job.

9. Do you believe there is a stereotype attached to being a Veteran in pursuit of a job?

While there are employers out there that try to meet you half-way and have Veteran-focused initiatives, I think more can be done to understand what servicemen and women bring to the table. I think at times there can be a stereotype of where a Veteran got their college degree, sometimes not realizing that they got this degree while working full-time, sometimes in austere environments. I also think there is a bit of a stereotype that lingers about PTSD as well and how it may or may not affect job performance though there have been several positive strides in addressing this concern.

10. What question(s) would you have liked to have known before taking your first job?

I wish I had done more research or asked my professional network on the art of salary negotiation including benefits. It is often the case when you are sent an offer letter, the company has put time into you and decided they want you, and they often have a salary range for total compensation that is expected to be negotiated depending on the industry and job. In hindsight, I wish I had understood that dynamic a bit more.

11. What are the most important lessons you can share on making a successful job transition from the military?

1. Network! You have platforms like Veterati and LinkedIn to connect with fellow Veterans and school alumni. This allows you to do get your resume in front of hiring managers and do informational interviews to find the right career path for you. Once you achieve success, send the elevator back down and help your fellow troops.

2. Take advantage of Veteran-focused platforms to help transition into careers. There are a plethora of free organizations and programs out there for you to take advantage of. I have mentioned a few, but to recap, Veterati, Candorful, Onward to Opportunity, Salesforce Military, Merivis, Microsoft Software & Systems Academy, Deloitte CORE, Hire our Heroes, Trade skills, and many more. They are the fire support you need to be successful in your transition, but you have to use them!

3. You are the CEO of your transition! No-one will care about your transition or your career more than you. If you don't put in the work, you won't see the result. Plan, Prepare, Execute, and never quit! Two of my favorite quotes are from Marcus Latrell, retired Navy Seal and lone-survivor of the Seal Team in Operation Red Wings, "You are never out of the fight!" and Sam Mills, a coach for the Carolina Panthers, "Keep Pounding!" and though not their original meaning or context, I think they can be embodied through the Veteran transition journey.

12. If you could do it again, what would be the one thing you would do (better) or not do to help in your transition?

I would begin networking earlier and put more importance on the value of networking. To be successful in either starting your own business or obtaining employment, it is more about WHO you know first, as opposed to WHAT you know. While the WHAT you know, and HOW you communicate it is certainly still important, WHO you know gets your foot in the door to have that critical interview.

Kadeame Houston

Service rank: Specialist, USA

Position: Sales Representative

Industry: Fleet Equipment - Construction

Biography

I was born on July 7th, 1991 in New Orleans, LA. I graduated from Baker High school in 2010 and went right in the Army Dec 2010. I attended basic training and AIT in Fort Leonardwood, Missouri. Shortly after graduating AIT, I was sent to my first duty station at Fort Sill, Oklahoma. After 5 years in the Army as a Motor Transportation Operator (88M), I decided it was time for a career change. During my transition, I figured using my GI benefits would be the best move for me. I attended and graduated from Thee Southern University at Baton Rouge with a B.S. in Business Marketing.

Questions & Answers

1. **Describe your journey from the service to your first job?**
IMy journey after the Army to find my first was pretty difficult. I wasn't too familiar with searching for jobs online and I didn't know exactly what I wanted to do. I thought the best option for me was to go to college.

2. **How did you find your first job? Describe the process.**
After college, my job/career actually found me. With my strong military background and previously being a SGT in the Army, it made me very

attractive to various fortune 500 companies.

3. When did you start planning your transition? What actions/ activities did you take?

I actually didn't really plan for my transition. I heard stories of people falling short but like many of those who failed to plan, I thought I was just the one.

4. Did you pursue any advanced degrees and/or certifications? Did they help?

While I was in the Army I pursed my Associate degree but never obtained it.

5. Why did you choose the work/career you are in?

I chose to work in this field because of its importance and rapid growth. Construction is one of the many fields that will not go away and will continuously grow.

6. Have you encountered any obstacles in advancing your career?

Yes, I have! The obstacles that I faced were the lack of transferable experience/skills.

7. What were the 2 hardest efforts about transitioning?

Dealing with civilians.

8. What do you think are the top issues for Veterans transitioning into a career?

I would have to say the top issue for transitioning veterans is getting used to a new world filled with its own type of order.

9. Do you believe there is a stereotype attached to being a Veteran in pursuit of a job?

I think the one stereotype that I heard a lot was that it is easy to find a job/career after the Army. That's false, you will have problems, it will take time, and don't think the Army on your resume gets you a guarantee at any job.

10. What question(s) would you have liked to have known before taking your first job?

I asked a lot of questions before I even wanted to interview for my career and I looked at the company. I would recommend any Veteran to do their research and still ask those questions just to vet the know of the company.

11. What are the most important lessons you can share on making a successful job transition from the military?

The three most important lessons I learned were:

1. Apply for college.

2. Figure out your field.

3. Don't stress anything.

12. If you could do it again, what would be the one thing you would do (better) or not do to help in your transition?

LOL. If I could do it again, I would have come out with a degree.

Joseph Isom

Service rank: Master Sergeant, USAF

Position: Senior Principal, Cyber Systems Engineer

Industry: Government Contractor

Biography

I entered the Air Force about a year after graduating from high school. I picked 5 jobs relating to electronics and got assigned to my 1st or 2nd choice. Basic training was an eye-opener for sure. The discipline was needed, but the heat of San Antonio in the summer was not.

Early on, I got the sense of a theme developing – "cooperate and graduate." After basic training, I was sent to Keesler AFB for 6 months of basic electronics training and then the Communications Electronics and Switching Systems Maintenance course. After technical school, I had assignments in California, Germany, South Carolina, Virginia, and Maryland. Throughout my military career, I progressed from an apprentice to journeyman to manager.

I always liked (and still do) the technical side of work and never strived to manage people or projects. After retirement, my transition to government contractor, then government civilian, and now back to government contractor has been a 38-year trip. I have worked for three defense contractors as well as Air Force and Navy Civil Service. I added my 20-year active-duty career to my civil service retirement and in a couple more years will retire completely.

Questions & Answers

1. Describe your journey from the service to your first job?

Following the Transition Assistance Program (TAP) briefing, about 4 months prior to retirement, I began looking for work as a government contractor at my last base.

SAIC and General Dynamics had openings in my field and I applied to both three months prior to retirement. I was hired by SAIC and began work immediately after retirement.

2. How did you find your first job? Describe the process.

I researched the local government contractors by networking with my peers and online resources. I looked through the email global address list and picked out individuals (based on their office symbol) and invited them to lunch. I studied information from company websites to learn more about their projects and/or contracts. Staying local and having a marketable skill made the process fairly easy due to the abundance of local defense contractors.

3. When did you start planning your transition? What actions/ activities did you take?

Six months prior to my retirement, I used an online resume training seminar to develop a tailored resume. I also attained an industry certification relating to my field.

Again, I studied information from company websites to learn more about their projects and ways to tune my resume toward them.

4. Did you pursue any advanced degrees and/or certifications? Did they help?

I did attain an industry certification for a computer operating system (O/S). Until then, my career was always related to computer hardware and networking. Having the additional O/S certification did enhance my marketability. I found that certifications are highly desired and can be obtained fairly quickly.

5. Why did you choose the work/career you are in?

■ I had a pretty extensive list of jobs starting in 9th or 10th grade and through high school working different positions in a restaurant, loading semi-trucks, paper recycling warehousing, and even an electrical apprentice. My father was an electrician and his advice was, "it's either too hot or too cold in this job…" Like many, soon after high school I joined the military and entered delayed enlistment.

I had to choose several options of career fields and the Air Force would put me where they needed me. I chose technical fields, looking for a career that would pay well after separation and where I would be working indoors.

6. Have you encountered any obstacles in advancing your career?

■ Probably the most prevalent obstacle in my career advancement has been keeping up with industry certifications. Certifications can become the proverbial "self-licking ice cream cone." If you pursue and attain too many, you can have issues with the continuing education and maintenance fees required to maintain them. Stay focused on what is required for the position you want. Also, the inevitable advancement to management was one thing I always had trouble with. Decide on your desired path.

7. What were the 2 hardest efforts about transitioning?

■ The first effort is learning to adapt to a less team-centric environment. The military is all about team effort. Early in basic training, I heard the term "cooperate and graduate." That came back during technical school and several times throughout my military career.

Outside the military, competition drives people to close ranks and not delegate or ask for help.

Another hurdle was reaching back to military colleagues for assistance with issues that may cross-over to a contract position. I had a certain animosity toward civilians and contractors while on active duty. You see people that may not show that they are pulling their weight and you form opinions.

After becoming a contractor and joining the civil service, I still saw those that don't pull their weight but, overall, the work ethic of individuals is replicated in all three scenarios.

8. What do you think are the top issues for Veterans transitioning into a career?

Having the certification and experience for the position you are looking for. In the military, my experience was always to get thrown into a position, get trained (either on the job or sent to technical training), then gradually (and purposely) fill the role you are assigned to.

Contract/civilian positions are looking for someone who can produce on day one. Having the certification will only get a second look at your resume. You need to show experience or enough knowledge to get further along in the hiring process.

9. Do you believe there is a stereotype attached to being a Veteran in pursuit of a job?

Typically, I associate the word "stereotype" with a negative connotation. In this instance, I'm going to say yes and explain that it is a positive. Military veterans are known for being self-starters, quick to adapt, and easy to train. Veterans also have a lot of training in treating others with respect (sexual harassment, ethics, etc.). I haven't encountered a negative stereotype associated with being a veteran.

10. What question(s) would you have liked to have known before taking your first job?

I think the military is great at identifying and explaining where your position fits into the mission. Contract positions, in my experience, seem to drop you in a role and expect results quickly.

Identifying my role in the overall mission and how it fits with other in the organization would provide clarity and purpose.

11. What are the most important lessons you can share on making a successful job transition from the military?

1. Start early. The military teaches preparation from day one. Remember that skill and it will help your transition. As an enlisted person, I learned that the more preparation I put into promotion testing, the better I did. You have control over your outcomes.

2. Be available to relocate. Being available to relocate, which was a core tenet in the military, can be very helpful to your bottom line. In my experience, your next job's starting salary is often based on your previous job's ending salary. So, if you have to relocate to take a higher paying job, that initial move can pay off in the long run.

3. Stay focused on the upcoming transition. I had success early in my search for a position and while that gave me security, it may have limited my early earning potential. While I was satisfied in that position, I think I took it to keep a level of comfort that I had on active duty. Keep your focus on what your goal is. Do you want to work technical type tasks or manage projects or people? The military tends to dictate to you, but in your post-military career you have control.

12. If you could do it again, what would be the one thing you would do (better) or not do to help in your transition?

I would take advantage of every opportunity for assistance/training/seminar that are available when you are preparing to separate. After separation, you can be too busy to focus on preparation. I passed on a few workshops that would have helped in the long run, because I had a position lined up at retirement. The more information you have before separation, the better off you will be.

Bill Johansson

Service rank: Commander, USN

Position: Clinical Physicist

Industry: Healthcare

Biography

After retiring from the US Navy as a Commander, Bill Johansson joined Moffitt Cancer Center in Tampa, Florida where he currently serves as an Assistant Clinical Physicist in the Radiation Oncology Department supporting Moffitt's mission to contribute to the prevention and cure of cancer. He is a former executive board member of Wheels of Success, a Tampa-based non-profit providing vehicles to working families in need. Together with his wife, he co-leads seminars and workshops to improve communication and trust for couples struggling with their marriages, in partnership with regional and international non-profit organizations. Bill is a 20-year veteran of the United States Navy where he served as a Submarine Officer and Operations Analyst in a variety of roles and leadership positions, to include a tour as second-in-command of the first U.S. submarine to integrate women onboard. He is blessed to have been a leader on teams who are six-time winners of national and regional awards for operational excellence.

Questions & Answers

1. Describe your journey from the service to your first job?

In 2014, I arrived in Tampa at United States Special Operations Command (SOCOM) having just been selected to command a submarine. I was planning to spend two years on the staff before attending the Submarine Command Course and taking command of a submarine. On Father's Day in 2015, I felt an unusual sensation run down my right side. While I thought I was simply dehydrated, I would soon realize I was having a stroke. I had lost 30% of the strength on my right side, and had to learn to walk and write normally again. After 18 months of rehab, and realizing I had lost some of the cognitive skills required to command a submarine, I faced a crossroads. Do I continue on in the military moving from staff to staff with two daughters approaching High School, or do I start working on a plan to transition out of the Navy? I had an incredibly uneasy feeling, as if I was on a barge that had just been released from its tugboat, drifting aimlessly down the river, being pushed by the current in a direction I could not control.

For me, the transition effort started early in 2018, about one year before I ultimately retired. Prior to accepting a Navy ROTC scholarship in 1998 to attend the University of Michigan, I had considered careers in Engineering and Medicine. The scholarship tilted the scales toward Engineering, but I had often wondered how a career in medicine would have turned out for me. I started looking at requirements to go back to school to become a Physician's Assistant (PA), but quickly realized I needed several prerequisite courses and hundreds of patient contact hours to even apply. How would I get there? I was a bit discouraged at first, but as I researched more, I started to build a plan. I was like a traveler in a foreign city without a map, starting to explore on my own – aware of the opportunity, but unsure of my direction or surroundings.

In April 2018, I was two weeks away from enrolling in a Nursing Assistant program in order to get enough patient contact hours to enroll in a PA program when I got a phone call from one of my former peers at SOCOM who had recently retired. He had transitioned into a strategic planning job at Moffitt Cancer Center in Tampa. Earlier that day, he had been in a meeting with the leadership of the Radiation Oncology department. The department administrator, a Medical Physicist, was telling a story about how early in his career when he worked in New York, he used to recruit new physicists from among the nuclear-trained submarine officers in Groton, Connecticut. My friend called me up. "You used to be a Nuclear Engineer on a submarine, right? You should talk to this guy and see if he could use your help."

He set up a call with the department administrator, and we talked about the possible opportunities for me in the Radiation Oncology department at Moffitt. We scheduled a time to meet, where I could shadow the dosimetrists and physicists in the department for an afternoon to see if I would be interested in clinical work. After a few hours, I knew this was exactly what I wanted to do. For me it was a perfect blend of leveraging my past experience, fulfilling a long-held desire to work a clinical environment, serving a worthy mission, and growing in a new career. The only problem… there was not a job opening. While I remained optimistic, I felt unsure, like climbing to the top of a ladder and not knowing if I can reach what I am grasping for without falling.

I spent the next eight months going through the formal Department of Defense transition programs, looking at other career opportunities, polishing my resume and LinkedIn profile, volunteering for various non-profit organizations around the Tampa Bay Area, attending networking events, but still no job opening at Moffitt. I was a little more than a month away from retirement and approaching the holiday season without a solid job opportunity in sight. The stress began to build and I shifted my focus to other career options. I remembered the last thing the department administrator had told me… he would love to have me as part of the team, but the hardest thing for him to do was add another position.

I applied for a few engineering jobs, to include a position at Tampa Electric Company, where I was told I did not have the experience they were looking for. I thought it was an obvious fit – I had the responsibility for running a 165-megawatt power plant as the Chief Engineer on the submarine, and oversight responsibility for six nuclear reactors as a submarine squadron Material Officer. Perhaps I did not effectively communicate my skills, but more likely it was risk aversion and a lack of someone on the inside advocating for giving me a chance. Then I applied to a government contractor who had a contract at SOCOM. The same afternoon I received an offer from the contractor, I also got a call from Moffitt. "Good news, the position is approved. You should be able to apply on the website within 24 hours." I felt a tremendous sense of relief and joy.

I was interviewing a week later, and received an offer within a few more days. I have been in the job for one and a half years, thoroughly enjoying every day of the journey.

2. How did you find your first job? Describe the process.

■ I found my first job through another veteran in my network. While the opportunity was quite serendipitous, my particular story illustrates the importance of networking. I have seen this with a number of my peers, spending hours online filling out applications without positive results, until they met the one person who could introduce them to a hiring manager inside the organization who gave them the chance to prove themselves.

3. When did you start planning your transition? What actions/ ■ activities did you take?

I approached every new assignment in the Navy with an eye towards transition. For any military family, the strain on home life is ever present. In our case, losing our son to SIDS early in my military career was a stark example of how hard active duty life can be with strife in the home. From that perspective, I always considered transitioning as an option, but did not start planning for transition in earnest until one year prior to retirement.

My first big step in transition preparation was to attend a LinkedIn workshop presented by Nancy Laine and Project Transition USA on MacDill Air Force Base. Everything really built from there. After I attended, I started coming back as a volunteer where I met more people, heard more transition stories, refined my LinkedIn profile and resume, and soaked up a whole host of lessons learned from other successfully transitioned veterans.

4. Did you pursue any advanced degrees and/or certifications? ■ Did they help?

I did not end up pursuing advanced degrees or certifications, but was in the process of doing so when the job opportunity as a Clinical Physics Assistant came along. Had my former colleague not connected me with someone who could use my skills in a clinical environment without further education, I would have pursued an advanced degree to become a Physician's Assistant.

5. Why did you choose the work/career you are in?

■ I have always been mission driven. It is the primary reason why I decided to join the Navy. I wanted to continue to contribute to an organization that served others after I retired from the military. Working in the healthcare industry, especially for a non-profit hospital, allows me to do just that; in this case, to be part of Moffitt Cancer Center's mission of "contributing to the prevention and cure of cancer."

6. Have you encountered any obstacles in advancing your career?

■ The primary obstacle to advancing my career is further formal education and certification. My manager is supportive of this effort, and the work I do on a day-to-day basis will help me pursue further education. Right now, I am somewhat limited in the scope of what I can contribute to the team without a license. However, with the volume of work, I can continue to make a valuable contribution each day without further certification.

7. What were the 2 hardest efforts about transitioning?

■ The two most difficult efforts about transitioning into the civilian workforce were first overcoming some broad stereotypes in the civilian sector associated with veterans, and second, translating relevant skills into a career field where it is not immediately apparent those skills apply.

With my specific employer, I at least had one proponent of giving me a chance to overcome the stereotypes AND translate relevant skills. I still encounter some who question my ability or credentials, but over the first year I was able to demonstrate my value to the team.

For other employers where I applied or interviewed, I met the most resistance with the recruiters and Human Resources – who I refer to as the "gatekeepers." In my experience, this is where the stereotypes and skill translation were the most challenging, which is why I am a huge advocate of networking. If you can meet the right person beyond the gatekeeper, you have a much better chance of being able to express your value to your potential future employer. The recruiter just doesn't want to strike out. Hiring managers are more willing to swing for the fences.

8. What do you think are the top issues for Veterans transitioning into a career?

I think the winds are changing on the top issues. I transitioned at an inflection point of this change, where veterans who transitioned before me did not always get much support in their transition journey, and those who transitioned after me have some wonderful opportunities through programs like DoD SkillsBridge and Hiring Our Heroes Corporate Fellowships to close the gap between skills they have and the skills they will need in a different career.

Right now, I think overcoming the view that veterans are rigid, unimaginative, or will not easily adapt to the culture is the biggest issue. In most cases, this could not be further from the truth. Anyone who has deployed has likely had the experience of needing to improvise to compensate for not having what they need. We have had to adapt to a number of new homes and workplaces, throughout the country and around the world. We have had to remain flexible while fighting wars and operating in very uncertain environments. These experiences provide immeasurable value that cannot always be easily demonstrated on a one or two-page resume.

9. Do you believe there is a stereotype attached to being a Veteran in pursuit of a job?

There are several stereotypes I have encountered throughout my transition process. A few of my favorites:

I went to a job fair wearing a Navy lapel pin, and someone at the registration desk directed me to a company looking to hire security guards, without ever asking what I did in the military.

I have heard numerous times how "veterans are too rigid and inflexible" to integrate into civilian life. My response is that perhaps the organization is too rigid and inflexible to consider hiring a veteran who may bring a different perspective or body of experience to the company.

Many envision the military as a black hole for creativity. To those, I would ask if one of your production machines went down on a Friday, what would you do. Wait until Monday? Call a contractor to fix it for you? What if you were hundreds of feet beneath the ocean, and your oxygen generating machine suffered a catastrophic failure thousands of miles from the nearest repair facility, and you NEED oxygen to live through the weekend. Well, I have been in that situation, and we found a way to make it work. That's creativity!

10. What question(s) would you have liked to have known before taking your first job?

How can I effectively negotiate higher salary/more paid time off/other benefits if I will not need employer-provided healthcare/dental/vision? This question is not one for the employer, but is an area which in hindsight I think was not well covered in any of the transition programs offered or required by the Department of Defense. Particularly for retirees who have the option of Veteran's Administration or Tricare healthcare benefits for them and their families, there may be more in the way of salary of paid time off if the company does not have to pay all or a portion of those costs.

What is your vision for me in five years? Ten years? What will it take for me to get there? In the military, most active duty service members have well-defined career paths and milestones. This is likely not the case with most civilian employers. There will probably not be someone managing your career path – that is up to you. If you don't ask, you will not know, or worse yet, may not be willing or able to do what is required to get promoted.

11. What are the most important lessons you can share on making a successful job transition from the military?

1. Figure out what you want to do, and what you need from others to help get you there. There are numerous veteran-focused organizations willing to help transitioning veterans, but it is extremely difficult for them to help if you don't have a clear idea of what you want. Be as specific as possible. As someone who wanted to continue to serve a worthy mission, I began volunteering in my last couple of years on active duty. Whether as a LinkedIn coach for Project Transition USA, as an executive board member for Wheels of Success, or for a number of other events, I was building my network in the non-profit arena. I gained valuable insight and met some great like-minded people who helped

me understand the differences between for-profit and non-profit companies. For me, that experience helped to show I would be a good fit at Moffitt Cancer Center, a non-profit comprehensive cancer center.

2. Spend time learning how to translate your skills from the military (hard skills and soft skills) into language civilian employers can understand, with a focus on how those skills can help them solve their most pressing problems. I accessed the services of a number of non-profit organizations to help translate my own skills, most notably: American Corporate Partners, Tampa Bay Job Links, Veterati, and Transition Masters. I also spent time reading articles and books on this topic, and taking advantage of LinkedIn's year of complimentary Premium access to take some online courses to be able to identify and translate my experience into something a hiring manager would understand.

3. Be humble, ask questions, and listen. While veterans have a great many skills, we don't know everything about the civilian world. First off, don't overstate what you did in the military. I have seen a number of veterans who had command at some level of the military refer to themselves as the "CEO" in a resume or in their LinkedIn profile. This is disingenuous. Unless you were a Service Chief and made enterprise-level decisions, you weren't the CEO. Second, ask questions and actively listen. My favorite question to ask someone I just met at a networking event: "Tell me about what you do?" My second favorite question when they got to something I didn't understand: "Tell me a little more about (thing I didn't understand)." My experience is that people love talking about what they do. After a while, you will find yourself slowly replacing military acronyms with civilian speak.

12. If you could do it again, what would be the one thing you would do (better) or not do to help in your transition?

The one thing I would have done better is to more fully trust the process and have patience. I was putting a tremendous amount of effort into self-discovery, research, accessing all of the local and national resources I could, and writing/re-writing/editing resumes and cover letters. I had all the help I needed, and all the drive to give the transition my best effort. I was working 20-30 hours a week on transition while still doing my Active Duty job for months before I retired, and 50-60 hours a week once I was on terminal leave. But I still let the doubt creep in… did I really make the right decision to transition now? I put myself through a lot of unnecessary stress and negative self-talk worrying about not finding the "right" job right now. I had a plan A, plan B, and plan C. Something was bound to work out for me, and it did. I just needed to work the process, trust the process and have patience.

Laurell Jones

Service rank: Lieutenant Colonel, USAF

Position: Consultant

Industry: Government

Biography

Multiple roles in financial management and financial analysis during a 23-year military career. Increasing levels of leadership in multiple international and US based locations. Served as a Squadron Commander twice (Turkey and Japan) and two assignments to the Pentagon including a Division Chief position. Over the span of 15 years as a senior managing consultant was a trusted business adviser to five federal government agencies. Managed projects and teams in the US and internationally. A strategic thought leader known for providing insight that unites project management and training strengths. Ability to drive project effectiveness across multiple government agencies and business units by tailoring executive level communication to obtain buy-in from diverse group of stakeholders. Branded as an approachable, collaborative problem solver leader who fosters a team environment that consistently led to the development of ideas and processes that yielded breakthrough results.

Questions & Answers

1. Describe your journey from the service to your first job?
■ With anticipation and excitement, I started planning my transition

about a year before my scheduled retirement. I recommend 12-18 months to start thinking about the logistics of transition and allow yourself adequate time if completion of additional education/certifications is in your plans. It took me about three months to find my position. While on terminal leave, I completed all applications and interviews.

2. How did you find your first job? Describe the process.

■ Once I announced my retirement, I was very fortunate that individuals whom I had worked for or I knew through mutual acquaintances approached me. My last duty assignment was at the Pentagon and I was remaining in the Washington DC metro so there were a number of job options available in the private sector and as a civilian in the Federal government.

I encourage members to use their entire network to include family, friends, church members, co-workers, current and past supervisors. An applicable saying is "a closed mouth doesn't get fed." Network, network, network!

3. When did you start planning your transition? What actions/activities did you take?

During the year prior to my retirement transition, I attended the two-day Transition Assistance Program (TAP) workshop. TAP was very helpful as a resource in resume writing. I also did some soul searching and conducted a personal skills inventory as I answered the question "What next". This exercise helped me identify my strengths, weaknesses, personal interests and professional passion. I was able to use that information to craft a resume that spoke to the positions I pursued in my job search.

4. Did you pursue any advanced degrees and/or certifications? Did they help?

While serving in the USAF, I completed a Master of Business Administration and later attended Air War College in residence where I completed a second master's degree. Additionally, I obtained a Certificate of Defense Financial Management (CDFM). During my transition period I didn't pursue any additional education, but I think the degrees and certification I already held were contributing factors to my successful job search because they were evidence of being on a quest for life-long learning. Most employers are looking for individuals who have demonstrated the ability to learn and interest in being knowledge seekers.

5. Why did you choose the work/career you are in?

■ At its heart consulting is about problem solving. I loved the possibility of using and adapting the skills I honed as an Air Force officer to a diverse set of problems. Consulting also offered the opportunity to support a number of different agencies. During my 15 years as a consultant while employed by the same firm, I supported five government agencies and held positions that ranged from Communications Director to Business Process Re-Engineering Analyst to Instructor to Project Manager to name a few.

6. Have you encountered any obstacles in advancing your career?

■ The expectation is that a senior consultant has grown up through the ranks and is very familiar with consulting methodologies and industry best practices. While this was a hurdle, I didn't see it as an insurmountable obstacle. Entering the consulting world at a senior level because of my military career experience definitely accelerated my "on the job" training and search for new mentors.

7. What were the 2 hardest efforts about transitioning?

■ The two hardest efforts about transitioning are deciding what you think you're interested in doing in the civilian world and translating your military experience into civilian need. Both of these efforts require time, but they are foundational to a successful job search. The good news is that resources exist to help with both of these efforts (e.g. skills inventory tools, What Color is Your Parachute – best-selling career book, VA military skills translator.) In my case, once I decided I wanted to pursue the path of being a consultant based on my skills and interest, it shaped my entire job search.

8. What do you think are the top issues for Veterans transitioning into a career?

Interview preparation and resume writing especially translating military experience and acronyms "jargon" into civilian language is an issue most veterans have to tackle.

Adapting to a corporate culture that is structured differently than the military. This requires you to watch and observe cues - not only what's written but what's done. That runs the gamut from appropriate work attire to job performance standards.

9. Do you believe there is a stereotype attached to being a Veteran in pursuit of a job?

A common negative stereotype is that veterans are autocratic leaders and not adaptable to a more democratic leadership style. Two positive stereotype which are actually true, is that veterans have high moral standards (integrity) and a strong work ethic.

10. What question(s) would you have liked to have known before taking your first job?

I did my research and used my network, so I felt prepared for life in the civilian world. I recommend transitioning veterans do some research on how to negotiate for salary in the private sector. In the military, obviously, that's not something that we do. One of my civilian mentors shared that advice and it emboldened me to ask for a hiring bonus. Without that advice, I wouldn't have known that was an option and would have left a five-figure signing bonus on the table.

11. What are the most important lessons you can share on making a successful job transition from the military?

1. Spend some time thinking about what you're passionate about and look for a career that dovetails. Do some "soul-searching". Consider your top drivers and motivation in the job search – location, work environment, professional interests, work life balance, do you want to continue doing what you did while in uniform – if there's a civilian equivalent or do you want to apply your skills in a new career field. Don't box yourself in narrowly based on your prior experience. Look at the common traits that transcend positions. Those traits include leadership, problem solving, team- work. Identify your skills, interest and see how that fits into a job not the other way around.

2. Don't be intimidated by the thought of writing your resume. Consider

using the LinkedIn Resume Assistant as a resource and inspiration in developing your resume. Use the veterans service organizations for free resume assistance and job posting boards e.g. AMVETS, VFW, MOAA. Ask for help -- definitely plan for a number of reviews and critiques.

3. Develop a timeline and personal checklist for your job search. Be proactive - start planning early for your transition (12-18 months is ideal). Make sure your planning and preparation extends to conducting through research about any company, agency where you interview. In the military, we always said if you're 15 minutes early you're on time. That embraced the philosophy that we tried to prepare for things to go wrong and mitigate that by prior planning.

4. Identify and obtain any additional education, certifications during your preparation time that make you a more competitive job candidate.

5. Seek out mentors – with military experience and steeped in the culture of your employer

6. Network, Network, Network!

12. If you could do it again, what would be the one thing you would do (better) or not do to help in your transition?

I can honestly say I wouldn't change anything that I did in preparing for my transition. The firm that I selected I stayed with for 15 years and continued to have challenging and enriching opportunities.

On a final note, I want to encourage all transitioning veterans to stay positive and remind yourself of what you've already accomplished.

Roger Jones

Service rank: Colonel, USA

Position: VP, Mission Support Operations

Industry: Defense

Biography

Anative of Hampton, Virginia, I graduated from a Historically Black College and University (HBCU), Norfolk State University, receiving my Commission as an Infantry Officer in 1985. I served as an Infantry Rifle Platoon Leader, Scout Platoon, Company Executive Officer, Company Commander and Ranger Instructor before going to the U.S. Army Special Forces Qualification Course at Fort Bragg, North Carolina in 1992. My Special Operations assignments ranged from Special Forces Operational Detachment (A) Commander at the 5th Special Forces Group (Airborne), Special Operations Forces Acquisitions Operational Test & Evaluator, through Special Forces Group Deputy Commander and Battalion Command at United States Army Recruiting Command. After my Battalion Command, I was assigned to Special Operations Command Central at MacDill Air Force Base where I deployed to Iraq in support of Operation Iraqi Freedom, and Pakistan in support of OEF-AFG. I used my 28+ years of experience as a foundation and transitioned to a career out of uniform where I first worked for Northrop Grumman and then two small companies supporting Special Operations Command Central, SOCCENT's Joint Exercises Planning cell. I went on to another small business – SHINE Systems & Technologies – to manage their SOCOM Wide Mission Support-B (SWMS-B) portfolio efforts.

That experience led to my recruitment to ARMA Global, a General Dynamics Company to manage their SWMS-A portfolio as a Senior Program Manager. I currently work at Spathe Systems as the Vice President of Mission Support.

Questions & Answers

1 Describe your journey from the service to your first job?

■ I mentally started my transition out of the military as soon a was promoted to colonel and six years before I separated from uniformed service. I knew I was not going to be promoted any farther and I had to start planning for life after the uniform. I made multiple lists and spreadsheets of jobs or careers I wanted to pursue. What was most important to me at the time centered around quality of life with my family and time spent with them. Two years prior to my actual retirement, I was approached by a Program Manager from General Dynamics, Ordinance and Tactical Systems (GD-OTS) who asked me to consider joining them after I retired. In 2013, General Dynamics was competing with other vendors to developing a new Ground Mobility Vehicle for the United States Army Special Forces. After visiting their GD-OTS HQs and talking to their Director of Operations and Director of HR, I decided to submit my application for retirement with a retirement date in the spring of 2014. I thought I had my post military career employment all lined up before I separated however, what I did not have in hand was a Contingent Offer Letter from GD-OTS. I was confident that GD-OTS as going to be awarded the $562 million contract to produce the new Ground Mobility Vehicle and my retirement date was set for March 2014. I was excited when I heard the announcement of GD-OTS' award of the GMV contract on the local news mid-2013. I did not hear from GD-OTS for weeks after they won the GMV contract. I called to re-connect with the PM and Operations Director. They both had a very different tone in their conversations with me post award. They told me that they could not hire me at that time. I had nothing from them that said they had to give me a position after I retired. So, it was back to the drawing board and I began networking within the building at United States Special

Operations Command. I quickly found a position with Northrop Grumman as a Joint Chief of Staff, Military Exercise Planner.

2. How did you find your first job? Describe the process.

■ I found my first job through networking inside the United State Special Operations Command prior to separating from service. Almost everyone around SOCOM knows that you are going to retire soon, and they are constantly asking, what are you going to do after you get out. Once my plans for GD-OTS disappeared, my story changed when folks asked about my future. There are defense industry companies that will scarf you up, but the key to getting the right position is timing. I informed a close friend and someone that I considered a mentor that I was looking for post-retirement employment. He was the Program Manager for Northrop Grumman and he said they were always looking for guys with a Special Operations background. They offer me a position and I quickly accepted with little negotiations. I wanted to start my civilian employment with no break or time off.

3. When did you start planning your transition? What actions/ activities did you take?

I was mentally prepared six years before I retired however, I did not attend the MacDill Air Force Base Transition Assistance Program until 9 months before my actual retirement date.   MacDill's TAP program was very enlightening. The course gave me the tools to get in the right frame of mind to prepare for post-retirement employment. Plus, it gave me the opportunity to network with other service members that were planning to retire. One of the best workshops in the course was the LinkedIn workshops. I then realized the importance of a digital resume online that recruiters could easily access 24-7.

4. Did you pursue any advanced degrees and/or certifications? Did they help?

For the level of work, I wanted after retirement, I needed a master's degree. Lack of the degree can be a major discriminator on a resume. I did not complete my master's degree until 2014 because a was undecided on whether to attend the Army War College. Once I declined to attend the War College in 2009, I committed to complete a master's degree in a discipline of my choosing. The Army War College's Master's program offered a degree in strategic studies. At the corporate level, most commercial employers do not care what your master's degree is in, however, I wanted a degree in Information Systems Management because I felt cyberspace was where our nation's future conflicts will be. My initial job out of uniform did not require me to have a master's degree, but once I started looking beyond working on site with a customer, a Masters' degree was a pass/fail as to whether they would accept me for a job at the corporate level.

5. Why did you choose the work/career you are in?

■ I choose to work in the Defense Industry because that is where former military professionals can put our experiences and acquired talents to immediate use. I did consider moving away from the DOD for post military service employment. I talked to a few companies about opportunities. But they wanted me to accept positions that a much younger officer with considerably less experience would take. The expectation was that I would work my way up once they recognized my knowledge, skills, and abilities. If I were 10 or 20 years younger, that may have been a serious consideration. But I wanted to go right to work applying my talents and not sit back and watch others learn lessons that I learned through out a 28-year Army career.

6. Have you encountered any obstacles in advancing your career?

■ I did encounter obstacles however I did not allow them to have a negative impact on my daily work ethic. I kept a positive attitude about doing my very best for the company and the supported customer. No one knew I was not satisfied with my position or any of my compensation. As a matter of fact, I would have been ok with keeping any of the past positions I held over the last six years since military retirement. Once I saw something or someone as an obstacle, I then began to consider alternate career opportunities. I believe it's human nature to overcome obstacles by changing yourself or adapting one's behavior.

7. What were the 2 hardest efforts about transitioning?

■ Some veterans find it difficult to transition to civilian work and leave their rank behind. We are no longer identified by the title and addressed as such with all the respect that the military requires. The transition from a uniformed Special Operator to positions of leadership out of uniform can be difficult. In civilian work, it's about the scope of work that you do, the responsibilities in your job and how well you take care of people around you that garner the respect and recognition. I have often talked about joining the United States Army Special Forces out of a sense of duty with a hunger for adventure. In time, adventure turns to a profession. Once a professional in your field, there is a thirst to master your craft and a quest for originality in your specialties. Moving up, you realize these positions are not about adventure or you anymore – the profession becomes a calling to get the mission accomplished and to take care of those around you. This step and transition is perhaps the most difficult for the professional operator to make as it requires you to elevate yourself from the crowd. I am proud to say that I feel right at home as I lead people out of uniform.

8. What do you think are the top issues for Veterans transitioning into a career?

I do not see many issues with veterans that transition into a career in the Defense Industry. Most veterans know what they are getting into because we get to observe Defense contractors up close by working side by side with them through out your career. The Department of Defense workforce is made up of uniformed service members, Civil Service employees and contractors with contractors making up 22% to 37% of the workforce based on service component. So, there are a lot of known issues in becoming a contractor. One unknown however is salary and knowing what your value in the industry is. Post uniform employment was the first time I had to negotiate my salary. I was very unprepared to have that conversation. It seemed selfish to ask for more money for your talents. No one told me about being prepared to negotiate my salary in annual income and/or hourly income. For almost three decades my talents and effort was all about serving my country, the constitution and those around me.

9. Do you believe there is a stereotype attached to being a Veteran in pursuit of a job?

Because I am in the business of recruiting veterans, I do not think there is a stereotype attached to veterans pursuing a job. I know the talented asset that is leaving the uniformed service. I know how much the United States service components have invested in its people. Outside of the Defense Industry, there may be stereotyping of our veterans. Our stereotype should not be that we all have Post-Traumatic Stress, or we are depressed. What we should focus on about veterans is character. Most veterans have an entrepreneurial spirit; we are fast lifelong learners; we are loyal and have integrity with a strong work ethic. That is the stereotype we should brand our veterans with.

10. What question(s) would you have liked to have known before taking your first job?

I wish someone would have told me about contingent offer letters before my first civilian job quest. I told you about how I was approached by General Dynamics, Ordinance and Tactical Systems (GD-OTS) who asked me to consider joining them after I retired. They convinced me to submit my retirement request however once they won a $562 million contract with USSOCOM, they told me they could not bring me on. I thought I had my post military career employment all lined up before I separated however, what I did not have in hand was a Contingent Offer Letter from GD-OTS as I separated from service. That is something I did not get in any of my formal uniformed education or from friends that retired before me. I think USSOCOM is doing better now by allowing service member at the end of their career to intern at perspective companies. It is enlightening to engage with people and ask questions with no retributions or judgement.

11. What are the most important lessons you can share on making a successful job transition from the military?

1. First, attend a Transition Assistance Program (TAP) workshop and take it seriously. You just don't know what you don't know, and you can learn a ton from people that have gone before you.

2. Second, make it your mission to analyze your transferrable skills and market them to a perspective employer or industry. Everyone has a niche and you should know yours.

3. Lastly, get out there and network, network, network. To rise above the noise of hundreds of people that are looking for jobs, start with veterans that are now in the corporate world. Do not rush to ask for a job. A lot of times there is no job available because timing is everything. Instead,

take time to know the person. Ask how they approached the transition from military to their civilian career. Only at the end of the conversation is it ok for you to ask whether they are aware of any job openings.

12. If you could do it again, what would be the one thing you would do (better) or not do to help in your transition?

If I had it to do all over again, I would start networking sooner, secure a position with a contingent offer letter and take some time off between careers. A couple of months' break would have recharged my personal battery. I would have given my family some quality payback time from all of those deployments and promised time "after I retire from the Army."

William E. "Bill" Kieffer

Service rank: Captain, USA

Position: President & Chief Advisor

Industry: Career/Management

Consulting

Biography

Bill is President & Chief Advisor of Kieffer & Associates Limited, an advisory firm specializing in Military Veteran Career Transition, Leadership Coaching, Strategic Talent Management (including military veteran hiring and employment) and Professional Speaking services. He also serves as a coach for "The Honor Foundation."

Bill is a senior human resource, talent management, and organizational development executive with over 23 years' experience in multiple large, complex, global companies. His broad-ranging work includes coaching/advising individual leaders and teams from the c-suite to the shop floor regarding talent strategies and practices that optimize individual and organizational capabilities, and enable mission success. This includes organizational consulting/development, strategy/program design, and implementation for full spectrum talent management (assessment, talent acquisition, performance improvement, talent & leadership development, succession planning, and transformation etc.).

Bill also served over 11 years as a United States Army Officer, in a variety of command and staff positions. Highlights include combat service in Somalia, support for the Panama invasion, operations in Central America, Hurricane Andrew relief operations, and being selected as "Instructor of the Year" while teaching at the US Army Logistics Management College.

Bill's education includes Harvard Business School's Strategic Human Resources Program; Harvard University John F. Kennedy School of Government's Leadership Education Program; a Master of Science, Administration from Central Michigan University, and a Bachelor of Business Administration from the University of Toledo.

He has earned "Marshall Goldsmith Stakeholder Centered Coach"; SHRM "Veterans in the Workplace Certification" and "Senior Professional Human Resources" certifications.

Bill is involved in a number of veteran, business, and community volunteer activities, including being elected to multiple terms as a councilmember in his hometown.

He has worked in / travelled to 32 countries, setting foot on every continent except Antarctica.

Bill was honored to present "Investing in the Middle" at TEDx Toledo in 2017.

Questions & Answers

1 Describe your journey from the service to your first job?

■ My journey was quite an adventure. My exit from the Army was due to an unexpected change in family circumstance. My military career had been fantastic with all the right assignments, schools and opportunities, and having been considered and selected for promotion to major.

When family life changed, I faced a tough decision – continue the great career I always wanted or have three young kids who knew who their dad was. For me there was only one answer – my kids.

Although I started 'planning' for my transition about a year out, I was not at all prepared for it. I really had no idea what to do or how to do it. For most of that year I focused far too much on my military duties rather than my transition.

Transition assistance was sparse in 1997. Precious little existed to prepare me for the strange new work world I was about to face. I was on my own professionally for the first time. There was no Army framework (or any other for that matter) to guide my transition efforts. There was no 'team' going through it with me. There was no 'battle buddy' or 'sponsor'.

2. How did you find your first job? Describe the process.

■ It was scary, frustrating and a hell of a learning curve.

I worked my tail off figuring out what I needed, wanted, was interested in and capable of.

I called friends. I called strangers. I read newspaper job ads, registered with job agencies, went to job fairs, had lots of coffee with new people and built up a network of people that were willing and able to help. Eventually a connection of a connection knew of an opening for which he thought I'd be a great candidate – despite it being in a totally different industry and career field. I did as much homework as possible to prepare, survived several interviews and eventually landed as the Deputy Director of Economic Development for the county in which I lived.

3. When did you start planning your transition? What actions/ activities did you take?

I started about a year out but only with a minor effort. I suppose I was in denial. I certainly underestimated how challenging it would be.

When I actually did take meaningful action, my first step was to figure out "Who I was, what I was bringing to the party, and how I define success." I figured that since I didn't know anything about the civilian work world, I better get clear on ME.

Next, I learned everything possible about the transition environment, what the 'career battlefield' looks like and how to 'attack it'. I learned the 'tools' of transition – how to network, where/how to search, how to build/use a resume, what an 'elevator pitch' is, how to interview etc.

4. Did you pursue any advanced degrees and/or certifications? ■ Did they help?

I already had master's degree and decided that additional certifications were not on the critical path to landing well. My first priority was cash flow, so gaining transition and job search expertise were higher priorities than additional degrees/certifications.

5. Why did you choose the work/career you are in?

■ The general career field aligns well with my undergraduate degree (BBA, Human Resources) and some of the best experiences I had while in the U.S. Army (Battalion S3, Company Commander, Officer Advanced Course Instructor, Recruiting Company Commander). The particular specialty areas I chose to focus on (talent strategy & management, learning & development, performance management, succession planning, employee engagement etc.) gave me the opportunity to leverage my military experience and make a value-adding impact on people and business, optimizing capability and results for each.

6. Have you encountered any obstacles in advancing your career?

■ Yes, especially early on. The civilian work world's culture is significantly different than the military and I was not prepared for the differences. Communication, decision-making, organization, profit focus, different understanding and expectations of 'leadership', office politics, and so many other topics were so different that I encountered obstacles that I didn't even know existed.

7. What were the 2 hardest efforts about transitioning?

1. Having virtually unlimited choices but little knowledge of how to make the best choice. For the first time in my professional career I was free to do whatever I wanted. There were no organizational expectations or limitations. On the one hand this was exhilarating. On the other

hand, it was scary as hell. There was no organizational 'momentum', no 'framework', no 'support structure'. I was now truly on my own. It took me a while to realize that my transition moved at the speed I moved it and there was no other 'engine' to keep it rolling nor 'tracks' for it to travel.

2. Learning civilian work culture and language. They are very different than the military and employers generally expect you to hit the ground running, capable of 1) doing the work they need done and 2) fitting in/adding value to the team culture. These are difficult to do when you are unfamiliar with civilian work culture and the 'language of business'.

8. What do you think are the top issues for Veterans transitioning into a career?

- Not knowing 'who they are, what they bring to the party, and how they define success'.

- Lack of familiarity with the civilian work culture and business language.

9. Do you believe there is a stereotype attached to being a Veteran in pursuit of a job?

Yes. There are multiple misperceptions that stereotype veterans and create negative bias. While this is unfortunate, when you consider that well over 90% of the population never served in uniform, it is somewhat understandable. Some of the more common misperceptions impacting the stereotype relate to PTSD and TBI, education levels, personal rigidity, ability to only follow orders, and military experience not being relevant to civilian job needs.

These unfortunate biases create opportunity loss for both veterans and employers. Thus, it is critically important for veterans to prepare thoroughly for their transition, so they are well armed to overcome the challenges.

10. What question(s) would you have liked to have known before taking your first job?

- How different is the civilian world and what do employers really expect?
- How much a difference being a veteran can make (positive and negative) to my success?

- What do I need to do to present myself as the best candidate (and once hired, the best employee)?

11. What are the most important lessons you can share on making a successful job transition from the military?

1. Start NOW.
2. Know YOU.
3. Understand the environment you are about to enter.

12. If you could do it again, what would be the one thing you would do (better) or not do to help in your transition?

I would have started earlier, recognizing that like investing for retirement, preparing for your transition is best done in little bits over time.

Dr. Gerald C. Lowe

Service rank: Lieutenant Commander, USN

Service rank: Specialist, USA

Position: Director of Operations

Industry: Government

Biography

Dr. Gerald Lowe is currently the Director of Operations at Arlington National Cemetery (ANC). He previously held the Supervisory Community Planner job at ANC in the Engineering Department. Before working at ANC, Gerald was the Deputy Director of Cemetery Operations for the American Battle Monuments Commission (ABMC) in their Overseas Operations Office in Paris, France. Prior to working at ABMC, Gerald worked as a Project Manager leading Bradshaw Construction Corporation's FL office. In 2015, Gerald completed an Executive Leadership program with Cornell University. In May 2019, Gerald completed his Doctor of Business Administration (DBA) at the University of South Florida.

Gerald is a native of Knoxville, Tennessee where he enlisted in the U.S. Army after high school and served as a forward observer, assigned to the 3rd Infantry Division - "Rock of the Marne," in Germany, and the 7th Infantry Division - "Light," in Monterey, CA. He then served in the TN Army and Air National Guards while attending college, and is an alumnus of Tennessee Technological University, in Cookeville, Tennessee where he was graduated with a Bachelor of Science in Civil Engineering and a Bachelor of Arts in German. He received his commission as a Naval Officer through the Officer Candidate School in Pensacola, Florida in April 1997.

After attending the Civil Engineer Corps Officer School's Basic class, Gerald spent six months at the Defense Language Institute learning Italian. He next served at Engineering Field Activity, Mediterranean Resident Officer in Charge of Construction, Aviano, Italy as an Assistant Project Engineer. Gerald's next command was Commander Special Boat Squadron ONE, later Naval Special Warfare Group THREE (NSWG-3) where he served as NSWG-3's Facilities Engineer.

Gerald's next duty assignment was graduate school at Florida Atlantic University where he graduated with a Master's in Ocean Engineering. Graduate school was followed by Naval Diving and Salvage Training Center in Panama City, Florida where he was certified as a Basic Diving Officer. Following Dive School, Gerald reported to Underwater Construction Team ONE (UCT1) as the Executive Officer where he deployed in support of Hurricane Katrina recovery efforts. Gerald next served as the UCT support officer on the Naval Facilities Engineering Command staff in Washington, D.C.

From D.C., Gerald deployed to Afghanistan where he served on the Combined Security Transition Command as part of the CJ-Engineering staff managing projects supporting the Afghan National Army (ANA) across Afghanistan. While in Afghanistan, Gerald was selected to transfer to the Foreign Area Officer community. Afterwards, he was assigned to the Defense Language Institute (DLI) where he studied French and was graduated with honors earning the Provost's Award. Before starting classes at Naval Post Graduate School (NPS), Gerald worked in Gabon with the Office of Security Cooperation. Upon graduation from NPS, Gerald received a Master's Degree in National Security Affairs.

Gerald's final tour was as the Arabian Peninsula branch chief in the J7, Exercises & Training Directorate, at U.S. Central Command from July 2011 – August 2013 as the lead exercise planner for exercise EAGLE RESOLVE and other regional exercises. In November 2013 after 27 plus years of military service Gerald retired from the U.S. Navy. From 2013-14 Gerald worked as a Joint Program Training Facilitator at U.S. Central Command.

Questions & Answers

1. Describe your journey from the service to your first job?

■ My journey was not planned. Truthfully, I landed in my first job as a default because I wasn't sure what I wanted to do, or where, or.... My transition preparation started, in earnest, when I was a mere four (4) months from retirement. Initially, I 'forgot' to stop and plan, a fundamental of project management – a task I had done the preponderance of my professional career. The turbulent adjustment I and my family went through is directly attributed to my poor planning. Military service, however, had prepared me in a beneficial way – being persistent. My persistence had exhibited itself negatively as I had persistently ignored planning. Eventually, however, I persistently planned for my next job and how to attain the rewarding work I wanted. Considering my transition holistically from when I started planning my transition, early days of retirement, through the period of my post-transition job it took me 1.5 years to find my first job that I was prepared to accept.

2. How did you find your first job? Describe the process.

■ I found my first job by responding / applying to an on-line job announcement.

3. When did you start planning your transition? What actions/ activities did you take?

When I started planning earnestly, I first considered what certifications / qualifications would be helpful. For me that meant using my experience and skills developed while in the military so I would not have to completely start anew. Project management was a clear choice as I had many years of experience managing projects (construction, exercises, equipment assessments and modernization to name a few). Leadership is another skill (many with military service have this skill as well). Considering that not just HR personnel lack military exposure and experience, but so do many hiring managers I sought to adapt, and translate my skills and experience gained from the military into attributes the civilian marketplace understands and desires. The process itself was long and challenging as I worked to re-define who I am, what my skills are, and what I bring to the table in a manner that HR personnel absent military experience or exposure could understand. It is important to note, the redefining, or translation of my skills and capabilities, was done with the help of friends and colleagues who had made this journey before me.

For leadership, I found an executive leadership certificate program offered by an Ivy League university as my first goal. Coupled with my years in uniform where I honed my leadership skills my newly acquired executive leadership certificate, I hoped, would carry significant weight. Next, and equally ambitious, I pursued and attained my PMP certification. My PMP certification gave me an internationally known certification that represents skills, experience, and abilities that are sought by the private sector across numerous industries.

4. Did you pursue any advanced degrees and/or certifications? Did they help?

Not immediately since I have two master's degrees. Certifications are what I pursued initially because I believed as a more experienced job candidate certifications would validate my hard-earned experience in a way that those in the civilian would appreciate.

5. Why did you choose the work/career you are in?

I chose my current work because of the potential to use, almost daily, more than one skill I developed or attained while serving in the military.

6. Have you encountered any obstacles in advancing your career?

Yes, there are obstacles to overcome when seeking to advance your career no matter what your new profession. The same challenges are more pronounced after you have already had one career, in my opinion, and are starting over again after transitioning from military service when you have no clear plan (there's that word again!). One example of an obstacle is regardless of your experience and skills (no matter how important and desired) you still have to prove yourself in your new job / profession; whereas, your new peers are already a known entity. There isn't a uniform business card that you wear that immediately indicates the experience and skills you have. Another obstacle is deciding do you work for a small business, start your own business, or work for a large corporation? All decisions are great options, but each has its own potential obstacles. Other obstacles that present themselves are whether to fully detach from any connection with the military / U.S. Government, or to continue the connection in some capacity. For example, you spend valuable time moving back and forth from working as a contractor, to government service, to working in private industry where inconsistency becomes your greatest obstacle to advancing. For some this approach works well and provides a variety of opportunities. For others, this approach is less productive and less rewarding. Bottom line, think through and plan which route you want to take so no matter the post-service career (or careers) you select you make the transition with your eyes wide open.

7. What were the 2 hardest efforts about transitioning?

■ Personally, the hardest efforts were leaving a profession and leaving people I enjoyed working with immensely, and finding a new career that was as rewarding.

8. What do you think are the top issues for Veterans ■ transitioning into a career?

Planning for what you want to do, where you want to live, and marketing those hard-earned skills and qualifications in a manner that even HR and hiring managers with little to no military exposure and understanding will want to hire you above all other candidates. Last (and this is not true for all veterans) realizing you don't need a uniform to make a statement, or to be your resume when you walk into a room – be confident that YOU and your skills will carry the day.

9. Do you believe there is a stereotype attached to being a ■ Veteran in pursuit of a job?

Often times, yes, there is a stereotype that because you are a veteran you cannot relate, communicate, and work with a civilian staff. Some even think you are too "rigid" because of military experience to learn something new. The other stereotype is more about ignorance of the multitude of skills that veterans offer. In this latter case, the stereotype is because such a large percentage of American society has no perspective or point of reference about military service and draw conclusions that are not founded on facts or experience.

10. What question(s) would you have liked to have known before taking your first job?

I would have liked to have known what level of responsibility I would be trusted with in my job, and if I would be challenged to grow.

11. What are the most important lessons you can share on making a successful job transition from the military?

For me, the three most important lessons on transitioning from the military successfully are:

1. Start to plan early (planning is an absolute must).

2. Pause to consider what I wanted to do with my second career that would be equally rewarding and challenging as military service.

3. Going outside my comfort zone when considering possible jobs for my second career.

12. If you could do it again, what would be the one thing you would do (better) or not do to help in your transition?

The one thing I would have done is take risks and make radical career changes that would have opened doors to new opportunities sooner than later.

Arthur Manansala

Service rank: Technical Sergeant, USAF

Position: Senior Manager

Industry: Utilities

Biography

I am a 9-year Air Force veteran, joining the service and 1983 and separating in 1992. The motivating factor for me to join the service was my poor discipline in my early college years. My great ASFAB scores really gave me the opportunity to have any job that I wanted and I choose "Open Electronics" because that fit my timeline to join as soon as possible (maybe not the smartest choice). After basic training, I was assigned to Keesler AFB and attended the Technical Controller tech school. As it turns out, Tech Control was a perfect field for me and really started me on a career path that I'm still on today. After tech school, I spent 2 years in McClellan AFB, 3 wonderful years in Bad Munder Radar Site in GE and my 4 final years in Onizuka AFB in California. These assignments gave me great experience in mobile, satellite, telecom and data communication – all very applicable to my transition to the civilian world. In my 9th year in the Air Force I made the decision to separate as I though the civilian world would be a better fit for me. I was hired immediate by Compression Labs Inc. as a QA engineer in software development and have been in the software industry for the last 28 years.

Questions & Answers

1. Describe your journey from the service to your first job?

■ I started interviewing for jobs in the private sector about 3 months prior to my separation. I targeted mostly telecom companies because that is where most of the previously separated people were successful at getting a job in the civilian world. I networked with passed Air Force employees, civilian contractors that worked in the same facility and went to job fairs.

2. How did you find your first job? Describe the process.

■ I was successful at getting one job offer from MCI (I was referred to this job by a former Air Force co-worker), but unfortunately, they wanted me to start right away so that I could attend one of their bi-yearly training sessions. Since I still had a few months left before my separation, I could not accept this job offer (they said they would make me another offer in 6 months when the next training session was scheduled). This was very frustrating for me.

Around 3 weeks prior to my separation, I was given a contact from one of my co-workers who had a friend who was looking to hire a tech support engineer. I called that person, was brought in for interviews immediately and was given a job offer in about 1 weeks' time. It was pure luck that this co-worker knew I was looking for a job.

3. When did you start planning your transition? What actions/ activities did you take?

I did attend a few job fairs in San Jose and participated in resume writing and interviewing seminars. I really didn't find these very useful to me. In the end, most of my leads came from networking and personal referrals. I find this to be the case even today.

4. Did you pursue any advanced degrees and/or certifications? Did they help?

No, I didn't take any additional courses. I also only had an AA degree – so this was somewhat of a roadblock.

5. Why did you choose the work/career you are in?

▪ Sheer luck – if that co-worked hadn't off-handedly heard that I was looking for a job, I would never had gotten that referral. The job I landed was in software development/engineering and I'm still doing that today.

6. Have you encountered any obstacles in advancing your career?

▪ Not really. I've advanced as far as I personally prefer. Any further and I feel that I would not maintain a good work/life balance.

7. What were the 2 hardest efforts about transitioning?

▪ First, not having a clear organizational structure. You really get use to this in the military. Second, understanding how the benefits worked and how to use them.

8. What do you think are the top issues for Veterans transitioning into a career?

Having the confidence to start something totally new. I hired 3 people right out of the military, and they all had issues with thinking they were the right person for the job. In the end, they all turned out to be fantastic and made it their new career.

9. Do you believe there is a stereotype attached to being a Veteran in pursuit of a job?

I do, and mostly a positive stereotype. Veterans are considered disciplined and organized who usually have great leadership skills. I have not come across any negatives so far in my experience.

10. What question(s) would you have liked to have known before taking your first job?

Tough question. I was so young at that point I'm not sure what else could have helped me. I guess if I were to give someone advise it would be to trust your own skills and be very flexible in what you pursue.

11. What are the most important lessons you can share on making a successful job transition from the military?

1. Network!! This is the most important. Tap co-workers, past co-workers,

make new connections, reach out to job site forums and participate.

2. Get professional help in resume/social media creation. A good resume makes a huge difference. I've interviewed 100's of candidates and reviewed 1000's of resumes – you need to be sure you can stand out in that crowd. Most recently, I was in the job market for 2 years and didn't find anything worth pursuing. Then I decided to get a professional redo my resume and LinkedIn profile. Within a month I landed a new job.

3. Look hard at your actual skills and highlight them. Sometimes it's not clear where your strengths are so you may need to interview past managers and peers to get their opinion.

12. If you could do it again, what would be the one thing you would do (better) or not do to help in your transition?

I would be broader in the job openings that I targeted. I really only targeted telecom jobs because that's what I thought I knew, but there was no reason to look beyond that. My last job transition was in a whole new technical domain – but my skills and experience made me a good fit (even though I didn't match many of the keywords in their job posting).

Patrick Morse

Service rank: Master Gunnery Sergeant, USMC

Position: Security Consultant

Industry: Compliance

Biography

I am a native of Kennebunk Maine. I joined the United States Marine Corps right out of high school. I went into the infantry, then later into Reconnaissance and finally into Marine Corps Special Operations. I have multiple deployments to Iraq and Afghanistan. I served in positions of increasing rank and responsibility from a small unit leader to a Battalion Current Operations Chief, I completed instructor duty with several professional development institutions. My final assignment was as the Senior Enlisted Advisor to the Director of Future Plans and Policies at Special Operations Command Central (SOCCENT). As I transition out of 24 years of service in the Marine Corps I was selected to attend and the Hiring Our Heroes Corporate Fellowship Program, where I am doing an internship with A-LIGN, a Tampa-based Cyber Security company. My personal decorations include, Bronze Star with combat "V", Navy and Marine Corps Commendation Medal, Navy and Marine Achievement Medal (4th award), Combat Action Ribbon, Meritorious Mast, and a Letter of Appreciation.

Questions & Answers

1. Describe your journey from the service to your first job?

■ I had wanted to retire in late 2014 and started developing my retirement plan two-years out from my anticipated retirement date. I utilized a Plan of Action & Milestones (POA&M) to track key events and submission dates for my Transition Readiness Workshop, to may Capstone Engagement, and initial meeting with the Veterans Association (VA). My fellowship with A-LIGN was scheduled for 12-weeks and included professional development courses and on the job training with experienced fellow employees.

2. How did you find your first job? Describe the process.

■ I attended a local networking social here in Tampa where I met the Program Manager for Hiring Our Heroes Corporate Fellowship Program. It was through her that I completed the application process and interviewed with A-LIGN. The whole process was a bit timely, considering the impact of COVID-19, but overall it felt very calming to meet other transitioning service members in my cohort and we all became familiar with the potential host companies for our fellowship. It allowed enough time and reflection for me to identify my next career field outside of the military.

3. When did you start planning your transition? What actions/ activities did you take?

I attended job fairs and social networking events. I also utilized transition workshops and workshops focusing on LinkedIn. In addition, utilized a resume coach to draft my targeted resume. I pursed training programs to gain certifications in Business Continuity and Project Management.

4. Did you pursue any advanced degrees and/or certifications? Did they help?

I I pursed a certification for Business Continuity because the intent of that career field married up closely with my jobs and experiences in the military. There is a specific security and risk/threat mitigation process that was remarkably familiar to me. In addition, I am currently pursuing a certification in Project Management. I highly encourage all transitioning service members to look into this field because it provided me with a fundamental view and approach of how the private/civilian business world views and executes projects. This helped me greatly to understand operations from a civilian perspective.

5. Why did you choose the work/career you are in?

■ Cybersecurity and business Continuity is service centric; so from a value stand point, it provides me with a greater work-purpose and with a focus on informational and operational security that matches with my experiences in the military.

6. Have you encountered any obstacles in advancing your career?

■ I would say getting a greater working knowledge of the technology side and tech-specifics concerning cyber security. It is no impossible, just a newer discipline to learn.

7. What were the 2 hardest efforts about transitioning?

■ First effort would be taking the time to pause and ensure that I am communicating effectively and clearly articulating my past experiences with my civilian employees' and not relying on military jargon. The second effort would be learning the different processes that the company utilizes.

8. What do you think are the top issues for Veterans transitioning into a career?

The biggest one would be finding your next "why?", purpose or drive behind your efforts. I think for military people, a career that serves others (customer/ clients) is a good start. Focus on what you are good at instead of your passions. Passions are often akin to hobbies; employers are more interested in what you do well which speaks to skill and capability.

9. Do you believe there is a stereotype attached to being a Veteran in pursuit of a job?

Yes. Employer's may view you as having a great work ethic and being punctual. But that doesn't speak to skill or capability. Just like in the last question, focus on what you do well; personnel management, resource management, effective communication, operations management etc.) everything that most transitioning service members have done in their careers fall in those lanes.

10. What question(s) would you have liked to have known before taking your first job?

Pursue some IT certification prior to retiring.

11. What are the most important lessons you can share on making a successful job transition from the military?

1. Find your next "why?".

2. Find and industry that interests you.

3. Decide on a retirement location/destination.

12. If you could do it again, what would be the one thing you would do (better) or not do to help in your transition?

Stay more actively engaged with my VA representative to ensure all medical documentation is submitted in a timely manner in response to a delay in the VA system from the impact of COVID-19.

Joe Motes

Service rank: Sergeant First Class, USA

Position: Diversity & Inclusion Program Manager

Industry: Health Care and Biotechnology

Biography

Joe Motes is a Diversity & Inclusion Professional passionate about creating inclusive workplaces for client companies. He works with small, mid-size, and large organizations in developing strategies and processes to create work environments of belonging for all their employees. He is an ally for all segments of diversity with focused attention and efforts surrounding gender equality, LBGTQIA+, Veterans, Underrepresented Minorities, and Individuals with disabilities.

Joe is the Host of The Inclusion Café Podcast and a 14-year veteran of the US Army. Link to The Inclusion Café https://inclusioncafe.buzzsprout.com/

Questions & Answers

1. Describe your journey from the service to your first job?

■ My journey into the civilian sector was hardly like those of my fellow sisters and brothers in arms. I have to say for me it was pretty seam less. My biggest challenge was deciding what I wanted to do after leaving the military. I started actively planning my transition about 24 months out. Once I made the decision, I knew I needed to start talking steps to preparing myself for a new direction. It took me about 1 year to properly prepare and around 1.5 years to actually get an offer from the time I started planning at the 24-month mark.

2. How did you find your first job? Describe the process.

Because time was a concern for someone like myself, I relied heavily on networking and virtual career fairs. I found the virtual platform extremely useful and ultimately attending virtual career fairs landed my first position. There are many of these platforms out there, I used: www.veteranrecruiting. com. It is free for the job seeker, and employers can pay a yearly fee for using the platform.

3. When did you start planning your transition? What actions/activities did you take?

I started planning 24 months out. I knew I had four more classes to complete my degree (it is a MUST to get your degree before you leave), as well as I needed to decide on what I wanted to do after service. I did not focus too much on resume writing because I felt that was a very small portion of actually finding a job. Resume seemed more like an industry buzzword. All my friends were landing jobs by networking. I HEAVILY ramped up my networking. Growing my LinkedIn network from 200 connections when I started to close to 2,000 in just a year. Making connections within companies I was targeting also assisted in connecting with them in a virtual setting at an online career fair.

4. Did you pursue any advanced degrees and/or certifications? Did they help?

Before leaving the service, I had completed an Associates and bachelor's degree. I am currently enrolled in an Executive MBA Program.

If I could go back in time and have the captive audience of ALL five branches of service and tell them one thing regarding transitioning it would be do not leave the service without your completed 4-year degree. Even if you just want to work in the family tire shop or feed and seed.

5. Why did you choose the work/career you are in?

I realized I wanted to continue to be a part of something greater than myself. My need to serve a cause and combine my profession with my passion lead me to the field of diversity and inclusion.

6. Have you encountered any obstacles in advancing your career?

■ I haven't but many have. I was very fortunate enough to crack the code of promotion in the civilian sector early on. This is something I counsel transitioning veterans on often. See, in the military you know from day 2 or 3 what you need to do to make it into the leadership ranks. Learn this, say that, be on time, press your uniform, shine your boots (well, back in the 90s you did), so on and so forth. It is part effort and part just waiting your time in service and time in current position/rank. In the business world, you have to be a lot more intentional about your career. First you have to ensure you are part of an organization that invest in its employee's growth. Second, you need to understand the structure of the company from an HR perspective and realize you may have to take some lateral moves before a vertical one. Last, and most importantly, they need to understand the Rule of 3 Influencers. This is something I personally crafted that has served me very well over the years. Every one of us need 3 people at all times in our professional lives, a mentor, a coach, and a sponsor. Each are different in their meaning and duties, but all three will ensure you progress throughout your career.

7. What were the 2 hardest efforts about transitioning?

■ The most noticeable is that transition programs do not really prepare you. Yes, they teach you about resumes, creating social media pages, dressing for the interview, but they teach you NOTHING outside of being a job hunter. They teach nothing on self-reflection, networking hacks, importance of influencers. This isn't necessarily the fault of the program or DoD, but the experience or say the exposure level of those involved in the program(s). See, a high percentage of the content and facilitation is developed and led by former career service members. Retirees who transitioned into the position, hardly any with job experience outside of the government and even a smaller number of those with actual corporate level business experience. This process needs a heavy dose of executive level (could be retired) professionals driving I would say 80% of its functions and operations. Especially in the classroom.

8. What do you think are the top issues for Veterans transitioning into a career?

One issue comes to mind and this is across all industries, especially for retirees is that very few know who to evaluate their worth $$. Most say things like, "I am retiring I ONLY need to make like 40K, and I will be good." As true as this might be, they are grossly selling their talent and abilities to the lowest bidder thinking it is a win for them. My mentor combined with my coach assisted me in understanding my value add to the organization hiring me which led me to making six figures my very first job out of the military. I have interviewed thousands of veterans who almost always under valuate themselves at the table. The solution could be addressed within TAP if classes were added that talked about talent market values, pay banding, etc.

9. Do you believe there is a stereotype attached to being a Veteran in pursuit of a job?

Not as much as the other segments of diversity that I have seen. There is one I have seen reoccur that all veterans will need to be given a learning curve. As this may be the case, I have never seen it any more or less than those who have never served in the military.

10. What question(s) would you have liked to have known before taking your first job?

I really didn't know what to ask, so knowing what questions would have been nice.

11. What are the most important lessons you can share on making a successful job transition from the military?

Rule of 3 Influencers, Start Early, Know Your Worth!

Degree, degree, degree, degree, degree.....LOL

12. If you could do it again, what would be the one thing you would do (better) or not do to help in your transition?

When I first started networking, I was reaching out to anyone and everyone. I did this probably for about 8 months. What I was left with were a lot of connections but no real meat in my connections. I wished I would have become a personal branding ninja and targeted markets that I truly could see myself in, and positions I wanted to do. It would have saved me a lot of time.

Larry Myers

Service rank: Commander, USN

Position: Research & Development, radar systems and test range equipment

Industry: Defense

Biography

I graduated from the US Naval Academy in 1973. I first served aboard a Navy Destroyer where I earned the Surface Warfare Officer Designation. I then went to Flight School and earned the designation as a Naval Flight Officer. I served in various Patrol Aviation and related squadrons. I flew over 3600 hours in the P-3 Orion Anti-Submarine Warfare aircraft. In 1983 I earned a Master's Degree in Business Administration (MBA) culminating two years of going to school at night. In 1984 I graduated from the US Naval War College with distinction. I later served for three years on the Joint Staff in the Pentagon. I worked in the Current Operations Division, J-3. I earned the Joint Specialty Officer designation. I completed my naval career as a program manager for the Office of Naval Research's (ONR) stealth technology and special programs office. I worked on research and development programs across the DOD and several Agencies. I oversaw the contracts we awarded to DOD contractors and government laboratories. I also worked with Intelligence Agencies relating to stealth technology development. I earned the Defense Acquisition Specialty Officer designation. At the end of four years in that position and over 21 years in the Navy, I decided to retire and transition to industry. I was hired by System Planning Corporation immediately after retirement. SPC was a small private firm who manufactured Radar Cross Section Instrumentation radar systems for stealth test ranges. SPC also provided expert technical consulting to government R&D customers. The Dense Advanced Research Agency (DARPA) was our biggest customer. I worked at SPC for 19 years.

Questions & Answers

1. Describe your journey from the service to your first job?

■ I had worked very closely with the office's chief scientist throughout my time at ONR. He had worked over 40 years for both government and industry in research and development positions. He had become my mentor and helped immensely navigate through my job search. I started about six months before my retirement date to start the process. It was probably two months before my retirement date that I actively started to have conversations with industry.

2. How did you find your first job? Describe the process.

■ I had spent four years working closely with industry. I had a fairly wide network of individuals who could potentially hire me. My mentor helped me identify the type of job I might want. Most of potential businesses were defense contractors but some like universities were not. When I announced that I was going to retire, some industry representatives contacted me.

3. When did you start planning your transition? What actions/ ■ activities did you take?

ONR asked me had to write a resume for myself when they were first looking at selecting me for the job. So I had a basic navy resume and only had to add the four years at ONR. I was a hiring officer for our ONR office so I saw many resumes over the four years. I held a designation as an Acquisition Specialty officer. I had headed contract selection teams to award contracts to industry and then managed the execution of the contracts. I understood the contracting process, from the government side. I also held many high level clearances due to the technical nature of our R&D.

4. Did you pursue any advanced degrees and/or certifications? Did they help?

In 1983 and '84 I attended college classes two nights a week to earn a Master's in Business Administration (MBA) in Management. I thought then that it would help me in the navy and my post navy career. I believe it helped me in personnel and contract management in the navy. I think it was a plus to have on my resume.

5. Why did you choose the work/career you are in?

I was very fortunate to be working closely with industry in my last navy assignment. I was working on cutting edge technology development. It was extremely interesting and very rewarding to know I was helping to advance the US defense capabilities. When I had the opportunity or transition to industry in a similar role, it was an easy decision.

6. Have you encountered any obstacles in advancing your career?

No. I only worked for one company for over the 19 years. I was steadily promoted and given greater responsibility. Ultimately I was head of the company's business development efforts. I was in charge of our strategic posturing with other contractors and government laboratories. I led our international efforts and was charge of export licensing. When the company opened a subsidiary in Adelaide, Australia, I was appointed to the president and ran the operation there.

7. What were the 2 hardest efforts about transitioning?

At first it seemed a lot slower than the pace I was used to in the navy. I think I was naïve because there certainly was a lot to learn. The second was understanding how company overhead impacted profit and loss and how to manage a government contract from the contractor's viewpoint. A big lesson was if you ran a cost plus contract out of money, you had to stop work and ask the customer for more money. No one was very happy.

8. What do you think are the top issues for Veterans transitioning into a career?

Today given the pandemic, it has to be the unemployment rate and the availability of jobs. Second would be health in the work place. It used to be the unknowns of the business cultures. There are a variety of cultures and they can be very different. In large businesses, it can be very structured and formal. In smaller business, it can be very laid back. On your transition check list, you need to ask yourself what culture would you most easily fit into.

9. Do you believe there is a stereotype attached to being a Veteran in pursuit of a job?

Yes, but I didn't realize it when I made the transition. I didn't personally know many others who left the navy and went to work in industry. I didn't know many hiring managers in industry either. I believed the company I went to work expected me to work hard. I also believed they expected me to open doors for marketing efforts. I did both and it worked well for me. Fast forward several years to when I was a hiring manager. I was constantly looking for bright military personnel who were making the transition. I recruited some of them. Once I hired these individuals, my observation was that that they transitioned one of two ways. Either they went gangbusters, immediately adapted to the company culture, and became part of the team or they weren't able accept the company culture. In some cases with senior officers they never, figuratively, left the military and in some cases had a sense of entitlement because of their previous rank.

10. What question(s) would you have liked to have known before taking your first job?

I was lucky to have a mentor help me go through the transition. We made up a list of questions to ask prospective employers. Examples included: what the company's business was, what employee benefits were offered, for what position they were hiring me, what did I need to do to be promoted, and what would my performance review entail. I had several interviews and I learned from each one. So I think I was ready when I started work.

11. What are the most important lessons you can share on making a successful job transition from the military?

When I graduated from the US Naval Academy, my Company Officer imparted these recommendations: Know your stuff, take care of your people, and (at that time) be a man. The later meaning be honest, be responsible, and be accountable. I believe these were equally applicable to my civilian job. You have to be technically sharp to know the product you are selling. Its strengths and weakness. You have be a head the game and know what the next step is if something goes wrong. People are number one asset of any company. You have to know their capabilities and weakness. Never put them in a position to fail. I am a big advocate of continuing education for employees. Lastly, accountably and honesty go hand in hand. You have to take responsibility for your actions. If you don't, you lose the respect of your seniors and subordinates.

12. If you could do it again, what would be the one thing you would do (better) or not do to help in your transition?

I think I would have taken more time off before starting work. I was excited at the prospect of starting a new career. At the time, I had no idea that I would only work for one company. It became harder to take more than two weeks off at a time.

Chris Newsome

Service rank: Sergeant, USA

Position: SVP, DoD Programs

Industry: Human Capital

Biography

As SVP of DoD Programs, Chris oversees RecruitMilitary's direct relationships with the Department of Defense at large, military garrisons, and America's military men, women, and their families with career access, and professional development resources. Following the attacks on America, on September 11th, 2001, Chris joined the US Army's illustrious 82nd Airborne Division. By June of 2002, Chris was shipped to Fort Benning GA., to completed Basic Training, Advanced Individual Training, and Army Airborne School. Within one month of arriving at Fort Bragg, NC (assigned to the 3/504 Parachute Infantry Regiment), Chris was sent on his first deployment, in support of Operation Enduring Freedom (Afghanistan). Over the course of his time in service with the Army, Chris would complete 3 combat tours- 1 to Afghanistan in support of Operation Enduring Freedom and two tours to Iraq, in support of Operation Iraqi Freedom. Throughout his time with the 82nd Airborne Division, Chris was placed in numerous leadership roles, working his way to the rank of Sergeant, and leading fellow paratroopers through the war-torn streets of the Middle-East. Upon returning to his home of record in Cincinnati, Chris acquired his education through the University of Cincinnati, and began working in the military space as a member of the team with RecruitMilitary, tasked with helping employers/recruiters more effectively connect with military talent.

Questions & Answers

1. Describe your journey from the service to your first job?

■ My story is one that should be used as an example of what not to do. I transitioned in the Spring of 2006. I had recently redeployed from my 3rd combat tour in 4 years with the 82nd Airborne Division, and all I could think about was returning to my home town. I was the ripe old age of 22 at the time, the weather was beautiful, and the last thing I wanted to do was sit in a classroom environment. Unfortunately, that classroom environment was where transition classes were held, and where the most important transition-centric guidance was/is given. With my perpetual distractions with thoughts of returning home and the "fun times" to be had, I simply "checked the blocks" during the process. I went where I was supposed to, made my appointments, and did what needed to be done in order to receive my Dragon stamp (the last formal step in transitioning from the 82nd).

I returned home with more than a month's worth of terminal leave stockpiled. I knew I would take a job, but I had no idea as to what I wanted to do. Having my Army income for the initial month or so after returning home tricked my standard approach to taking initiative, and I found myself pushing it off to later. Fast forward 5 or 6 weeks and "Later" was upon me and I had to scramble to find work. I ended up taking a temp-to-hire job at a factory that manufactured single-serving condiments for restaurants. I was in a low-paying job, wearing a hairnet, working 2nd shift, surrounded by people I could not relate to. This was a far cry from leading paratroopers in Afghanistan and Iraq, and the immense sense of purpose that came with it. I now had a job that I did not like. And it was entirely on me. My circumstances were the product of the work I had put in (little-to-none).

2. How did you find your first job? Describe the process.

■ A family member mentioned that he knew of a temp-to-hire agency that staffed many reputable companies. I started there.

3. When did you start planning your transition? What actions/activities did you take?

It is hard for me to say that I planned my transition. As a junior NCO, I knew how to navigate the world around me, but I did not invest much forethought into the process. Transition was already mapped out for me. I was provided with a list of places I needed to go and things I needed to do in order to complete the process. There was a bounty of invaluable information bestowed upon me through these transition classes. However, I had not reached the personal maturity level that I needed to truly retain the information being given to me. I was distracted.

4. Did you pursue any advanced degrees and/or certifications? Did they help?

Once home, and after taking a couple "dead-end jobs", I began my pursuit of higher education. While I possessed many traits from my time in service that Corporate America seeks, I struggled to articulate them on a resume or in a professional setting. I knew that this would be my key to more professional options. I started taking classes at a local community college and worked my way into the University of Cincinnati. As I was nearing graduation, I started working for the company that I am currently with. While the degree did not get me the job, it absolutely helped me advance in my career.

5. Why did you choose the work/career you are in?

I chose my work/career as the industry allowed me to pursue a personal passion and turn it into a profession.

6. Have you encountered any obstacles in advancing your career?

I have certainly encountered obstacles in my pursuit of professional advancement. Beyond, economic ups and downs, business/industry phenomena and the like, many of them were simply learning opportunities disguised as obstacles. Progress and advancement are never guaranteed or assumed to be gifted simply because one has served in their station for a certain period of time. The professional world is a meritocracy. Time in service and time in rank hold no bearing. I had to identify ways by which I could uniquely contribute to the mission, while lifting others along the way, while working to master my lane, and learn the lanes in which I wanted to operate. Your professional life should be one of constant evolution. When you stop evolving, you stop advancing.

7. What were the 2 hardest efforts about transitioning?

■ The single hardest element of transitioning was the culture shock. Outside of the military, it is not common for people to work is as unified of a manner as the military. Humans are egocentric in nature. It is less common to experience selflessness or somebody working hard if there is no personal reward. It makes one miss the comradery that goes hand-in-hand with military service. You will likely not encounter the same level of brotherhood or sisterhood that you experienced while you served.

Another difficulty was simply navigating every element of your life by yourself. The military simplifies many aspects of life. Pay is consistent, Dental and medical appointments are scheduled for you, you are told when you are going to the promotion board, you are given the materials to study for advancement, first call and COB are firmly established, and so on. When you transition, you must learn and navigate the world around you, and do so with minimal guidance if any.

8. What do you think are the top issues for Veterans transitioning into a career?

- Understanding how to articulate one's military background in civilian terminology is #1. For example: If you led troops at any point, you have management experience. It is not always about technical skills. The soft skills are what are hard to come by in Corporate America. Leadership is hard-earned, not created on a college campus.

- Understand that you cannot expect the same level of standard from non-military peers. Their experience has been different than yours. You cannot bark orders at them or talk to them with a knife hand. You must always be empathetic. Relax your demeanor a little.

- Understand how promotions and upward mobility work at your workplace. Again, time in service and time in rank mean very little now.

You are not there to fill a seat. You are there to advance the company's mission.

9. Do you believe there is a stereotype attached to being a Veteran in pursuit of a job?

I have seen some with a sense of entitlement. Just because you served, it does not mean you are not still competing for the job. Nothing worth having comes easy. You must stand out from the herd. Filling out an application and submitting your resume are things that everybody has to do. If you think a recruiter will put you on a pedestal because you served in the military, you are wrong. You get preferential consideration in some cases, but that may mean you get an extra few second look at your resume. The best candidate gets the job. Find ways to stand out. Perfect your 30 second elevator pitch, make sure your resume speaks for the job you are applying to, interview with confidence.

10. What question(s) would you have liked to have known before taking your first job?

- What do employees who have worked [here] for years' love about working here?

- Where do you see my background making the most impact on [the business]?

11. What are the most important lessons you can share on making a successful job transition from the military?

1. Be prepared for the difference in culture. Manage your own expectations.

2. Don't treat your colleagues as though they are your peers from when you served.

3. Understand what your personal professional progression goals are. Know how to advance.

12. If you could do it again, what would be the one thing you would do (better) or not do to help in your transition?

I would pay close attention to each and every word that was spoken to me during transition. If I can throw out a second top important thing: get a mentor!

Kent Paro

Service rank: Captain, USN

Position: VP Operations

Industry: Financial

Biography

Kent joined Grow Financial Federal Credit Union as Vice President (VP), Enterprise Risk Management, in June 2017. In July 2018, he began a one-year job rotation that turned permanent as the VP of Retail Operations where he is responsible for the day-to-day performance of almost 200 people in 25 branches across Central Florida and South Carolina.

Kent retired from the US Navy after more than 30 years as a Navy SEAL Captain with the following service highlights: Aide-de-Camp for the Commander of US Special Operations Command (USSOCOM); the single Assignment officer for all SEAL officers; the Operations Officer for an overseas Unit responsible for SEAL operations in the Pacific and a Group responsible for all east-coast SEAL Team operations; and former Commanding Officer of a SEAL Team, a Special Boat Team, and an overseas Unit.

He served as a staff officer on the Joint Staff in the Pentagon during 9/11 and had multiple deployments in support of combat operations in Kuwait, Bosnia, Afghanistan, Iraq, and numerous lesser-known operations and conflicts.

Hand-picked for most assignments, his last assignment was as the Lead Assessment Director at USSOCOM where he led a team of ~300 people around the world to develop recommendations for the Commanding General on how to spend the >$42B in a five-year period that began two-years in the future in order to get the best mix of special operations capability that our nation could afford. Kent also served on the USSOCOM Parachute Team, the Para-Commandos, and performed for more than a million citizens around the country in dozens of NFL and college football stadiums.

Kent is a 1986 graduate of the United States Naval Academy with a BS degree in Engineering and received a MA from the Naval Postgraduate School in Monterey, California, in National Security Affairs: SOLIC.

Questions & Answers

1. Describe your journey from the service to your first job?

■ Luckily, I had a hard date to backwards plan from as I approached 30 years of service. I started to plan for the transition in earnest, about 18 months before my 30-year date when I was asked by the SEAL community to request retire-retain status from the Navy which was granted and took me out to 31 years of service (giving me an extra year to plan and work, I had a total of approximately 30 months to prep). My timing was perfect, and I was retired 6/1/17 and started working 6/7/17.

2. How did you find your first job? Describe the process.

■ I worked hard at networking and as it turned out, one of my contacts used my name as part of his "make-himself-feel-better" plan. He had been hired by Grow Financial as their first military hire when he got an offer he could not refuse about a year into the job. He told leadership that he was leaving, and they might want to meet me as a potential replacement. I had a breakfast meeting with the Chief of HR and the Executive VP, it went great. I had several phone calls with other members of the staff and then had dinner with the CEO. After that I sent in my resume, filled out all the official application paperwork, and then had an interview with a 5-person panel. From my perspective, it was relatively easy.

3. When did you start planning your transition? What actions/ activities did you take?

I was a "plank-owner" with a local group of civilians who were interested in helping Special Operations service members transition and this was a Godsend. Over time I became the leader of the military side of this organization and we worked hard to provide training and education, along with networking and job-shadow opportunities. I attacked the transition like it was a mission and did all I could to prepare. I had a resume that took 97 iterations with a professional to get as right as I could get it; she kept asking me, "ok, great, so what, what was the impact, why do I care?" A friend put me in touch with a headhunter who ultimately helped me craft my answer to what I cared about and what I wanted the environment I work in to be like. This helped frame a lot of my "why," and helped as I started to get serious about the transition. I worked hard on my elevator pitch and used it whenever I could to get my name out there and meet as many businesspeople in the Tampa area as possible.

4. Did you pursue any advanced degrees and/or certifications? Did they help?

I had a bachelor's and master's degree before I started the transition. I entertained getting a PMP Certification and used the Syracuse Program to go through all the material. I started this about one year before my transition and could have taken the test right around my transition but chose not to. I do believe a degree and an advanced-degree are helpful.

5. Why did you choose the work/career you are in?

I was mostly focused on the culture of where I would work and the impact I could have on co-workers, our customers (or Members in the Credit Union world), and the community. All through my pre-employment phase with Grow Financial, and even up to six months after being hired, I kept thinking, 'ok, when is the other shoe going to drop? These people can't be this way for forever.' I was wrong and now realize that I was fortunate to go from one incredible culture (SEAL Teams) to another and make impacts in all the areas I cared about.

6. Have you encountered any obstacles in advancing your career?

■ I'm fortunate that since day one, my boss told me and continued to tell me that they didn't hire me for my financial industry knowledge because they knew I had none, they hired me to be a leader. My boss told me that he could teach me the industry knowledge. The only obstacle in my mind, is my knowledge of the financial industry. I clearly "get" the leadership portion of the job and can see myself moving 'up the chain,' but not before my knowledge and understanding of the financial industry reaches an appropriate level. I know that I'm harder on myself and my expectations are higher than those of my boss, but nevertheless, that's what I have encountered.

7. What were the 2 hardest efforts about transitioning?

■ Understanding the idiosyncrasies of the industry you enter and getting your foot in the right door to begin the transition. I still work with Veterans in the transition and these themes seem to be consistent. The hardest effort I see, is the determination of what doors you want to get in and then enabling or being ready to go through that door when it appears or is offered. I think that's where proper preparation pays off. When you finally do enter another industry, and especially in a leadership position, it pays to learn and understand the culture and what makes it tick. Even though we all have experience going to a new/different assignment (like the Joint Staff), the things that matter in the new industry take time to figure out. Your basic ability to assimilate will always be useful, but if you are patient and focused on learning your way around, it pays dividends.

8. What do you think are the top issues for Veterans transitioning into a career?

Opportunity. Not all employers are going to go with the philosophy that they do not care about your industry knowledge and all they want you to do is be a leader because they can teach you everything else. So, getting the opportunity to prove that your leadership really matters and improves their organization can be tough. If in your preparation, you figure out how to translate your abilities into those leadership qualities that matter to them, you are on your way to making your opportunity.

9. Do you believe there is a stereotype attached to being a Veteran in pursuit of a job?

Yes, and it is always fun to turn those stereotypes on their head. Most Americans do not know anyone in the military and all their perceptions come from Hollywood or media; they generally believe in the rigid, tough, inflexible version. Many believe that we all have PTSD and that everyone has been in combat. I enjoy the surprise I see on their face when they learn that I was a 31-year Navy SEAL veteran and I am a reasonable leader that everyone generally likes and respects. I do the best I can to show them I am a normal person and educate them that most of us are normal. I carry the message that we do not expect any handouts in terms of employment, but we can be extremely valuable to an organization just by virtue of the character and ethic we generally bring.

10. What question(s) would you have liked to have known before taking your first job?

I wish I knew how to prepare for my industry; what to study, read, and learn. Three years after starting here I'm still piecing together all the important elements I need to be a professional in the financial industry.

11. What are the most important lessons you can share on making a successful job transition from the military?

1. Understand your "why" and what you care about; how do you want your life to be day-to-day and how will that be satisfied?

2. You are NEVER too early to start preparing. Treat the transition like a mission, take ownership of your future and move out. Take all the mandatory classes and then some. Learn about LinkedIn and how to maximize that platform. Get help with your resume, either professionally or from your network of civilians and transitioned veterans. Make sure your resume translates all the incredible experience and capability you bring to any organization in their terms. Ask yourself "so what?" "what's the impact?" "why does a civilian employer care about this?" for every word you write on your resume. Prepare and rehearse your elevator pitch, make sure it leaves whoever you give it to wanting to know more about you and continue the conversation or help you.

3. Build your network. Meet people from different industries and learn from everyone you meet. People are willing to help; all you must do is ask. Take any opportunity you have/make to shadow someone in their industry. I shadowed a contact in the construction industry as my first job shadow and once we got on sight and I met his team in their project trailer, I realized that a Team Room is a Team Room, and I had all the skills I needed to survive and thrive in that environment, a good confidence builder for me at the early stages of my transition.

12. If you could do it again, what would be the one thing you would do (better) or not do to help in your transition?

I wish I had moved out with greater confidence from the beginning of my transition. I wish I fully realized that the 31 years I spent on active duty taught me invaluable lessons and gave me a hefty toolbox that worked in the military and works in the civilian world. When I was first put in charge of 200 people, I made it a point to go and meet each person. I asked each person the same four questions (when did you start here? Did you come from a financial background? Where did you grow up? And what do you do for fun?) and wrote down the answers in my book—obviously, nothing earth-shattering. Once I got to everyone, I built on the initial conversations and learned more about them and what made them tick, I also asked them questions that helped me understand my job better, and I built solid relationships with them. The impact was palpable, and morale surged within the organization. My peers were curious about what I was doing, and I was shocked that this was something that not everyone did… Any one of us would have done the same thing, get to know your people before you try and lead them. The bottom line is that your military experience has prepared you well to add value to almost any organization. Be humble but confident in that knowledge! I wish you all the best as you transition to the next phase of life.

Shaunna Patterson

Service rank: Staff Sergeant, USA

Position: Program Manager

Industry: DoD

Biography

Shaunna Patterson is married to William Patterson and have 3 children (Jay, Christopher, and Derek). She and her husband are both Army veterans.

Shaunna has over 16 years of experience in the Project management industry. She began her career as an Assistant Project Manager and evolved into positions including Senior Program Manager of Project Controls, Senior Project Manager and Project Executive for notable Firms.

In her role as Senior Program Manager at TMPC Inc. Shaunna fosters an environment of teamwork and ensures that strategy is clearly defined while overseeing performance and maintaining morale. Her strong communication and client service skills enhance Compass' process-driven management philosophy.

Shaunna is a graduate of Kaplan and Purdue University, holding a Master's in Business Management with a focus on Project Management, Master's in Business Administration, and a bachelor's degree in human service.

Questions & Answers

1. Describe your journey from the service to your first job?

■ My tenure with the United States Army ended in December of 2007. I honestly did not know what I wanted to do after the serving 10 plus years so I begin to research careers about 3 years before I transitioned out of the military and ran across the Project Management field. I then realize that I needed a college degree in that field to be successful, so I enrolled in college and received my Masters' degree in Business Management with a focus on Project management and that was the start of a beautiful work-life.

2. How did you find your first job? Describe the process.

■ Finding a job after serving can be frustrating depending on the industry. I found my first job online using various job search engines like Indeed and LinkedIn. I noticed that USA Jobs were not very responsive and that it was very hard to get into the GS system which was disappointing as one would think that veterans would be one of their first choices; and while military have preference, it's still hard to get into that system. This made job searching for permanent roles within DOD frustrating, so I turned to the civilian sector. I found that the civilian sector is less stressful as it's not focused on the "who you know" system, but more on the technical knowledge of the candidate.

3. When did you start planning your transition? What actions/ ■ activities did you take?

I started planning my transition 3 years out. I knew I needed a Masters' degree in my field to make e competitive with the rest of my peers and so I enrolled in college. After I completed college, I knew I needed a really good resume that would tell my story and so I hired a resume writer to convert everything that I had done in the military on a resume so that hiring managers who have never served would understand my work history and skillsets. I then begin to network through various channels and was able to land my first job 3 months after leaving the military.

4. Did you pursue any advanced degrees and/or certifications? Did they help?

I pursued my master's degree as I knew it would give me an advance over all my peers. I also ensured my Security clearance stayed active, which allowed me to be more marketable in the contracting world. Any degree, certifications, or security clearance makes an individual extremely marketable and that is the name of the game, stay marketable, stay relevant to employers.

5. Why did you choose the work/career you are in?

I choose Project/Program Management because I like to be a part of building something great from start to finish. As a project manager, not only do I get to be a part of building something, but I am managing it from cradle to grave. Project management is a field where one is continually networking and talking to people to get the job done.

6. Have you encountered any obstacles in advancing your career?

I think if one plans everything in advance it reduces obstacles, however, planning does not eliminate obstacles. The obstacle that I ran into the most was just being able to get an opportunity to interview as I found that people were hiring people they knew and so it was really important to have the degree and the certifications a that was the only way I was able to get my foot in the door.

7. What were the 2 hardest efforts about transitioning?

The two hardest efforts concerning transition from military to civilian are networking and finding a job. It is hard to do anything if one does not know the right people.

8. What do you think are the top issues for Veterans transitioning into a career?

The top issue is planning; I don't think military personnel think about life after the military until it is too late. Then they find themselves scrambling, rushing trying to make opportunities happen. One must start planning at 2 years before transitioning and all military should take advantage of college while serving so that they are prepared academically.

9. Do you believe there is a stereotype attached to being a Veteran in pursuit of a job?

Being that I have been out of the military for more than 13 years, it's easy for people to see me as more than just a veteran. I am a Mother, I am a Wife, I am a Program Manager, I am a U.S. Army veteran. I am all these things and more.

Yet, I feel that many people — including business leaders, hiring managers, and CEO's, primarily see veterans one-dimensional armed services veterans.

As a veteran seeking to transition into the corporate world, I acknowledge that my military experience is an important piece of who I am, but it does not define me. I share this with you because it's important for employers and colleagues to recognize.

We all have biases — conscious and unconscious. It is important that we recognized them.

10. What question(s) would you have liked to have known before taking your first job?

The question I would have had would be salary. I did not know that one could negotiate one's salary. I was worth way more than what I was paid. I quickly learned the art of negotiating salary and now I can demand what I am worth.

11. What are the most important lessons you can share on making a successful job transition from the military?

Three lessons that I take away with me are:

1. Planning- One should start planning at least 15 months out. This includes picking a career field, figuring out where one wants to live, saving money, and know all the resources that are available to you. One should also attend the transition assistance Program workshop offered by the military. TAP was created to give employment and training information to armed forces members.

2. College- It is important to have the right credentials when searching for a job. College is necessary as all jobs are starting to require a college degree.

3. Network- Start going to job fairs, getting online, find military-friendly employers, connect with recruiters and headhunters who focus on military to civilian transitions.

12. If you could do it again, what would be the one thing you would do (better) or not do to help in your transition?

If I could do it all over again, I would have planned better. I would have saved more money, attended as many transition workshops that I can attend, and picked a career field sooner.

Leslie Picht

Service rank: Major, USAF

Position: Global Cybersecurity Incident Response Team Manager

Industry: Manufacturing

Biography

In 1993, Leslie Picht entered the U.S. Air Force as a Communications-Computer Systems Officer. After six years in the Communications-Computer field, Leslie attended Undergraduate Pilot Training. She spent the next 14 years conducting global KC-135 aerial refueling operations for Operations SOUTHERN WATCH, IRAQI FREEDOM, and ENDURING FREEDOM. In 2014, Leslie retired as a Senior Pilot with over 1,200 combat hours and over 2,900 total flying hours.

Leslie has a Bachelor's in Computer Science, Master's in Business Administration, and a Master's in Cybersecurity specializing in Threat Intelligence. In addition, she is a Project Management Professional with over 25 years' experience in Program and Project Management. She is also a Certified Scrum Master and Certified Scrum Product Owner. Leslie is an active member of the Project Management Institute.

In 2019, Leslie completed the SANS VetSuccess Immersion Academy, an intensive, accelerated scholarship program for veterans transitioning into cybersecurity.

She earned the following GIAC certifications: Security Essentials (GSEC), Certified Incident Handler (GCIH), and Windows Forensic Examiner

(GCFE). She is a member of the GIAC Advisory Board. Leslie is currently the Global Cybersecurity Incident Response Team Manager within a Global Security Operations Center. She also serves as a SANS Institute Mentor.

Questions & Answers

1. Describe your journey from the service to your first job?

■ After 20 years, I retired from the Air Force in July of 2014. My transition may be considered non-traditional. I received great advice from a veteran friend before I retired. He said I had no idea how tightly wound military members are. He recommended taking time off to decompress. So, I decided to take a year off completely. I wanted to vacation in Germany for a month, raise a puppy, and travel to see family and friends. All these things are challenging in the military.

Several people warned against taking this time off. What about the much-feared resume gap? Your technical skills might be outdated. You won't get hired if you've been out of the market. While these things might be true in some fields, I valued peace more. In my mind, what other time in your professional life will you make such a large shift in your career path and lifestyle? Take time to consider what will make you happy. I also believe it is easier to explain the resume gap as a veteran. Many employers understand and appreciate the deployment stress and demands on military members and their families. If a particular employer does not understand this, it may foreshadow how well you may expect to fit into their corporate culture. The year off was a wonderful time in my life. If possible, I highly recommend a similar phase for anyone. I feel too many jump straight into the civilian workforce and miss this wonderful grace period.

Planning to transition after a year off from work required financial planning, research, and networking. Ultimately, I began planning my transition two years before my retirement. During my year off, I networked and refined my resume. I bridged the resume gap with a volunteer position associated with the career path I intended to pursue. Overall, I was hired into the first position for which I applied. I applied for the position in July of 2015, exactly one year from my retirement. The application, screening, and interview process spanned three months. I started my first day of work near the end of September 2015.

2. How did you find your first job? Describe the process.

■ During my year off, I volunteered with my local Project Management Institute (PMI) chapter. I served as the Director of Strategic Projects. The chapter had several unfilled leadership positions that year. I intentionally selected a position with a title aligned with my desired future corporate role and involved extensive networking. The role required community outreach with numerous local companies. Companies with Project Management Offices (PMOs) frequently asked the chapter to come onsite and give presentations on the project manager career path, certifications, and available resources. The company I eventually hired into requested one of these chapter presentations. When you are potentially seeking employment opportunities, you can tailor a presentation to include information using your own path and experience as an illustration rather than using a generic description or example. After the presentation, the Director of the PMO pulled me aside and asked what type of position I was seeking. We had a lengthy, candid conversation. He stated he did not have a position meeting my desires currently. The next day, I followed up with an email thanking him for his interest in our PMI chapter and offered our chapter's assistance with future training for his staff. Of course, I included my personal contact information.

Three months later, he emailed me with a position he thought I might find interesting. He did not have an approved requisition number yet. So, he was reaching out directly before anyone else could even see the job posting. I provided my cover letter, resume, and contacts via email the next day to express my interest. A week later, he emailed me with the job requisition number so I could officially apply. In the end, a volunteer position directly led to my first civilian position. I did not specifically find my position. I was asked to apply through a networking connection.

3. When did you start planning your transition? What actions/activities did you take?

My transition planning began two years before my retirement. However, it was not a full-throttled effort, but a series of small, incremental steps. In 2012, I joined a local PMI chapter to network and learn about the profession and opportunities. I enrolled in a Project Management Professional (PMP) Bootcamp with a PMI registered education provider. I earned my PMP certification a month later. In 2013, I attended the Transition Assistance Program at my base. I did not have a retirement date yet, but you are encouraged to take it well in advance. I continued to network at monthly PMI chapter meetings. In July 2014, I retired from the service. During my year hiatus, I refined my resume, established a full LinkedIn profile, paid for a professional headshot, and purchased a few power suits for interviews. In January 2015, I started my volunteer role as the Director of Strategic Projects with the PMI chapter. Through a networking connection, I applied for a Project Manager II role in July 2015. I was hired into the position and started work in September 2015.

4. Did you pursue any advanced degrees and/or certifications? Did they help?

I did pursue the PMP certification as this is a common certification for professional project managers. Although my military experience included extensive project management, this is not what the military calls it. You show up to work one day and the commander says you're planning and running the base airshow in six months. That is all. I wanted to balance my experience with an industry-recognized certification. In August 2015, I also enrolled in a Certified Scrum Master course. This agile training became a topic of discussion in my actual interview process. I believe this was a factor in my hiring decision. The specific position they were hiring involved the management of a distributed agile team and sprint management for a software development proof of concept. I did not know this at the time. By already pursuing the certification on my own, I demonstrated my commitment and willingness to extend personal time and money toward my professional development.

5. Why did you choose the work/career you are in?

While in the service, I enjoyed managing complex initiatives requiring extensive cross-functional integration. The challenge of solving a complex problem was fun. However, the true synergy came from building relationships with people. I was commonly tasked projects which failed previously or no one else wanted to handle. Many times, these were perceived as "dead on arrival" because of previous animosity between teams. I thrived on working through the distrust and quirks of people.

6. Have you encountered any obstacles in advancing your career?

I have not truly experienced an obstacle in advancing my career. The path varies in the corporate world. However, if you maintain the basics you learned in the military, you will still control your own destiny. Pursue continuous education or technical training. Build an active network of professional relationships. Keep your commitments to yourself and your supervisor. These will maintain your relevance in the industry and keep your options open. Outside of the military, you now have the ability to change your position or location when you choose. Your limits are based on how well you maintain your skills and networks.

7. What were the 2 hardest efforts about transitioning?

Whether in a resume or an interview, translating military language into equivalent civilian terms is a significant challenge for veterans. We tend to underestimate certain skills because they are expected or common in the military environment. The level of direct supervision, decision making authority, and scope of control for military members can be larger and far earlier in a career than the civilian community would expect. Describing your military job on a resume may not have an equivalent in the corporate world. They don't drive tanks or diffuse bombs daily. They may be impressed by the job, but they don't understand what you can bring to their organization. However, all employers need people with an ability to analyze complex data, make decisions in a dynamic environment, lead people, and achieve results.

Once hired, I was stunned by the lack of specific accountability, organizational structure, or clear line of authority. When I asked questions in these areas, other employees didn't even understand the concepts. They'd never seen it, so they didn't miss it. It was extremely frustrating until I had an epiphany. They don't know what's going on either. Now, I can just move to the front and lead before they even know what's happening. It's like a blank check.

8. What do you think are the top issues for Veterans ■ transitioning into a career?

I think far too many people just try to get a job, not the job. This is a major transition in your life. It's a whole new chapter. Maybe a little self-reflection is appropriate? You have an opportunity to completely change your path. Who are you outside of the military? What do you want to be when you grow up? What would you choose if you weren't afraid? What do you love? Why drives your passion or peeks your interest? Some have never slowed down enough to even ask these questions. Maybe you are fortunate to already know these answers. If so, share this with others as we are in the minority.

The transition will be more difficult if you have not researched the current industry expectations of your chosen career. What does the typical career path look like? Where are you in that path currently? What education or training is expected? How do you connect with people in the industry? What are the different job roles and their salaries? Do your homework in advance.

9. Do you believe there is a stereotype attached to being a ■ Veteran in pursuit of a job?

Many employers respect the commitment and service we've made to our country. They just don't always know what to do with us. This is where stereotypes get traction. How you communicate can be the difference in bridging the gap. On the negative side, some may see veterans as blunt, brash, aggressive, and un-polished. On the positive side, we can be viewed as decisive, leaders, and highly trained. So many other facets are missed. Veterans can build complex plans, speak in public, conduct efficient meetings, perform under significant stress, conduct professional training, set and manage priorities, coordinate large teams, and drive results. Every company values these attributes, but they usually don't instill them in people so young.

10. What question(s) would you have liked to have known ■ before taking your first job?

In my transition, I did not understand how to gauge the different levels within a company based on the job titles they used. Industries can vary. For example, in the banking industry, everyone seems to be a Vice President. Is this a Director role in other industries? There can be a large variance between companies within an industry as well. How do you determine equivalent positions? How do you know where your experience fits? This gap in my knowledge led to entering the company at a level lower than my experience.

11. What are the most important lessons you can share on making a successful job transition from the military?

1. Spend time, even a little, thinking about what path will make you happy.

2. Research the prerequisites and industry expectations for this career.

3. Build a transition plan and network when you don't need something. In other words, plan in advance. People can tell when you are networking with your hand out wanting something. Network with the intent to offer something to others. The difference in tone is palpable and completely changes people's response to you.

12. If you could do it again, what would be the one thing you would do (better) or not do to help in your transition?

In hindsight, I would research salary negotiation in more depth. In the later phase of interviewing, I was asked for a desired salary range. Fortunately, my hiring manager selected the highest salary of the range I provided. This was nice, but a clear message I left money on the table.

James Quilty

Service rank: Sergeant, USA

Position: CEO

Industry: Government/
Commercial IT

Biography

James Quilty is the Chief Executive Officer and founder of Sofia Information Technology Consulting, Inc. (SofiaITC) on June 21, 2012. He has a rich background in Information Technology with over 20 years in Information Technology Program/Project Management, Systems Engineering, and Information Security supporting military and law enforcement missions both as a Non-Commissioned Officer in the U.S Army (Military Intelligence) and as a government contractor at the Pentagon, FBI, and USSOCOM. James is on the Board of Directors as President for the Central Florida Chapter (CFC) National Veteran Small Business Coalition (NVSBC) and on the Advisory Counsel for Global SOF Foundation (GSF).

James' experience in information technology includes project management, providing managerial oversight, collaborating with teams to provide vision and strategic direction in enterprise environments, coordinating, investigating and resolving network/service incidents, and leading ad-hoc engineering efforts to solve critical IT system and network problems in short lengths of time for sensitive U.S. government agencies.

James holds a Master's in Business Administration with a Graduate Certificate in Information Security, with Distinction, from Keller Graduate School of Management and was inducted into the Sigma Beta Delta International Business Honor Society. Additionally, he holds a Bachelor of Science in Information Technology where he graduated with great honor (Magna Cum Laude) from the American Inter-Continental University.

James is a U.S. Army Service Disabled Veteran, recipient of the Korea Defense Service Medal, Meritorious Service Medals, Certificate of Appreciation from Lisa Costa, CIO USSOCOM, NSOCC-A/SOJTF-A Certificate (received Flag flown in AFG), Certificate of Appreciation (for outstanding dedication to duty during the 9/11 terrorist attack on the Pentagon), and a Certificate of Appreciation from Madeleine Albright, Secretary of State. An active member of Project Management Institute (PMI), AFCEA of Tampa – St. Petersburg Pelican Chapter, the National Defense Industrial Association (NDIA), Women In Defense (WID) and Veterans of Foreign War (VFW).

Questions & Answers

1. Describe your journey from the service to your first job?

■ My journey to transition out of the military and into the corporate workforce began 5 to 6 months prior to my re-enlistment date in 1999 as an E-5/SGT in the U.S. Army (98J20: ELINT/SIGINT Analyst). As I started researching and asking questions of what was required in transitioning, I quickly realized that this required the assistance of several friends and co-workers as there wasn't a solid transition assistance program at Ft. Meade, MD. During out-processing, there was a resume writing class as one of the options to attend on the out-processing checklist, just nothing else that assisted anyone in landing an opportunity. Based on recommendations from friends and peers, it was highly recommended to attend as many and upload my resume to the following job search sites: clearancejobs.com, monster.com (favorite), and dice.com. These are still great options to add to your arsenal, along with attending a LinkedIn course (today at MacDill AFB) that shows you how to capitalize on using it as an opportunity resource for a job, sales, consulting, etc. Additionally, there are better resume writing tips such as short-form (commercial) verses long-form (government), tailoring the resume to a specific opportunity (not just a canned version for all), and the appropriate formatting which includes what and what not to place in your resume.

2. How did you find your first job? Describe the process.

■ I wouldn't say it was painful, I'd say it was a bit unnerving waiting for responses to opportunities I had applied for. Believe it not, an opportunity came to me through Monster.com from a company that had a contract at the Department of State (DOS) as a Lead Technical Installer for CAT5/Fiber; completely not what I had in mind as it was outside the scope of ELINT/ SIGINT. However, I took that leap of faith and haven't looked back. It was the right move going into the Information Technology field as 20 years has just flown by with the great opportunities of work for the Department of State (2000), Pentagon (PTSC/OPNAV-TCC: 2000-2006), Federal Bureau of Investigations (2004-2009), Federal Aviation Administration (2009-2011), and U.S. Special Operations Command (2011-2020).

3. When did you start planning your transition? What actions/ ■ activities did you take?

I didn't have a degree or certifications at the time of separation, however, after working at the Pentagon for a couple of years under Northrop Grumman, I applied for the opportunity. Unfortunately, I was passed over for this opportunity due to not having a degree. So...what came next...most definitely the pursuit of a degree! I chose a Bachelor of Science in Information Technology and opportunities started rolling in!

4. Did you pursue any advanced degrees and/or certifications? ■ Did they help?

Let me just say...Most definitely! There is no question in my mind that for one to climb the ladder, it most definitely requires three realms of accomplishments (if only I knew this coming out of High School; but never too late!): degrees, certifications, and years of experience. Over the years, one of these three will be your challenge or saving grace. Let's talk about personal experiences:

1. My first experience, in order to be promoted from Senior Engineer to Project Manager (2002) within Northrop Grumman, the number 1

requirement was a bachelor's degree. Well, I didn't have a degree yet and so I was passed over for this opportunity. So, what did I do? I pursued a Bachelor of Science (BS) in Information Technology as I knew that any future opportunities, whether as a contractor or Civilian employee, would be dependent upon having a BS or higher.

2. My second experience with one of the three was when I was offered an opportunity at USSOCOM as a Data Center Engineer. However, I had two weeks to pass the Security+ certification exam prior to the opportunity coming to fruition. I took a gamble, studied, paid for and passed the exam…Yes!!! However, what I'm about to say, actually scares me. By passing this exam, I beat out two other applications…wait for it… that had PhD's! Yes, I have a Master's degree as well in Business Administration, but to have a $250 Security+ exam (now $349) afford me that opportunity over others with higher education is definitely questionable in my mind. So, prepare yourselves by having in your arsenal, a degree, certifications, and years of experience which will come soon enough.

5. Why did you choose the work/career you are in?

■ Technically I didn't choose the IT career path, the career path chose me! I have an amazing 20 years in this field and quite a few more years to go. The Information Technology and Cyber Security fields have so many dynamics to it, is lucrative, and will always have a deficit in numbers versus the number of available opportunities.

6. Have you encountered any obstacles in advancing your career?

■ Of course, who hasn't experienced or who will not experience some type of obstacle while advancing in one's career. If the world was perfect, then we would not experience some type of speed bump, roadblock, re-direction, personal challenges, financial challenges, or others. Nothing worth achieving is accomplished overnight and without putting in the work.

- Choose something you love.

- Research what it requires to reach your goal: degree, certifications, years of experience, financial backing, etc.

- Everyday work towards that goal; even if it's an hour.

- Never give up! You will succeed. You'll be blessed for putting in the hard work. These are my favorite reminders:

    o Proverbs 13:4 Lazy people want much but get little, but those who work hard will prosper.

    o "There is no substitute for hard work." Thomas A. Edison.

- If your goal is in Cyber Security, then here's a good resource for additional training and education:

    o Jün Cyber (juncyber-ed.com).

- If your goal is to pursue building your own company, then there are a few resources I'd highly recommend:

    o Bunker Labs (bunkerlabs.org).

    o Action Zone (actionzonetampa.com), powered by Veterans Florida.

    o JULO Strategy (julostrategy.com).

At one point in my life, I was a full-time student, a full-time job employee, and a husband and father. Talk about being stressed, but well worth it!

7. What were the 2 hardest efforts about transitioning?

1. Figuring out what to do since my line of work at the NSA was limited to majority military personnel, a few GS's, and a couple contractors. Where else could I work with my ELINT experience or do I go after other opportunities? How do I capitalize my experience on my resume? How do I write the correct resume for the opportunity I'm going after?

2. Taking that leap of faith from a known, secured job (military) to hoping I'll find the right opportunity for my family and I. First, I'm very grateful that I fell right into an opportunity working at the Department of State installing Fiber (including polishing the ST connectors) and CAT 5 cable. This opportunity set me on the course towards Information Technology Administration, Engineering, Architecture, Cyber Security, and Program Management to CEO of SofiaITC.

8. What do you think are the top issues for Veterans transitioning into a career?

- Timing -timing is everything from an opportunity aspect from contract renewal/re-compete to workforce increase/decrease.

- Expectations: Your "Dream" job may not be available at the time of your transition. What are you going to do? Will your retirement funds hold you over for a couple months until the opportunity becomes available, will you need to accept another opportunity until it becomes available, or are you working towards your own pursuit of by creating your own dream job (i.e. Consultant or President of your Company)?

- Preparation: Start at least six months out on creating your resume (multiple versions) for a few different types of jobs (i.e. Director, Program Manager, Project Manager, etc.). You need variations to get your foot in the door. Take as many online courses and certifications as possible within your area of expertise to show continuing education; employers love and appreciate this. Apply on clearancejobs.com, monster.com, dice.com, and linkedin.com/jobs (tons of opportunities). Go to networking events in your local and national career fairs sponsored by Northrop Grumman, SAIC, CACI, L3, Raytheon, GDIT, Raymond James, Microsoft, etc. Attend Expos where you can meet various company's you're interested in working for due to the products and services they offer to clients. Basically, network, network, network (and that includes with me.

9. Do you believe there is a stereotype attached to being a Veteran in pursuit of a job?

There are those occasional companies that just don't want to bring on a Veteran for a few reasons. 1.) We've (Veterans) been molded already into something that just doesn't quite fit their way of doing business. 2.) They had a bad experience with a previous Veteran that may have displayed some level of PTSD. Or 3.) They just don't hire Veterans because they simply don't want to. But don't let that stop you in pursuing your dream!

10. What question(s) would you have liked to have known before taking your first job?

- What is my worth in the corporate arena based on current military experience, skillset, achievements, clearance level, local area verses other cities, etc.?

- What resume building classes do you offer?

- What are some of the upcoming career events are scheduled over the next few months?

- What job boards are there for our local area or government entity?

- Can you proofread my resume and make suggestions?

11. What are the most important lessons you can share on making a successful job transition from the military?

1. Don't go it alone; use your resources and those that are willing to assist you. To get anywhere in life, one can't go it alone, but accomplishes it with strength in numbers. Or as Helen Keller said, "Alone we can do so little, together we can do so much."

12. If you could do it again, what would be the one thing you would do (better) or not do to help in your transition?

1. I should have worked harder at pursuing my degree and a few certifications while in the military versus after getting out.

2. If you have a clearance, validate the Clearance level and poly in JPAS prior to leaving the military...get a copy! Also, have an agreement with your SSO that they will maintain your clearance in JPAS for a few months until you transition into an opportunity with a contracting company.

Sarah Rendon

Service rank: Master Sergeant, USMC

Position: Senior Manager

Industry: Government

Biography

Hello – I am Sarah Rendon. I grew up outside of Chicago, Illinois, in a sleepy but pleasant suburb. I joined the Marine Corps directly from high school. I had no idea how much the decision I was making would impact my life!

I was blessed with a 23-year career as a Ground Electronics Maintenance Chief, where I was primarily stationed on the west coast (and yes – Twentynine Palms, CA, where I spent almost ten years, is considered west coast). I retired as a Master Sergeant in September of 2018.

My best accomplishments are my children. I have a son who has also chosen to serve (in the USAF). He is currently stationed in Charleston, SC. My daughter, now 10, wants to serve her community as a teacher when she grows up.

I currently work as a Project Manager providing Financial Improvement and Audit Readiness and Logistics Management solutions to our clients. I directly attribute my successes in my current role to the skills ingrained in me during my tenure as a Marine.

Questions & Answers

1. Describe your journey from the service to your first job?

■ I knew in September of 2017 that I would be asked to retire due to overseas orders I did not feel were in the best interest of my family. I retired a year later in September 2018. That last year was tough, and my lack of embracing the journey only made it worse. I enjoyed my job and was finally going to be in the zone for Master Gunnery Sergeant after 6.5 years! My denial of the path I had chosen definitely hindered my progress. It was not until I was within six months of my End of Active Service that I truly started to make an effort towards my own success.

I attended the required separations classes and the specialty Executive Separations classes for senior enlisted/officers. My transition was made easier because my OIC at the time set a drop-dead date for tasks. He first established a date where I was no longer allowed to take on new projects. Later, he took all responsibilities from me, as my replacement was not expected for another two months. Although this was very difficult for me to handle, in retrospect, it is what I wish I had done for others before me. It allowed me the time I needed to decompress and to take part in job fairs and other transition classes. I used that time wisely, conducting position description research, which is how I found myself in Project Management.

2. How did you find your first job? Describe the process.

■ Finding my first job was a painful experience. I spent six months (after my EAS) unemployed. I ended up getting hired in much the same manner as anyone else (or about 85% of new hires) - through networking. My husband knew someone at the company I now work for, and they had an open position. Although they did offer me a contingent offer letter in October of 2018, the company never won that contract. Later, when they won a different contract in the same geographical area, they asked if I would be interested.

3. When did you start planning your transition? What actions/ activities did you take?

I took every class I was authorized to take. This included the standard Separations class, the Executive Separations class, Sandlers Sales course (to learn how to sell myself!), the federal resume writing class, the DoD Skillbridge Program - Onward to Opportunity Program Management Course, and the Hire Heroes National Career Coach Program. I started attending the job fairs on base, but usually left there feeling a little letdown. It seemed that the police academies were overrepresented at many of these functions, instead of more private companies. The San Diego military Mojo hiring event was very worthwhile, however, with representatives from some big names and very few Police Academies. Some of these companies were even conducting on the spot interviews. I also hired a resume writer (worth every penny!).

4. Did you pursue any advanced degrees and/or certifications? Did they help?

I did a lot of reading of Position descriptions before applying for jobs or deciding what certifications to pursue. This research led me to believe obtaining my Project Management Professional Certificate would give me an edge and possibly make up for my lack of networking by ensuring my resume was seen by a person when weeded out through the automated recruiting systems. Before I was hired, I also started (and later completed) my Data Analytics Certificate from Cornell University. I believe that my degree, combined with these certificates, directly contributed to obtaining my initial position and subsequent promotions.

Data Analytics is a highly desirable skill set in a myriad of industries. Everyone wants to see the newest and prettiest graphs and drill-downs. We all want those decision-makers to be in a position where they have the necessary information in front of them to make the best decision for all stakeholders—understanding the basics of KISS (which we all learned in the military) can help in this technology driven endeavor.

5. Why did you choose the work/career you are in?

This job chose me, and I am grateful for it. I did not initially want to be a government contractor because I feared I could not let go of my active duty. Instead, I have found it to be pretty freeing. I can look at my Active Duty counterparts, and instead of wishing I was still in, I find myself grateful that I am not. Meanwhile, I am still part of a great team that cares about what they are doing. Being part of a great team can make up for being in a position with which you are not particularly thrilled.

6. Have you encountered any obstacles in advancing your career?

I have not previously encountered any obstacles, as I have been promoted twice in the last 1.5 years. Unfortunately, this early propulsion has left me where I will now struggle for any further promotions. As my responsibilities increased, they have also shifted away from being a Subject Matter Expert and a "doer" to business development and "management". This is a significant transformation with which I find myself grappling. Part of what I loved in the USMC was that I knew I was an expert after 20 years of performing a particular job. I enjoyed teaching those I worked with and the (positive) stress of managing the administrative versus the operational sides. Moving to the business development side is difficult because I do not enjoy networking, and I am out of my comfort zone. I know I must continue to push myself in these endeavors; however, knowing and doing are rarely the same.

7. What were the 2 hardest efforts about transitioning?

I know this will not speak to everyone – but I miss cammies!! I spend a lot of money on work clothes that I cannot wait to get out of at the end of the day. I also spend too much time figuring out what to wear and doing my hair. It seems trivial, and I thought I would enjoy wearing nice clothes and doing my hair, but ironing my hair every day is simply not happening. It is also next to impossible if I want to do a workout before work.

More importantly, the vernacular is also very difficult. Every industry, down to the different companies, have their own language. Acronyms no longer mean what they meant to you for years. You have to make a concentrated effort to sound like you belong. How long can you use the excuse you used to be in the military?

8. What do you think are the top issues for Veterans transitioning into a career?

I think one of the issues facing Veterans is probably a lack of knowledge of what is happening in corporate America. We have no idea what life is like in the private sector. For so long, we have been doing what we are told. Now the world is ours, and we do not fully understand the ramifications. There are plenty of mentoring venues out there, and you need to find one that works for you. You do not have to have a veteran mentor. You can find someone practicing in the industry you are targeting. People want to help you; you need to seek out and further, accept the help.

Another huge issue is the lack of savings. Without an appropriate safety net, many veterans are forced to take the first job they are offered. In my separations class, I was taught that I can pick 2 of three sides of the triangle – location, position, or salary. I understand this concept, but disagree with the premise. I may be forced to choose only two of these, to begin with; however, if someone wants all three, they need to put in the work.

9. Do you believe there is a stereotype attached to being a Veteran in pursuit of a job?

I feel that we (Veterans) use this as an excuse. I did not run into any negative attitudes towards me or my service during my job search. The stereotype is perpetuated by veterans and veteran groups, which are all making excuses for why we cannot get jobs. The reality is WE (individual veterans) do not do enough to put ourselves in a good position for when we leave the service. We live in this world where we believe our SERVICE is enough to get us a job. The adage "What have you done today?" is everything. If you are not making the efforts to have a successful career after the military, your life will generally be more difficult, but even with doing the "right" things, there is no guarantee life will be easy.

10. What question(s) would you have liked to have known before taking your first job?

What do you want to do? This is something we are not used to asking ourselves or even thinking about much while we are serving. Shifting your focus to yourself can be challenging for anyone, but I think in particular women. We generally spend a lot of time worrying and shaping our soldiers, Marines, Sailors, and children, often to our own detriment. Only recently has "self-care" become acceptable and even applauded.

I also would have benefited from speaking to people in different size organizations and asking, "What does your company's size mean to your benefits, workload, promotion opportunities, etc.?" As Active Duty, we tend to complain about the quality/quantity of the services the DOD provides us. We were often spoiled. Most companies cannot offer you 30 days of paid vacation a year. Nor can they offer you free healthcare or a career ladder with SMART goals leading to promotions. I expected that every place in the civilian world ran more efficiently than the military, but I quickly found out that was not the truth. Knowing what type of benefits were available (FTO/PTO, gym memberships, 401k matching, etc..) and what company size means to the different benefit packages and promotion opportunities can be meaningful and were a knowledge deficit for me.

11. What are the most important lessons you can share on making a successful job transition from the military?

1. Do not wait for someone else to do anything for you. If it is important to you, you will find a way to get it done.

2. Take some time to find what you enjoy doing. Although you may not be able to wait to get that dream job, you can better shape your future if you know what you want to be doing.

3. Do not network only with prior military. My LI feed is full of veterans and those trying to assist veterans. After taking some time to figure out where I want to head, my feed is now becoming filled with information more pertinent to where I see myself in the future.

12. If you could do it again, what would be the one thing you would do (better) or not do to help in your transition?

Much like high school, I would not wish to go through this experience again. To look back with my hindsight glasses, I would try to embrace the journey this time. I would find more things to be grateful for each day instead of letting my lack of a job define me and dictate my self-worth.

I would have pushed harder for an internship (another DoD Skillbridge Program) as well. This program can be tough to get, and I took no for an answer too quickly.

Rick Rogers

Service rank: Command Master Chief Petty Officer, USN

Position: Military Leadership and Professional Development

Industry: Federal Civil Service

Biography

Rick was born in California and raised in Washington state; in France; and in southern Illinois. He enlisted in the U.S. Navy in 1972 and graduated from Basic Underwater Demolition/SEAL (BUD/S) training in 1973 (Class 71). Over the next 31 years he deployed to over 30 countries, serving at SEAL Team ONE, Underwater Demolition Team ELEVEN, SEAL Team FIVE, and Naval Special Warfare (NSW) Development Group; as the Command Master Chief of NSW Unit EIGHT in Panama and of NSW Group ONE in Coronado; as the Senior Enlisted Leader of Special Operations Command Europe in Stuttgart, Germany, and of United States Special Operations Command in Tampa, Florida. He retired from active duty in 2003.

Starting in 2004 as a government employee, Rick helped develop Navy ratings for SEALs and Special Warfare Combatant-craft Crewmen (SWCC). In 2006 he was project lead for the NSW Alternative Final Multiple Score (AFMS) pilot to improve the eligibility process for SEAL and SWCC for the Navy's Chief Petty Officer Selection Board; the NSW AFMS was approved for implementation in 2010. Starting in 2012 he helped facilitate NSW leadership courses, particularly the 4-day NSW Command Leaders Seminar for NSW prospective COs and CMCs. He retired from civil service in March 2019.

In April 2019, he had the privilege of being inducted into the USSOCOM Commando Hall of Honor.

Rick has earned a B.S. in Liberal Arts from Excelsior College and a M.A. in Performance Psychology from National University.

He lives in Bandon, Oregon, with his wife Trish, dogs Lee and Kolo, and several cats. He has three grown step-children and two step-grandchildren. He enjoys trailer trips, craft beer, red wine, sunsets, and dancing on tables with Trish.

Questions & Answers

1. Describe your journey from the service to your first job?

■ I started planning to move back to California (from Florida) about a year before I retired from the military; however, that planning concentrated on the logistics of moving and on preparing my application for VA disability. I did not prepare at all for finding a job in California. When asked, I said I would "figure it out when I got back there [California]." I had no plan for finding a job.

2. How did you find your first job? Describe the process.

■ Dumb luck. I had moved my then-wife back to California a few months prior to my retirement in order to get her reestablished there and to find us a place to rent once I got there. While surfing one day, she ran into two people we knew. When asked what my plans were for after I returned to California, and discovering I was a "free agent", one of them, an active-duty Naval officer, said he had a project he wanted me to take the lead on. The other one, a retired Naval officer who was the regional manager for a company that provided contractors for government projects, said he wanted to hire me as a contractor. My wife relayed this information to me, and ultimately, a few months after I retired, I began work on that project as a contractor. About a year later I transitioned to civil service, still working on the same project.

3. When did you start planning your transition? What actions/ activities did you take?

I did practically nothing, regarding job/career transition planning, in the last years of active duty service. I'd sat in on a VA seminar several years before retirement just to see what info was disseminated, and I took a short resume writing seminar offered at that same VA seminar. But that was it.

4. Did you pursue any advanced degrees and/or certifications? Did they help?

I didn't finish my bachelor's degree or earn my master's degree until long after I'd retired from the military, and I did both of those for intrinsic reasons rather than from any perception that having those diplomas would advance my civil service career.

5. Why did you choose the work/career you are in?

Obviously, in my case, the work/career chose me (see answer to Q2). Having said that, I was ecstatic that I'd still be working for the Naval Special Warfare community that I loved. I was passionate about continuing to serve in NSW in whatever value-added capacity I could, about helping NSW operators and enablers do their jobs better, and ultimately contribute to mission success.

6. Have you encountered any obstacles in advancing your career?

No. Again, some of it was just being in the right place at the right time when a different position became available at the command I worked at.

7. What were the 2 hardest efforts about transitioning?

Not to sound simplistic, but one challenge was acquiring a civilian wardrobe suitable for a civil service supervisory position. I didn't have to wear a coat and tie – an open-collared shirt and slacks was an accepted professional look – but for 31 years I only had to know which uniform to wear on any given day. Didn't really have to think much about it. Now I had to plan farther ahead on what I wore, and to have enough combinations of shirts and pants and even shoes and belts so that I wasn't wearing the same stuff three times per week. It took a little while to get used to doing that.

8. What do you think are the top issues for Veterans transitioning into a career?

I suspect anxiety could be one issue, and that can lead to stress, which if unchecked can become a negative. Anxiety about being able to find a job, a good job, to be able to continue to provide for their family, maintain or even improve their standard of living, have job satisfaction. I had some anxiety in the months right before I retired, particularly because I had not planned well for any post-military career. I suppressed that anxiety by telling myself I was too busy, and too far away, from San Diego to do anything productive about job searching while still on active duty. I was foolish, and I got lucky. Proper planning, thoughtfully executed, should inspire self-confidence that might mitigate anxiety.

9. Do you believe there is a stereotype attached to being a Veteran in pursuit of a job?

From my personal experience, no, but then I was interacting with current and former military to finalize acquiring my post-military job. Others who interacted with civilians in the corporate world may have a different opinion.

10. What question(s) would you have liked to have known before taking your first job?

How exactly is my pay calculated? Since I started as a contractor for a year before transitioning to civil service, my contractor pay was based on hours worked over a given period of time. Sounds simple, but I didn't understand the nuances, so in the beginning I was working (and submitting the hours worked) more than 40 hours per week because when I was active duty I always worked long hours. It was just a habit. It took a few months for me to realize that the contract was for a specific number of hours, and by working more than 40 hours per week, I would expend all the hours in the contract sooner than everyone anticipated. That meant I'd be out of work, and therefore not receive a paycheck, unless the company assigned me to some other contract – which was not a guarantee. Once I figured this out, I just worked 40 hours per week – or at least only submitted for 40 hours per week, even if I worked a few more than that. Those of you who are more familiar with contract work might object to this simplistic view, knowing that a contract can be re-negotiated if the work turns out to require extra hours, or even more than one person. However, the Navy command paying for the contract agreed to pay more than they originally wanted to in order to secure me, personally, as the contractor. I was grateful that they did that, and didn't want to risk the whole deal by raising any issues of possibly needing extra hours to finish the contract. Remember, NSW is like my family, so I had no problem working a little beyond the set schedule. But I almost dug myself a deep hole by not completely understanding how contractors are paid. Ignorance is not bliss in the area of compensation.

11. What are the most important lessons you can share on making a successful job transition from the military?

Networking, protecting your reputation, and did I mention networking?

My experience confirmed that the cliché "It's not what you know, but who you know" still holds an underlying truth: The more people aware of your skills and reputation, the more likely that someone who knows someone who is looking for a person like you. When I retired, Internet networking platforms and social media were in their infancy, so I got lucky through word of mouth. I suspect the challenge today is that there are so many job applicants flooding cyberspace that it can overwhelm corporate human resource departments trying to sort the wheat from the chaff. Personal networking - through phone calls and emails to your immediate circle of family, relatives, friends, and colleagues present and past, and asking them to socialize your status to their personal circle – might be considered antiquated these days, but also might touch someone looking for you but didn't know how to find you. The critical component of personal networking is that your immediate circle knows you personally, and can therefore offer something that a sterile resume cannot: An informed opinion of your character and reputation.

Which brings me to my second lesson, protecting your reputation throughout your military career. While luck was a key factor in my job acquisition, it just enabled that fortuitous meeting in the surf zone. I believe my reputation was the critical variable - that I was offered work on a significant project because of their belief that I had the combination of personal integrity, work ethic, and professional expertise that they were looking for, even though they might not have directly worked with me before. That belief was the product of my work in Naval Special Warfare over three decades, in positions of increasing responsibility, where I always tried to do the very best job that I could, made sacrifices, earned trust, and very much believed in being a team player. I made mistakes, but tried hard to not repeat that mistake. Ultimately, I believe that a person's reputation is defined by others (co-workers, supervisors, friends, family) from their direct observation of how you go about your daily work, how you live your life. You don't get to say you have a certain reputation; it's built brick by brick by what people say about you. You earn it, good or bad, by your daily actions, by the behavioral choices you make. Just like trust, it's hard to earn a good reputation, and it's harder to repair it once it's been tarnished. Do everything you can to earn and protect your good reputation, because people who don't know you personally will pre-judge you based on it. It could make the difference between you getting a job over someone else with similar skills.

12. If you could do it again, what would be the one thing you would do (better) or not do to help in your transition?

Since I fell into a great job, doing worthy work I was passionate about, it would be easy to say that I wouldn't do anything differently if I had a do-over. However, as I've already indicated, I got very lucky. But luck is not a strategy, and it would've been much smarter if I'd started contacting people I knew in San Diego several months prior to my retirement, instead of relying on a chance encounter in the surf zone of a Coronado beach.

Russell Smith

Service rank: Colonel, USAF

Position: VP, Cyber Practice

Industry: Federal Systems Integrator

Biography

I retired in the summer of 2016 after 30 years of service; 5 years enlisted and 25 years as an officer. After retirement, I moved to Northern Virginia, both in pursuit of job opportunities and to move closer to my in-laws. My enlisted years were spent in law enforcement and then, after receiving a commission, I moved into information technology. I approached my AF career as something that was temporary until I could find a "real" job. As is normal, I think, there were always times when I contemplated getting out, but no opportunity outside ever appealed to me the way continuing to serve this great country did. I was also fortunate that my children were still young and very tolerant of the frequent moves, and my wife truly enjoyed each assignment we were blessed to get. During my career, I received the opportunity to work at a Federally Funded Research Development Center (FFRDC) called the Institute for Defense Analyses (IDA). The assignment planted a seed in me of a possible civilian job, since I really enjoyed the work and I would be able to continue contributing to the Department of Defense (DoD) mission. Once I became focused on my military transition, I narrowed the potential employers to three FFRDCs. Finding folks on the inside that could help me navigate the hiring processes were critical. In each company I interviewed with, there was someone advocating for me. I was hired by

IDA and had a great 2 ½ years, but another opportunity presented itself at Science Applications International Corporation (SAIC) that became too good to pass up. I have been with SAIC for almost two years. During my time at SAIC I have been promoted and am now the Vice President for SAIC's Cyber Practice providing cyber solutions, products, and capabilities for our DoD and other federal customers.

Questions & Answers

1 Describe your journey from the service to your first job?

■ I started planning for my transition about two years prior to retirement. In some ways, however, I knew my military career would come to an end and I would have an opportunity to start a second career in the private sector. I was fortunate that my role in the military would carry over to my second career. In other words, I felt that continuously learning in my military career, including achieving civilian certifications, would not only benefit the military organizations I was assigned to but a future civilian employer. I often mentored members of organizations that I led to consider and take advantage of all the amazing training and education opportunities in the military. I found the best NCOs and officers were committed to personal growth which would not only set them up for success after leaving the military, but cemented their success in their military careers.

2 How did you find your first job? Describe the process.

■ I learned about my first civilian employer when I was selected as a National Security Fellow for Senior Development Education (SDE). During this time I was assessing different SDE opportunities one of the options was Institute for Defense Analyses (IDA). At that time, I had not heard of IDA, but fortunate for me, my boss had and worked with them while at CENTCOM. He spoke very highly of the quality of their work and so after a little research I chose IDA and fortunately for me was selected for a one year fellowship there. I enjoyed the work and the people at IDA, which led to me to put IDA on a short list of potential civilian employers.

3. When did you start planning your transition? What actions/ activities did you take?

When I decided it was time to retire and actually set a retirement date, I projected a full one year out. Logging into the personnel system and setting that date became a forcing function to focus on the future. The act of setting the date a full year out is a tremendous benefit that the military allows. At that point I ensured I was enrolled in the Transition Assistance Program and took advantage of the guidance provided through that program.

4. Did you pursue any advanced degrees and/or certifications? Did they help?

Yes, I pursued a Certified Information Systems Security Professional, Project Management Professional and National Defense University's Chief Information Officer. These certifications were valuable during my career. Military leadership has recognized the value of these certification and has provided the training dollars to offer service members these certification opportunities. As I look back on my military career, one of the many aspects of service that I enjoyed was the emphasis on personal and professional growth. Early in my career so many training courses were designed specifically for the military members by military education and training organizations. Over time and because of the DoD's reliance on civilian information technology, civilian certifications have become a critical part of active duty training and education. I do believe that taking advantage of the professional development opportunities helped me in getting my civilian jobs. Obviously, the knowledge, skills, and abilities that the certification represents are important to a prospective employer, but there is also the demonstrated quest for professional growth and potentially learning new skills that is very important.

5. Why did you choose the work/career you are in?

The Air Force pointed me toward the career field I am in. I started my Air Force career enlisted in Security Forces. During my first four years, I knew I wanted to get commissioned. When I signed up for ROTC in college after my enlistment, I was told the best chance of getting commissioned was with a technical degree. I took a chance that I could handle the academics, and fortunately I could and found a new calling in information technology. I went from being a software programmer to leadership in base communications units to tactical communications units to cybersecurity. All the while, I enjoyed the new opportunities and the amazing people I was fortunate to lead. I guess I didn't choose the career field I ended up in, the Air Force chose it for me.

6. Have you encountered any obstacles in advancing your career?

In the private sector, I have found technical expertise is incredibly valuable. Therefore, there are obstacles constantly being put in front of you, because technology is constantly changing. Additionally, leadership in the private sector has a slightly different focus than military leadership. All the leadership training we get in the military is definitely applicable and valued in the private sector, but there are two primary areas of focus: business acumen and technical competence. I have found that my military leadership is a great starting point, but I still need to develop business acumen to truly be successful. One area that comes to mind, and is a common requirement in business leadership positions, is managing Profit and Loss (P&L). Demonstrated success in managing P&L in increasingly larger portfolios is the equivalent to demonstrating increasing leadership responsibilities at the flight, squadron, group, etc. level.

7. What were the 2 hardest efforts about transitioning?

I went to work for a civilian employer with a sizable retired and former military workforce. IDA's culture made transitioning very easy. However, the most challenging aspect of moving into a civilian workforce was the need to generate your own work. After spending an entire career in the military, the idea of finding profitable work was very difficult. Civilian companies exist to make money, and everyone, no matter what their role is, must contribute to the success of the company by growing the business. The idea of filling out a time card and accounting for work in terms of how it contributes to the "bottom line" required a mind shift.

8. What do you think are the top issues for Veterans transitioning into a career?

A good friend of mine gave me some advice transitioning into the civilian workforce. He wanted me to understand that while we feel a very strong sense of loyalty to our military service, and the military leadership culture focuses on "taking care of the force", that is not how the private sector operates. Understanding the transactional nature of the private sector will help a veteran's transition. In the private sector, it's perfectly acceptable to seek out other opportunities if you feel there are better opportunities. The only way to know about those opportunities is to make sure you maintain your network of fellow veterans after you move into the private sector.

9. Do you believe there is a stereotype attached to being a Veteran in pursuit of a job?

Veterans are known for their mission focus and outstanding work ethic. I have never experienced or heard of a negative stereotype about veterans. That may be because of how many veterans work in the NCR.

10. What question(s) would you have liked to have known before taking your first job?

How do you effectively negotiate your salary? This is completely foreign to a veteran if they are transitioning into the private sector. There are also some negotiations that take place within the federal job search around Step level, but the GS pay scale, and the other federal pay scales, are a matter of public record. Each company has its own way of stratifying positions within pay scales and pay bands. It's also very important to think about other forms of compensation; bonuses, stock options, etc. that are part of your pay "package". Having a network contact at that company is invaluable if they are willing to share how compensation is evaluated in the hiring process.

11. What are the most important lessons you can share on making a successful job transition from the military?

1. Know what you want to do. This question may be easy to answer if you're looking in an industry where your skills are easily transferable. There are TAP resources that will help line up military skills into civilian job requirements, if you need that help. If upon leaving the military you feel like it's a great time for a change, that's ok. Most employers value military service and know you're willing to work hard and learn. Make sure you highlight your breadth of experience and success no matter what you've been called upon to do. If you are changing career paths it's important to know that you are starting out knowing as much as you

did coming out of tech school, and your status as a senior NCO or field grade officer will not mean anything. Moving into the corporate world makes every veteran, as a friend of mine told me, a corporate 2LT!

2. Start early. The sooner you can answer question #1 the better. Once you've decided where you want to take all your great knowledge, skills, and abilities, you should immediately begin building up your network. Looking into potential jobs or employers or industries when you've got plenty of time before making a decision is easier and a whole lot more fun. Even if you're a couple of years out, having a conversation with potential employers can be very insightful, and will also potentially get you on their radar. However, employers are rarely in a position to make a real commitment until you are ready to make a real commitment and the hiring timelines are typically measured in weeks not months.

3. Go to where the jobs are. In the post COVID world this may be much easier. Teleworking is going to continue to grow and everyone expects the remote worker to be the norm. However, many jobs are not knowledge worker positions where working from home is possible. If you want to live in Cedar Rapids, there's no reason to look for jobs that are not in Cedar Rapids. I know that's obvious, but it's important to think about where you want to live and maybe more importantly where you absolutely do not want to live. If you have no interest in living in the DC area, but want to be a GS-15, you will have less opportunities. If you want to live in rural Tennessee, but refuse to do corporate business development (which is often easy to do remotely), you will have less opportunities. Aligning your geographic requirements, with your network and connections, with the type of job you want to do will make the transition very smooth.

12. If you could do it again, what would be the one thing you would do (better) or not do to help in your transition?

I consider myself very fortunate as I entered my final military assignment. I entered into my transition period with a good sense of where I wanted to work, a solid network in that area, and the type of work I wanted to do. However, there were plenty of dead-end roads I traveled looking for the right position. That was all part of the process. Never be discouraged when something doesn't work out. Companies, especially in the federal government contracting space, are always shifting their hiring focus based on work won and lost. Federal hiring practices can be extremely hard to navigate, especially at the Senior Executive Service (SES) level, but don't be discouraged. Most importantly, remember that the transition is a journey and as you learn more, even after you leave the military and work in the private sector for a while, you continue to get closer to your ideal position.

Clif Stargardt

Service rank: Colonel, USAF

Position: Program Manager

Industry: Defense

Biography

Air Force meteorologist for 10 years, left active duty and joined the Reserve. Spent 3.5 years as a laser system test engineer and deputy program manager with Boeing in Albuquerque, NM. Returned to full-time duty for 5 years as a space operations officer in Colorado Springs. Left full-time Reserve and worked as a program manager for Harris Corp, leading a space electronic warfare sustainment program for a year. Returned to full-time duty again to stand up and command a new squadron. I was then selected for Colonel, attended Air War College in Alabama, and then moved to Tampa to command all the individual Reservists assigned to Special Operations Command, Central Command, Southern Command, Air Combat Command, and Air Force Special Operations Command, about 1300 total. I have Bachelor's degrees in Math and Meteorology, and Master's degrees in Meteorology, Engineering Management, and Strategic Studies.

Questions & Answers

1. **Describe your journey from the service to your first job?** I The first time I left active duty in 2002 I had no idea what I was going to do. I didn't want to be a meteorologist anymore (which at the time seemed like the only thing I was qualified to be) and my wife (who was active duty) and I were moving to Albuquerque. I went through the Transition Assistance Program (TAP) and hired a resume' writer, and started researching what was available in Albuquerque. I really figured I might be working at Home Depot while I finished my Masters in Engineering Management to make myself more marketable.

A month or so before we moved to New Mexico I had reached out to the senior Reservist on Kirtland Air Force Base looking for a new Reserve position. This was in fact my first foray into networking without knowing what networking was. She asked if I was in the market for a civilian job, which indeed I was. She pointed me to the website for Boeing-SVS, a small subsidiary of Boeing that built laser control systems. I literally thought, "There is no way on Earth I'm qualified to work there." But the company was growing and they were looking for technically-capable young people they could grow and train (and who had security clearances). The company was 50% PhDs in electro-optics and control systems, but I would have mopped the floors if that's what it took. I did a phone interview before we moved, and then another in-person interview when I arrived; then, it took about 6 weeks for on-boarding. The whole process took about 3 months. I spent 3.5 wonderful fun years at Boeing, working hard to cover up the fact I wasn't qualified to be there. Along the way I was actually part of a team that won an award for making scientific history.

When I transitioned from full-time Reserve duty the second time, I had established a close working relationship with the Harris General Manager in Colorado Springs, so it was 100% the network. He and I actually started talking about a position with the company for about 9 months before I transitioned out of full-time duty. I had expected to stay in that job a very long time, but less than a year later the military came knocking with an opportunity of a lifetime.

When I finally retired from the military in 2018, as a Colonel, this transition seemed, at the time, the most difficult. First off, I was more senior and had expectations that the civilian world would welcome an established leader such as myself like Caesar riding into Rome. To a certain degree achieving that rank is a detriment. I was also doing it in Tampa, which has zero space industry presence. Retiring in Colorado Springs would have been easy. Tampa, not so much. But I spent the summer of 2018 trying to build a network outside of the defense industry, since I didn't expect to return to that in Tampa. In the end, it was passing my resume' to one of my Reservists in SOF AT&L who passed it along to Booz Allen Hamilton, who deemed me qualified to work there based on my experience with Boeing and Harris more so than my military experience. At the end of the day I was only retired for about 3 weeks before I received an offer from Booz, and then I came aboard about 4 weeks after that.

2. How did you find your first job? Describe the process.

Networking isn't the most important thing in the transition job search. It's the only thing. I am 3 for 3 where networking was the only factor in gaining employment. The older and more senior I got the harder the transition due to my level of expectation and employers' level of expectation. But in my experience, it's all about the network.

3. When did you start planning your transition? What actions/ activities did you take?

I hired resume' writers, gained new marketable degrees (education), earned the Project Management Professional (PMP) certification, and networked, networked, networked. I can't say any of those were deciding factors, but they all made the job search easier.

4. Did you pursue any advanced degrees and/or certifications? Did they help?

I pursued advanced degrees and the PMP certification because they were directly applicable to the field I was looking in (program management). And I know they helped because the people hiring me told me they liked me having those qualifications, given I didn't necessarily have directly-related experience.

5. Why did you choose the work/career you are in?

Because I'm not sure what else I'm interested in doing, nor what else

I'm qualified for. I've never been passionate about any career except being an officer in the Air Force. And I couldn't do that forever. I didn't have the talent or technical background to be a pure engineer. But I found I had a knack for planning and solving the complexities that come with program management, so that's been where I've gravitated. If I could find a job in the civilian world that directly equates to "command" in the military that would be wonderful, because command in the military is where you make the most difference in peoples' lives. But getting there requires working your way up in the civilian world, even for retired Colonels. Someday I would like to teach in semi-retirement.

6. Have you encountered any obstacles in advancing your career?

Nothing that's not self-induced. I've only been in my latest civilian career for 2 years, so I'm concentrating on learning the business of DoD acquisition and being good at the job I have. I'm in no hurry to try and start leading teams or moving up in management of the company.

7. What were the 2 hardest efforts about transitioning?

For me, the hardest part, all 3 times, was coming from a position of rank and granted authority (officer) with an institutional subordinate workforce (enlisted), to a position without that institutionalized authority. In my mind, I would sometimes think, "Hey...I was a big deal in uniform!" as I'm working for someone younger and less experienced than me, or where my peers were my subordinates a couple months ago. I won't lie, it takes getting used to, and the quicker you get used to it, the easier the transition. Some will never get used to it and they'll always have a hard time, perhaps never fully transitioning out of uniform.

8. What do you think are the top issues for Veterans transitioning into a career?

Civilian companies do not understand and do not appreciate the leadership and responsibility military members get at much younger ages than their civilian counterparts. Civilian companies also have a stereotype of military members being rough, impersonal, and doing nothing but barking orders to subordinates. Perhaps some in the Army and Marines are like that, but it's less so in the Navy and certainly not in the Air/Space Force. There is simply a large cultural divide between the civilian and military worlds, making it difficult for that first transition.

9. Do you believe there is a stereotype attached to being a Veteran in pursuit of a job?

Definitely. See above

10. What question(s) would you have liked to have known before taking your first job?

In my first job with Boeing I had a salary number in mind that I would accept. After being a Captain in the Air Force I was willing to settle for about $45K. The offer came at $63K and I jumped at it. I had no idea I could negotiate and a peer of mine, who knew the ropes, negotiated to around $75K very easily. By the second and third time I transitioned, I knew the ropes.

11. What are the most important lessons you can share on making a successful job transition from the military?

1. Figure out what you want to do.

2. Start building a network early around what you want to do.

3. Utilize that network. Network, network, network.

12. If you could do it again, what would be the one thing you would do (better) or not do to help in your transition?

In my first transition, I just bumbled into it and, other than my salary negotiation, it turned out to be a wonderful experience. My second transition was well-planned and executed, although I didn't really explore other potential options. In my third transition, I let a little bit of desperation creep in. I might have come up with a different outcome had I been more patient and worked my network harder and longer. But in the end, I'm happy where I am.

Kanessa Trent

Service rank: Sergeant Major, USA

Position: Leadership/Organizational
Resiliency Coach

Industry: Education/Credentialing

Biography

Kanessa Trent hails from Fort Wayne, Indiana and served in the U.S. Army for 29 years as a public affairs professional and educator. Kanessa retired from the US Army September 30, 2020 as a Sergeant Major having served in a variety Public Affairs positions from brigade to four-star command. She served on numerous deployments including tours in Haiti, Panama, Bosnia, and Afghanistan as well as to more than a dozen countries across the Indo-Asia-Pacific region. She was stationed in South Korea for three years and in Hawaii for a total of seven years during two separate assignments. Kanessa spent the final four years of her career teaching at the at the Sergeants Major Course, United States Army Sergeants Major Academy in the Department of Joint, Interagency, Intergovernmental and Multinational Operations.

She holds two graduate degrees; a Master's Degree in Adult Education and Lifelong Learning from Pennsylvania State University and a Master's Degree in Leadership Studies from the University of Texas – El Paso. Kanessa earned her Bachelor of Science Degree in Journalism with a double minor in Marketing and Mass Communication from Thomas Edison State University. Kanessa was the Department of the Army's 2002 Journalist of the Year. Kanessa has made her forever home in El Paso, Texas. She has one son and enjoys traveling, reading and anything that involves sun, sand and surf.

Questions & Answers

1. Describe your journey from the service to your first job?

■ I began my transition officially 19 months prior to leaving the Army. I wish I had started sooner. Once I made up my mind that I would retire rather than take one more final assignment, I began thinking about what I wanted to do. Almost everyone I spoke to assumed I would go after a GS or contractor position doing what I had done for the majority of my career, which was Public Affairs. And I wasn't completely opposed to that, but I also recognized I had the opportunity to do whatever I wanted at this stage in life, so I began thinking about every option.

A coworker asked me what I truly wanted to do. I told him that if I had my way, I'd find a job that allowed me to teach online from home. I had a certification in distance education and liked the idea of being at home for a year but still working as I enjoyed my transition from the Army. I spoke with my Alma Mater and many other universities and colleges but finding an adjunct professor position seemed highly unlikely.

And then I struck up a conversation with someone I saw on LinkedIn whose job title I liked. I wrote to him and asked if it was a real job or just something catchy to get noticed by employers. It was then I learned that he worked for a company that taught leadership and organizational resiliency. I was intrigued enough that I signed up for the course myself and felt immediately connected to the curriculum and the mission of the program. Months prior to my signing out on transitional leave, the company offered me a job. I said yes, of course, and began coaching and facilitating clients just as my final days in uniform occurred.

Not only had I been hired to teach online from home, but the sessions are conducted in a one-on-one setting using a video chat media platform. For me, it is the ideal fit. I've been able to bring in an income all while enjoy the summer months on transitional leave at home with my son. Coupled with the COVID-19 pandemic when many of the full-time career positions I'd applied for were put on hold, this job opportunity was a blessing to me in so many ways. No matter what I end up doing in the future, I can't imagine a time where I'm not affiliated with this company. Its ethics and its values align with my own, and its mission is one that I wholeheartedly, 100% believe in. I get paid to help others learn, grow and develop their own leadership philosophy to better their teams. It's been a real gift to me.

2. How did you find your first job? Describe the process.

■ I found my first job through LinkedIn, when I wasn't even looking. I think that's the lesson many don't consider. Your next job or your next career may present itself in a way you do not expect. I initially asked someone on LinkedIn, who I was not at that time connected to, about his job title. It read "Resiliency Coach" and I thought that sounded so interesting. I asked him if it was a real job title or just something to get recruiters to notice him. What I learned was that he was the Vice President for People and Policy for the company that now employs me. I am so glad I thought well enough to follow up on my instinct when his job title so interested me.

3. When did you start planning your transition? What actions/ ■ activities did you take?

Having two graduate degrees already, I thought it was important to pursue certifications, so I began researching what to take. Ultimately, I decided to leverage the Onward to Opportunity program that IVMF through Syracuse University offers transitioning military members (and their spouses). I chose to get my Project Management Profession certification. Knowing now what I know, I would have chosen a different certification, but nonetheless I have only glowing reviews for O2O. The four-day workshop they put us through was PHENOMENAL. It was like SFL-TAP (Soldier for Life Transitional Assistance Program) on steroids.

I also signed up for American Corporate Partners, which was so valuable. I deliberately chose a woman, 10 years + older than me and in a different discipline. I wanted professional career advice, not "how to get this particular job" advice. What my ACP mentor did for me was help me to realize what I didn't want before I could decide what I truly DID want. I'd had several military retirees who call themselves "transition experts" tell me that I had to choose EXACTLY what I wanted to do after the Army and brand myself that way or else I'd fail (their words). I never bought into that and still don't. I knew my education and skills could land me a good job with a good company doing what I'd always done for our United States Army, but I was also sure of my many soft skills. What I needed to figure out was what I was willing to do, what I wasn't and how I would go about finding my dream job. My ACP mentor was fantastic in helping me sort through the emotions of it all initially and then considering jobs that I wasn't necessarily considering but was clearly ideal for. That mental shift opened up so many doors for me as I started widening my interests. I've applied for and been interviewed for positions that I ultimately was not offered or didn't accept all because I was willing to give myself permission to go for what I wanted.

I began attending two networking events each month. At first, those were job fairs, but I quickly learned that wasn't where I was going to find my next opportunity. Many of those job fairs are focused on entry-level positions that I was not going to consider. I then decided to put four hours on my calendar each week dedicated to networking and attending community events. I did this with purpose and rigor. I created and maintained a document with the names of each person I met and spoke to. I followed up with emails, requests for coffee and tagged them in LinkedIn posts. After a while, I continued to run into the same people at various events and the conversations were significant, meaningful and interesting. I made friends with some of those contacts and others became important key leader contacts. I was authentic in my approach to networking, as I feel everyone should be. I didn't network just to shake hands and move on to the next person; I was deliberate about establishing connections and developing relationships. That served me well. I now sit on two committees in my community that allow me to give back. They aren't paid positions, but they are important organizations that truly help those in El Paso. I'm able to do this because of my purposeful approach to networking.

4. Did you pursue any advanced degrees and/or certifications? Did they help?

Yes. I've always been a lifelong learner. I left the Army with two graduate degrees and earned two certifications in the last 6 months of my career.

5. Why did you choose the work/career you are in?

■ My passions include education, helping others and being able to give back. I'm in my current position because I get to do all three of those things.

6. Have you encountered any obstacles in advancing your career?

■ COVID-19 clearly presented some real challenges. I was in the final round of two separate positions, one local and one in another state, when COVID hit. Both companies wrote to tell me hiring actions were on hold. That was in April 2020. It's now September and I've not heard back.

7. What were the 2 hardest efforts about transitioning?

■ One thing I had to learn and tell myself is that it's ok to pursue more than one job, one position, one opportunity at a time. I initially felt disloyal when I considered applying for more than one position at a time. I'm not sure why. It sounds ridiculous to me now. But then, the idea that if I were offered two jobs and had to choose seemed to be a loyalty issue. It took several conversations with friends and family before I realized how dumb, and how pompous that sounded. First, why would I think out of hundreds of candidates I would be offered two positions? And second, if by some grace of God, I was offered two positions, I had the option to say no. I'd never said no to any job the Army offered me and willingly took on additional duties to help others. That was a lesson I had to learn and thankfully I recognized this and got over it sooner rather than later in my transition process.

I am not sure if this is considered "hard," but I expected to at least receive notification from a company when I applied and some sort of timeline. That's not the case in the civilian world. You apply, get an automatic notification thanking you for the application and that's it. From there it's a waiting game. The first job I applied for that I really wanted, I assumed I would never get because I didn't hear anything for months. Five months after I applied, I got an email inviting me in for an interview. I then did a series of three more interviews that same month. The same thing happened with another job I really wanted and that's when COVID-19 hit and the interviews and the hiring process froze. To this day, I've still not heard anything from that company in another state.

8. What do you think are the top issues for Veterans transitioning into a career?

I think veterans leaving the service either have a lack of confidence or are completely overconfident in what they bring to the civilian workforce. The first is true when soldiers don't take the time to prepare for the transition and are unsure of their own worth, experience or what they want to do next. The latter is true of a lot of troops who feel entitled to step right into a job that pays equal to what they were making on active duty just because they served. In either case, soldiers are usually wrong. While no company owes a veteran a job, it is absolutely true that veterans bring incredible skills – especially soft skills – to the civilian workplace. Many times, articulating those skills is what holds someone back. And a bit of humility goes a long way.

I also think that most people don't understand what it means to network. It's not enough to click on "connect" on LinkedIn. Developing meaningful relationships is what matters. I now receive phone calls and emails regularly from people I've met asking me if I'm interested in one job or another. Most of the time those jobs haven't even been announced yet, but my colleague is thinking of me and what a good fit I'd be. That's because I developed true and lasting relationships with people in this community who know me and are willing to vouch for me.

9. Do you believe there is a stereotype attached to being a Veteran in pursuit of a job?

Sure, I think there are some employers who stereotype those who serve in the military. But those stereotypes are easily overcome with preparation and a lot of it. When I hear veterans say they can't find a job or they haven't been offered anything meaningful, often what I also hear is that they are waiting for someone to do the work for them. Finding a job is a full-time job. Disputing stereotypes is easily done once a well-prepared former service member is sitting in front of an employer. A person must be poised, dressed well, have researched the company and be prepared to explain why his or her skills – hard and soft – are valuable to that company.

10. What question(s) would you have liked to have known before taking your first job?

I don't know how to answer this question. I felt prepared.

11. What are the most important lessons you can share on making a successful job transition from the military?

1. Network, Network, Network.

2. Educate yourself.

3. Be humble. Be hungry. Be honest.

12. If you could do it again, what would be the one thing you would do (better) or not do to help in your transition?

Two things I would have done if I had to this over. I would have started a full year earlier and I would not have worried so much about having the perfect resume. I spent SO much time worrying about having the perfect two-page resume. Had I to do over, I would have put everything down on a master document and used that to create the perfect resume for each and every job I applied for. When people said in the beginning, "you have to cut and paste your paragraphs" or that type of thing, I couldn't fully envision what they meant. I wasted A LOT of TIME and EFFORT and stressed a great deal over the perfect resume when many times the company had their own portal for applications (even for senior executive positions).

Andrew Vasquez

Service rank: Major, USAF & Reserves

Position: Financial Advisor

Industry: Financial

Biography

Drew Vasquez is a financial advisor who serves his clients with passion, honesty, and love. As a fiduciary, utilizing his life and health, Series 66, and Series 7 licenses in 6 states serving approximately 300 clients, Drew serves his clients face-to-face and provides analysis and recommendations catered to each client/family uniquely based on their financial status, goals, risk tolerance, time horizons. Prior to his career as an advisor, Drew was an active duty Air Force officer for 6 years after graduating from the US Air Force Academy in 2007 where he enjoyed playing baseball, the relationships he built, and snowboarding. His final position on Active Duty was the Budget Chief for global unconventional warfare programs at Headquarters, US Special Operations Command at MacDill, AFB, Fl. Drew continues to serve in special operations as a reservist a couple weeks a year as the Deputy Comptroller at the Headquarters, Special Operations Command Central located at MacDill AFB, Fl.

Drew enjoys spending time with his wife Jessica and his 3 daughters Kennedy, 8, who enjoys playing piano, singing, and gymnastics, Kallie, 6, who enjoys playing softball and gymnastics, and Kruze, 1.5 years old, who keeps everyone on their toes. On his off time, Drew enjoys playing golf, the beach, and coaching/practicing his daughters' interests with them.

Questions & Answers

1. Describe your journey from the service to your first job?

The transition was intimidating because there is no chance of a success as a financial planner. I wanted a firm that would pay for my licensing and provide training which First Command offered and looking back is probably one of the best at on-boarding, training, equipping, and helping advisors succeed. It took my wife and I 6 years of active duty military service to prepare for the transition I made because it required us to save 6-12 months of living expenses to protect our family's income needs should I not succeed at a the primarily commission based industry I was entering as a financial planner.

2. How did you find your first job? Describe the process.

I was confident I wanted to be a financial planner, just not sure with who. When USAA did not react as expected to my inquiry to work for them as a financial planner, I was excited to accept an opportunity with First Command who was going to train me, pay for my licenses, and help me succeed with a team/mentor/coach at my office in Tampa along with all of the materials and resources necessary. The scariest part was the unknown of success or failure. Additionally, I was not sure if I had secured a reserve job yet so my medical coverage would have been much more expensive and a new dynamic to our finances if I did not stay in the reserves.

3. When did you start planning your transition? What actions/activities did you take?

Went to the Service Academy Career Conference (SACC) in San Antonio, TX to find a career/financial planning firm and ran across First Command at the end of the last day of the job fair and had already been recommend them back in Tampa by my military mentor.

4. Did you pursue any advanced degrees and/or certifications? Did they help?

Series 7 and 66 FINRA licenses.

5. Why did you choose the work/career you are in?

■ Had to have them to continue a career with First Command and/or to become a financial planner anywhere for that matter.

6. Have you encountered any obstacles in advancing your career?

■ Everyday there are new challenges because we are dealing with system and regulatory limitations and humans who are ever-changing, come with different moods, personalities, perspectives, and desires/priorities – I am always on my toes! The biggest challenge is keeping everyone happy.

7. What were the 2 hardest efforts about transitioning?

■ Lack of guaranteed pay and focusing on intentional efforts to earn income and grow my business instead of slacking off (being lazy).

8. What do you think are the top issues for Veterans transitioning into a career?

- Lack of education and knowledge about the careers available that mesh well with their experiences and/or desired career

- Lack of confidence in the ability to earn similar income

- Insecurities about not having the government pay and benefits

9. Do you believe there is a stereotype attached to being a Veteran in pursuit of a job?

I believe that generally most employers give veterans a benefit of the doubt ahead of others who have never served.

10. What question(s) would you have liked to have known before taking your first job?

- What is the average timeframe for advisors to earn $XXX amount (whatever my desired amount is annually)?

- How can I position myself to delegate administrative work as quickly as possible so I am focused on my skill set which is financial planning and advisement.

11. What are the most important lessons you can share on making a successful job transition from the military?

1. Be disciplined, do what you say you are going to do.

2. Always be honest.

3. Never stop working hard until you have earned the ability to take breaks/vacations.

12. If you could do it again, what would be the one thing you would do (better) or not do to help in your transition?

I would have watched/listened to successful people in my career field more, taken better notes, been more organized, and not been as anxious/nervous when things did not go my way.

Ryan Walters

Service rank: Chief Warrant Officer 4, USA

Position: Business Development Manager

Industry: Defense

Biography

Ryan Walters, Chief Warrant Officer 4 (retired), served as U.S. Army Special Operations Helicopter Pilot. He currently serves as a Business Development Manager for Thales Defense and Security, Inc. His primary focus is on the Rotary Wing Defense and Civil aviation market. Prior to this role, Ryan served with the Veterans Health Administration Louis Stokes VA Medical Center in Cleveland, OH; one of the largest VA healthcare systems in the country. While with the VA, Ryan worked in healthcare administration and medical supply chain management. Ryan helped the organization successfully navigate a complex global supply chain that was constrained by the global COVID-19 pandemic.

While in the Army, Ryan spent most of his 20-year career as a Special Operations Aviation Chief Pilot and flight instructor with the 160th Special Operations Aviation Regiment. He was also previously enlisted, serving with the 2nd Ranger Battalion, 75th Ranger Regiment. Ryan has spent four years' cumulative time deployed to combat zones and other conflict zones around the globe.

Ryan holds an undergraduate degree in Business Management, a MA in Diplomacy from Norwich University, Northfield, VT, and is completing his capstone for his MS in Project Management and Organizational Leadership with Northeastern University, Boston, MA. Ryan and his family reside near Cleveland, OH, where they spend their free time supporting Equestrian events.

Questions & Answers

1. Describe your journey from the service to your first job?

■ I started my deliberate preparation for retirement in the Summer of 2017. This placed me roughly one year out. I had made up my mind that I was going to retire right at 20 years in. Upon retiring, in 2018, I was only 38. I was hopeful that I would capitalize on my outside of the cockpit "soft skills" that I had developed as a Battalion Senior Warrant Officer and Chief Pilot. Admittedly, I think that I should have started the networking portion of my retirement preparation a little earlier. If I could suggest an ideal period to start, 18 months out is nominal, I think. Now, I understand that there are unique circumstances that do not allow such a generous timeline. I did have quite a bit of support from my leadership.

I was extremely aggressive on LinkedIn. I set up my profile for the area and markets that I was going to target on my profile. I began to send innumerable personalized connection requests with a condensed elevator pitch, and that I was planning on moving to Cleveland, OH, and that I would love to connect, network, and even grab a call. This served me well, as I was introduced to countless people. Understand that not everyone you connect with will be in the market for you. They may, however, lead you to other people in their network that would be interested in your skills. It is important to always stay professional and to never demand anything from these early connections, other than the ability to connect with them. My approach has created many friendships with many great people that I still talk to all the time. It is important to build those bridges with folks and to always be prepared to support the next veteran.

My strategy quickly turned into me wanting to spend time, and money, on traveling to Cleveland to meet people in person. This was something that I was comfortable with. I elected to do this, instead of pursuing other qualifications that I thought would make me more marketable. There are cases where you must have specific certifications/qualifications, but, I elected to submit for four day passes (Thursday-Sunday), and I worked to set up a full days' worth of meetings, breakfast meetups, cups of coffee, etc. This served me well, as this led to my first job working at the VA Hospital in Cleveland. I had also interviewed with a few other companies. Essentially, I had three decent job offers in front of me, and I chose the best one at the time. This was all attributed to investing in meeting people and developing a network that continues to function today.

2. How did you find your first job? Describe the process.

■ My first job, with the VA, was through a networking referral. Through my previously mentioned strategy, a person, with whom I networked with early on in my transition, and is now a great friend of mine, offered up his extensive network to me. Through dozens of introductory emails, he connected me with the Medical Center Director, and I was able to meet with her and her staff. A word of advice—anytime you meet people, and especially senior executives, dress for the role that you think you may want. Be prepared. I had resumes (printed on quality resume paper), business cards, and I was prepared for anything. I wanted to be interviewed on the spot! Now, this is not always the case, but this is the mindset that I had. With a nice suit on, I was ready to go, wherever I was, and at whatever time. I treated all networking sessions, cups of coffee, lunches, dinners, etc., as opportunities for people to get to know me, my background, and why I could make an impact in their organizations. Again, this all started because of the aggressive, professional strategy of networking on LinkedIn, and countless phone calls.

3. When did you start planning your transition? What actions/activities did you take?

I entered the Army right out of High School. It was the best option for me, and in hindsight, it was the best choice that I ever made. I did not go to a particularly good High School, and I was, admittedly, unprepared for College, academically, mentally, and fiscally. It was not until later in my career that I pursued my undergraduate degree. However, I did start eight years out. In 2010, I started the pursuit of my Undergraduate Degree in Business, using

Tuition Assistance. I enjoyed getting back into school. It was challenging, as I was deployed, a lot, as a Special Operations Helicopter pilot in the Army. But I made it work. With a young daughter at home, and the desire to do well in the future, I made the commitment. That morphed into me using my Post 9/11 GI Bill for two Graduate Degree programs: one in Foreign Policy; the other in Organizational Leadership and Project Management. Academia certainly helps, and if you are serving in the military, and you complete a degree program, that shows a lot of dedication and focus. You, arguably, have a more difficult personal and professional schedule to work around than most people, and as someone that has served as a senior supervisor and manager, outside of the military, I value to work and effort that goes into pulling that off while also serving your country, and others will as well.

However, networking is king, and you must do it. Resume writing is not something I would suggest. There are many people out there, and many free resources, that can help you do that. You need to do that—that is, translating those skills and accomplishments into vernacular that is easily understood by hiring managers who do not know what your military skills translate into. You must do this, and it is ok to ask for help. Use the free resources that are out there, as many are available through transition assistance programs.

4. Did you pursue any advanced degrees and/or certifications? Did they help?

I did, because I felt that it would make me more marketable, and personally, I enjoyed being a student, albeit an older, adult learner. I think that, aside from making yourself more marketable, that pursuing advanced degrees, such as a Graduate Degree, can expose you to different perspectives, different groups to network with, and opportunities that you may not have considered. Many Graduate programs have robust alumni programs that also support transitioning veterans. Or, they have veteran student groups. This is another important element to consider. And, honestly, I think it is good to continue your studies. What do you have to lose, especially if you have the benefits that you have earned, other than your contribution of time? It is worth it, and can help you, in the long run.

5. Why did you choose the work/career you are in?

■ I chose my first career (I have been retired for two years now) because, at the time, it was the best combination of rewarding work, pay, and benefits. It was not the offer with the highest salary. However, the position provided me with incredible experience, and in a career field that was entirely different than being a Special Operations Aviator—healthcare administration. I enjoyed this vocation because it provided me with a new set of challenges. Honestly, I would encourage dabbling in different fields/vocations than what you are used to. I think it helps you become more marketable in the future, and it shows that you can successfully adapt to changing environments. I ended my time at the VA as a Deputy Chief Supply Chain Officer. I elected to get involved with the defense industry and to get back into working on projects and programs related to military aviation. Personally, I think it is ok to change up vocations every few years. There is nothing wrong with being a little uncomfortable. That means that you are learning.

6. Have you encountered any obstacles in advancing your career?

■ I have. Working in the Federal Government, the speed at which you can progress/promote is exceptionally slow. I understand that I had to prove my worth and show my value. However, there are few options to accelerate time in grade requirements as a Federal employee. The private sector is much different. Both avenues provide an incredible experience and competitive benefits. Federal employment can offer a higher degree of stability and security. However, the private sector can offer faster promotions and greater benefits. The bottom line is that you must overcome barriers that are self-imposed by you, the veteran. You have to accept that you may need to enter into an organization at a lower level than what you are used to, and you have to have a growth mindset so that you learn. You must develop relationships and trust, no different than you did in the military. You must have realistic expectations and you must constantly work to prove your value to your organization.

7. What were the 2 hardest efforts about transitioning?

1. If you have a family, you must focus on the family transition too. You, the veteran, maybe entering the workforce right away. However, your

family will also be going through a transition. Gone will be the safety net of other benefits, tax incentives, etc. Plan accordingly for the transition in pay and benefits. Be sure to have everything lined up so that there is not a gap n coverage for healthcare, dental, and vision. The last thing you want to do is increase the stress and burden on your family.

2. Be proud of your military background and experience, but do not wear it on your sleeve. You left the service because you chose to. Be proud of your service, as it shaped and defined you for a period. However, you need to redefine what it is that you desire to become, rooted in your military experiences. Understand that there are also amazing people out there who have done incredible things too, and they are not in the military. Be humble, have some humility, and build on the experiences that you had in the military. And one bonus tip—do not compare your new organization to your military unit. More succinctly, do not try to look for what you had in the military. The camaraderie, dedication, and willingness to put your own life on the line for others as others do the same for you—is unique to only a few vocations in the world. Although you will see and work with many people dedicated to a cause, to their organization, and to their job, you won't find many who would put it all on the line for you, to the same order of magnitude as military service.

8. What do you think are the top issues for Veterans transitioning into a career?

I think that effectively translating military skills and experiences, into comparable skills and experiences for the public and private sector, remains a singular challenge. Most organizations do not understand rank structures, military schools, or what it means to, say, lead people and teams in combat. Furthermore, your rank is generally going to be foreign to employers. They will not be too concerned with how senior you may be, or how prominent that was. They want to know how you can contribute to their team, solve problems, and help them generate profit.

9. Do you believe there is a stereotype attached to being a Veteran in pursuit of a job?

I do, and I did experience this personally. Now, I must add that this is not always the case. It all depends on what organization and line of work you are pursuing. However, in many cases, there are stereotypes. Personally, I have encountered folks who, in the interviewing process, had concerns with me being military, and possessing the inability to be an outside the box thinker, only able to function when told what to do. This is entirely not the case, and quite the contrary. Most military personnel are very capable self-starters who need extraordinarily little guidance to get the job done, and often do so without direct supervision. Once they know the requirements and expectations, they get the job done. Again, you will have to sell this in the form of being a self-starter who knows how to function, independently, in a decentralized environment and that military personnel are not blindly following orders all the time.

10. What question(s) would you have liked to have known before taking your first job?

In my first vocation, I would have liked to know what a true progression timeline looked like. I would have appreciated more insight into the latency in the promotion and competing for more complex and challenging roles and responsibilities. I would have also liked to have known more about the organizational structure, etc. The more information that you know, before taking a position, the better off you will be when you onboard and start.

11. What are the most important lessons you can share on making a successful job transition from the military?

1. You must start early, and you must own the process. You must have a plan. This is your transition, and not anyone else's. All transitions are different. Be transparent with your leadership. Tell them what you're doing, and present them with a strategy that afford you time to focus on the mandatory tasks that you have to accomplish, while also focusing on the personal time that you will need to make this a smooth process.

2. I would encourage anyone to first identify where it is that they desire to move to upon separation. I understand that in many cases, you must

go where the work is. But, as a retiree, we sat down, as a family, and decided where it was that we wanted to retire to. Once we pinned that down, I focused on the job market and my aggressive networking.

3. You must network and you must sell yourself. Do not sell out! But you must tell me why I should hire you. What makes you different that your peers? This takes us back to being effectively articulate with your experiences. I want to know what it is that you did, why did it matter, and what was the outcome. Show me time, money, percentages, and resources. Qualify your statements and qualify results.

4. Understand that your first job will likely not be your last job. You will change jobs, and that is ok. You are in control of your own life now. Set your compass and do the things that you love.

5. Lastly, take time, if you can, between your separation and the start of a new job. Decompress and spend time with family and friends.

12. If you could do it again, what would be the one thing you would do (better) or not do to help in your transition?

I think that I had an exceptionally smooth transition. I was in the right mindset early in the process. If anything, I would have started even earlier. You cannot make up for lost time, as it is your most precious resource. Own the transition, as it is your transition, and not anyone else's.

Daron Weishaar

Service rank: Major, USAF

Position: Program Manager

Industry: Defense

Biography

I am a retired Air Force Major and certified Project Management Professional (PMP) with over 40 years of DoD experience as both a defense contractor and Active Duty Commissioned and Non-Commissioned Officer in the U.S. Air Force. I have in-depth Operations, Program, Project, and Quality Management experience leading programs providing professional services capabilities, products, and technologies to a diverse set of customers operating from locations throughout the world to include: USSOCOM, JMISC, SOCCENT, NAVSPECWARCOM, USCENTCOM, 26NOS, AFLC, DISA, 388FW, AFOTEC, and USSTRATCOM. My experience includes over 13 years of providing support to USSOCOM and its components as a Program Manager, Director, and Active Duty Airman under ACAT-I Acquisition, Multi-Award IDIQ, FFP, and CPFF programs to include the: V-22 Osprey Operational Testing and Evaluation Program, Positive Threat Target Tracking and Identification Program (PTTIT), the JMISC Global Media Support (GMS) Program, Global Battlestaff Program Support (GBPS) Program, SOCOM IT Enterprise Contract (SITEC), SOCOM Wide Mission Support (SWMS) Program (Groups A & Group B), and the NAVSPECWARCOM Personnel Services Support Program. I am well versed in all phases of program, project, and operations management and have extensive experience in industrial and systems engineering and the test and evaluation process. I hold multiple MS

Degrees in Industrial and Systems Engineering and Business Organizational Management, a Bachelors in Computers Science, and am a Graduate of the Connecticut School of Broadcasting. I have held an active PMP certification since September 2006.

I also perform Public Address Announcing and Master of Ceremonies for sporting events, formal ceremonies, farewells, or any other activity where you are needing a "voice".

My wife Krista and I have been married for going on 35 years and have two sons Matt (28) and Josh (24). I enjoy all kinds of sports and travel.

Questions & Answers

1. Describe your journey from the service to your first job?

■ My journey from the service to my first job started in January 2004 when I, ok our family, had made the decision we were going to retire from the USAF. We were within a year of having to PCS once again and I knew I was likely headed for a tour in the desert. I had yet to serve an unaccompanied tour since my entering the Air Force in 1979 and could read the tea leaves and knew where I was headed. The time was perfect for a brand-new Major to experience his first field grade assignment serving somewhere downrange far, far away. The Air Force had recently changed the time in grade requirements to retire as a Major from 3 years to 6 months so I decided to take them up on their offer. While I wasn't pinning on my new rank till March, I made the decision we would retire effective 1 September. March 1st, 2004 saw me pin on Major, get a new ID card, and file my retirement paperwork all on the same day. I was also "automagically" registered to attend the Transition Assistance Program (TAP) Class. I received a date sometime in March from what I could remember.

With a 1 September retirement date, I knew I needed to have a job by then. I was very antsy about doing what I could do to have a job secured BEFORE my retirement ceremony in July. In looking at the calendar I essentially had all of 4 months to prepare and find my first job. Back then, it may have seemed like a lot of time. Looking back on it, it probably wasn't near enough time to prepare for the "first" job.

2. How did you find your first job? Describe the process.

■ I was VERY fortunate in finding my first job. Recruiters from several of the "beltway-bandits" took part in the TAP class either as instructors, resume writer assistants, or mentors in assisting with the transition. A recruiter from BAE Systems helped me get my resume together. Turns out he was actually looking for someone with my skillsets at the time and I was essentially interviewed on the spot during TAP class for a position with BAE Systems. A few weeks later I was called in for a second interview with hiring managers about a position they had opening up the first of August. The timing was perfect! From what I can recall, I got a call back in May saying I was going to be offered a position. So, in short, it was easy. The pain came in the waiting to see if I was going to be offered the position.

3. When did you start planning your transition? What actions/activities did you take?

My planning really didn't start until I entered TAP class. I had absolutely no idea what life outside the uniform was all about. I entered the Air Force 3-weeks after high school graduation. I was fortunate that I had a Bachelors, a Masters, a Top-Secret Clearance, and 25 years of military experience. Defense contractors would be standing in line to get the skills I had to offer.

4. Did you pursue any advanced degrees and/or certifications? Did they help?

I didn't pursue any advanced degrees specifically as part of my transition process, or in preparation for my transition. There was an unwritten rule that the only way to obtain Major in the Air Force was having an advanced degree. Didn't matter what field the degree was in, you just had to fill the square. Since I had a technical undergraduate degree, I felt it best to get a Masters with a Management focus. As you progressed in rank, you ultimately took on more business management type positions and stepped away from the technical side.

My second Masters came courtesy of the Post 9-11 GI Bill in 2013. I had always been intrigued with Systems Engineering so I sought colleges that offered such a program. I considered myself somewhat of a problem solver. You bring me the problem, tell me the resources I have at my disposal, the constraints I have to operate under, and I go out an solve the problem. This is after all the systems engineering process. Fortunately, UF had such a program, was more than happy to accept the Post 9-11 GI Bill, and 20 months seemed like time I could put forth to obtain the degree. The great thing about UF's Outreach Engineering Management program was it gave me the engineering coursework, while at the same time additional business related classes that helped me as the business responsibilities of the positions I held and programs I managed continues to increase.

My PMP certification, obtained in 2006 as a contractor, is perhaps the most important certification I hold, and maintain as a Program Manager. Every program I have managed since 2008 has mandated the Program Manager hold a Project Management Professional certification or it's equivalent Defense Acquisition University (DAU) certification. While I was able to complete DAU both on active duty and as a civilian contractor, I do not hold any "official" certification through DAU because I have never been in a formal acquisitions billet. I simply say on my resume I have satisfied requirements for Level II Certification in Program Management and Level III Certification in Test and Evaluation. DAU provides a transcript of all coursework you've completed with them so I can back this up with documentation.

The ITIL Foundation certification I hold came courtesy of the company I was working for as a result of the government making it a requirement for personnel on the contract. Since the Government levied the requirement, they ultimately reimbursed our company for it's employees obtaining the credential.

I was also required to obtain a Security+ CE certification as a result of leading a Network Operations and Infrastructure Solution Contract because the Gov't specifically wrote in the contract it was a requirement. Fortunately, I had enough of an information technology and computer background that allowed me to attend a boot-camp type class to brush up on the skills and then pass the certification exam. Once again, I leveraged by Post 9-11 GI Bill to offset some of the cost associated with the boot camp and the certification exam.

As the Government continues to levy more hard requirements on key personnel not only managing programs, but filling more senior roles on the programs, advanced degrees and certifications are going to be essential if you desire to hold the senior level positions. Anything you can do while on active duty to utilize the resources you have at your disposal would be beneficial. After leaving the service, take advantage of your Post 9-11 GI bill for certain. While I understand a lot of folks transfer this benefit to their spouse or children, it also warrants some consideration in using the benefit to better yourself and your credentials.

5. Why did you choose the work/career you are in?

It aligned with what I was doing on active duty. I started filling Project/Program Management type roles when I earned my commission. The Project and Programs I was managing on active duty directly carried over to the Project and Programs I would run during my first position after retirement and continue to be in line with the types of programs I am overseeing today some 15+ years later as a DOD contractor.

6. Have you encountered any obstacles in advancing your career?

The obstacles come when the programs end. As a Contract Program Manager, you don't have much to fall back on once your program ends. If you don't win the follow-on work, you are likely let go since you won't have a contract to bill your time to anymore. Businesses, especially small businesses, aren't going to carry you on overhead very long if you can't bill time against a contract. This is the nature of the business I choose to enter. Unfortunately, I've been let go multiple times since my retirement because a program came to an end. I was able to bounce back, sometimes quicker than others. There are always programs that need to be managed.

7. What were the 2 hardest efforts about transitioning?

First, knowing what to wear first and foremost. Am I underdressed, am I overdressed? Dress shirt, polo, tie, jacket, suit? I had worked with some contractors in the past and some dressed more casually than others. I was always impressed by the Booz-Allen-Hamilton folks I worked with at DISA. They were always in suits! That's how I wanted to dress when I went to work. Second, you didn't have to stay 12-16 hours a day! You worked your eight hours and then you went home. It was OK to go to lunch. People "punched" out. And what do you mean I have to fill out a timecard at the end of the day!

8. What do you think are the top issues for Veterans transitioning into a career?

You are not going to start at the top. Unless you know someone really well in the company you are starting your civilian job with, you must work your way to the top. It's OK to take a step back, and work your way up. Unless you go to a defense contractor some companies you work for may not know the first thing about the military. Your "boss" may have never served a day in the military.

9. Do you believe there is a stereotype attached to being a Veteran in pursuit of a job?

Absolutely! Veterans don't know the first thing about how things work in the "real" word. If you think you should be given a job just because you are a Veteran, you would be mistaken.

10. What question(s) would you have liked to have known before taking your first job?

The salary impacts and tax implications of getting out. What health care was going to cost if you didn't retain your military health care.

11. What are the most important lessons you can share on making a successful job transition from the military?

1. Start early.
2. Be prepared for an eye-opening experience.
3. No one is simply going to give you a job because you are a veteran.

12. If you could do it again, what would be the one thing you would do (better) or not do to help in your transition?

Talk to folks that had recently gotten out to learn from their experiences. Maybe worked harder to get a Civil Service (GS) Position when I retired.

Donn Westerhoff

Service rank: Sergeant First Class, USA

Position: CTO

Industry: Defense/Federal Contracting

Biography

Unavailable.

Questions & Answers

1. **Describe your journey from the service to your first job?**
■ My retirement from the service came about unexpectedly, so planning was minimal. Although I had explored the necessary certifications and credentials, those were a relatively new phenomenon when I was retiring so I did not pursue any certs prior to retirement. I did however, manage to leverage networking opportunities allowing me to obtain employment immediately upon retirement.

2. **How did you find your first job? Describe the process.**
■ Leveraging network opportunities allowed me to transition directly to a position upon separation.

3. **When did you start planning your transition? What actions/ activities did you take?**
In expectation of retiring on a normal timeline, I researched my chosen career path and the requirements to move into that career field. I researched compa-

nies and began to build a network of former military friends in the field. I did attend TAP classes, however, found it insufficient. I did employ the services of a professional resume writer.

4. Did you pursue any advanced degrees and/or certifications? Did they help?

Prior to retirement, no. Certifications like CCNA and Microsoft were just beginning to make an appearance. I did obtain, existing certification from the FCC, ISCET and NICET, relevant to the industry I was entering. Later in my career, these certifications carried more weight and became more vital to obtaining positions of more technical responsibility.

5. Why did you choose the work/career you are in?

Natural transition into the telecommunications industry from the signal corps.

6. Have you encountered any obstacles in advancing your career?

Yes, as an enlisted member, senior opportunities are not as readily available as those afforded for commissioned officers upon retirement. Additionally, many civilian employers feel that as a retiree that the compensation need not be as rigorous due to the retirement annuity and benefits afforded retirees.

7. What were the 2 hardest efforts about transitioning?

Secondly, the camaraderie that is often found amongst military is lacking in most of the civilian sector; a significant lack of operational focus, mission accomplishment.

8. What do you think are the top issues for Veterans transitioning into a career?

A solid resume that discusses your military functions in relatable civilian terms is important. Networking is key; use social media and other resources to locate your next job. Your military retirement is and should be separate from any compensation or benefits you are offered. Beware of resume writers, recruiters, and job search companies- there is usually a hefty price tag attached. Research and engage with reputable resume writers with actual military experience. Headhunters are an awesome resource, however, be certain of how they market you and what they are getting out of the deal. Beware of committing to any agency that wishes to represent you.

9. Do you believe there is a stereotype attached to being a Veteran in pursuit of a job?

Yes. I think it is safe to say that most employers that are truly civilian based (not government contractors) have many concerns about hiring veterans from a transition perspective; veterans are disciplined, work towards standards, understand a chain of command. In terms of enlisted personnel, we are not afforded the senior positions at transition that many officers are afforded, even if our education and credentials are equal or exceed those of transitioning officers. Oftentimes, employers believe veterans are not savvy to civilian technologies or business practices since we have never been in a civilian company, and frankly, veterans do not often success in translating their experiences into civilian speak; perpetuating the employers' concerns. There are also concerns about our ability to adapt into the civilian culture and workforce. I think too, that many companies feel that veterans ask for more in salary than the company believes we are worth; again, a function of the inability to translate both in your resume and in your oral interviewing skill s an effective translation of military to civilian skills.

10. What question(s) would you have liked to have known before taking your first job?

None.

11. What are the most important lessons you can share on making a successful job transition from the military?

1. Research industry and applicable certs-obtain what you can.

2. Solid resume relating military experiences into civilian terms, highlighting value—money savings, building teams, opportunities, leadership. If technical, state accomplishments in these terms.

3. Research and Network; use social media to find contacts, and reach out.

12. If you could do it again, what would be the one thing you would do (better) or not do to help in your transition?

The resources that are available now, weren't available when I retired, but I would have definitely told my younger self to make a harder push to complete higher education. Although many jobs, particularly in the contract world will say "BA or equivalent", true civilian jobs do not make that comparison. When I retired, Military transition assistance was virtually worthless at the time. Use networking skills, reach out to people on social media like LinkedIn. Do not be afraid to use placement agencies like TekSystems or InSight Global. Be prepared to describe your value in terms your employer will understand.

Michael White

Service rank: Major, USA

Position: Instructor

Industry: Academic/IT

Biography

I entered the Army in January 1987 and attended One Station Unit Training (OSUT) for Basic and Advance Training as a Military Policeman at Fort McClellan, AL. Afterwards I was sent to Fort Benning, GA for Airborne Training and then on to my first Duty Station at Fort Bragg, NC. While at Fort Bragg, NC served as a M60 Gunner, Driver and RTO. As an enlisted soldier, I served in Panama, Haiti, Fort Bragg, and Korea. I held leadership positions as a Team Leader, Squad Leader, Platoon Sergeant, Operations Sergeant and Acting First Sergeant. I was selected for Officer Candidate School in May 2002 and was commissioned a 2LT on 8 August 2002 and branched as Quartermaster. My first Officer assigned was assigned to the 2nd BCT 225th Support Battalion on Schofield Barracks, Hawaii. While assigned to Schofield Barracks I deployed twice to Iraq, and served as a XO, Transportation Platoon Leader, Assistance Support Officer and Logistical Advisor. I was then selected to a Functional Area 53 Automation Officer and sent to training at Fort Gordon and then follow on assignment where I assigned as the G35 System Branch Chief, Camp Arifjan, Kuwait. Then I was assigned to my last duty station as the J6 Director, Information System for the Joint Communication Support Element on MacDill AFB, Tampa, Florida. I retired 28 Feb 2014 after 27 years of service. My awards are Bronze Star with oakleaf cluster, Defense Meritorious Service Medal, Meritorious Service Medal 2 oakleaf clusters, Army Commendation Medal 5 oakleaf clusters, Joint Army Achievement Medal, Army Achievement Medal 2 oakleaf clusters, Master Parachutes Badge, Air Assault Badge, Combat Action Badge.

Questions & Answers

1. Describe your journey from the service to your first job?

■ I first started my transition around the November timeframe as I was dealing with a terminally ill mother, I was starting the process of looking for my new civilian position. I knew that my transitional date was 28 Feb 2014 around the July 2013 timeframe. I started preparing for my departure but due to my mother's illness I did not take good advantage of the outside resources and tried to attempt job interviews and resume preparation on my own.

2. How did you find your first job? Describe the process.

■ I did many other interviews for other positions, but this position that was to be my first job I kind of stumbled upon. I close friend that was working at Special Operations Command suggested that I look at a position as a Project Manager. The first position that I was to interview for was with another sub to the prime on the contract. Shortly after I did the interview, my mother had died due to her battle with cancer and I needed to return home to tend to her affairs. I was called and offered the position, but I could not commit at that time due to my situation. The hiring manager informed me that another position as to open in a few weeks and that he was forwarding my information to the hiring manager.

3. When did you start planning your transition? What actions/activities did you take?

I submitted my retirement package in May of 2013, so you could say that I started my planning at that time. I waited to do any official research until I was given a transitional date. I had attended a resume writing class on base and as part of the transitional training that I received. But I used a lot of my retired friends who were program managers to review my documents. I had already achieved most of my certifications and I had completed my degree in 2011 as part of my functional area training. As for my networking process, I had been building my LinkedIn profile and branching out by networking at professional conferences over the prior four years.

4. Did you pursue any advanced degrees and/or certifications? Did they help?

I did not attend any advance schooling during my transitional phase as I had already completed my degree. I did attend some Microsoft training on servers, and it was more for my personal benefit. I do believe that my prior education and project management training benefited the most in my transitional phase as many jobs that I applied for where searching for this training or certification.

5. Why did you choose the work/career you are in?

It was a choice that I made many years back when I was a young logistical officer deployed with some special operations soldiers. I was there watching them send data over a radio channel and thought to myself, computers have always been interesting, but they just got more interesting. So, when I returned I looked into it and found a functional area that would work with me. I loved being a logistical officer, but I knew that more was better. Once I got into the automation and signal field is when I found out how project management truly work. I found that project management can go hand and hand with almost any project that I would have to take on. It was not until I was in Kuwait and I had to run large projects that I was more interested in how the functionality worked in all aspects. I found that there are so many rights and wrongs within the field that I knew I was going to need that specialized training.

6. Have you encountered any obstacles in advancing your career?

At first it was not easy to advance as the hard projects were given to the more seasoned project managers. But I used my smaller projects to fine-tune my skill set. I approached it like learning to walk or talk. Learning from the seasoned project managers and taking from them there takes on how to approach more complicated projects. I also used that time to assist in building a rapport with key stakeholders and functional managers so that I could get them to work together when it was my time to lead a larger project. I also went back to my engineering days and learned how to work outside of the box to keep a project on time and on target with cost and equipment issues. And I learned to overcome these obstacles by learning from other mistakes and my own. You must be humble at times and be willing to help others. I learned that in project management if you are less willing to be a team player you will find it harder to accomplish some of the major tasks.

7. What were the 2 hardest efforts about transitioning?

■ One of the hardest parts was learning how the system works, many civilian organizations are not as military-friendly as they seem. I went to many job interviews where the job description was not what was being looked for. Second was learning that those training holidays, military leave, and other little benefits are not always translated into simple transition tasks. Your flexibility is also not an easy approach in taking time off for appointments. But in the end, you must train yourself to understand the transition approach and learn that it was great while in the military, but it is not always going to be that easy afterwards.

8. What do you think are the top issues for Veterans transitioning into a career?

handle these types of positions. They forget fast how they had the ability to get things done on the sheer will of having resources or unlimited resources. Now they are the outside man or woman looking in and hoping they can get the task accomplished. You must work together with people who are not militarily tuned or have never been a leader. It's harder trying to motivate individuals that are not willing to go the extra mile.

9. Do you believe there is a stereotype attached to being a Veteran in pursuit of a job?

At the beginning of my transition I would have said no, but after several attempts and searching I found that many organizations are leery of pursuing veterans. Expecially those who are my field of IT or project management. They believe that we are overachievers or very rough around the edges. I had some companies that would not even consider my application for the fear I was overqualified. So even though you have minimal skills they view you as a threat in some ways. I found this out with the medical field for IT support. They rather hire younger less qualified and train them up.

10. What question(s) would you have liked to have known before taking your first job?

At that time, I had none, even after it I was fortunate of having a great hiring manager and supervisor. For some military transitioning, the biggest issues are when you go to work directly into a civilian position that has no affiliation with the military. But for myself, I went to work with individuals that I knew or had lots in common. Therefore, the transition was a bit easier.

11. What are the most important lessons you can share on making a successful job transition from the military?

1. Ensure that you take the transition part seriously. Ensure that you attend training and use the resources that are provided. Be humble in the fact that you might be a great leader, but you are not always the best learner. The way that you write your resume, the way you prepare and the mentality that you are better than everyone is not going to get you a job.

2. Expect failure and learn from it. You may go for job interviews and stack the deck as we say, but organizations are looking for more than the best qualified, they are looking for someone that will blend with the current team and organization. Do not go in over cocky and display a negative vibe that you will regret later.

3. Start preparing for your next position in the civilian sector two to three years out, network, educate and attend those training courses that will help you advance or get noticed when your applying for positions. Do not just rely on the fact you are a Senior NCO or Senior Officer; most organizations want more than your military experience they want follower more than a leader at the beginning.

12. If you could do it again, what would be the one thing you would do (better) or not do to help in your transition?

I would say if I could do anything over again it would have been to use the free time that I had during the transitional time to obtain the certifications that I needed. Rather than working and trying to squeeze it in after I got the job. I would have also looked more into different fields to ensure that I was pursuing the right job set. Although I believe I choose correctly, I really did not look at anything else but project management. Just ensure you are ready to leave and prepared for it. One of the biggest concerns I had was the money issue, and most of my friends were chasing the dollar and not the correct job. Just remember to use a checklist and start early.

Dave Whitley

Service rank: Master Sergeant, USAF

Position: IT Manager

Industry: Defense/Federal
Contracting

Biography

MSgt Whitley retired from the US Air Force in September 2000 after a well decorated and illustrious career. MSgt Whitley held a variety of assignments, to include strategic aircraft maintenance technician on multiple airframes (B-52D, KC-135A, KC-10, F-15C/D, F-111D, T-37, T-38 & T-43). He was selected for a special duty assignment as a Tactical Air Command Non-Commissioned Officer Leadership School Instructor. His most recent assignment was the Superintendent, Air Mobility Command, Heavy Aircraft on the Staff for the Air Force Reserve Command.

Upon his retirement, Dave pursued a new career path as an Information Technology Technician. After seven years as a Network Administrator at companies in industry, Dave was selected for the position of Directorate Trainer for the U.S. Central Command where he increased the USCENTCOM Staff curriculum from three classes to nine. He also supported the U.S. Special Operations Command as a Knowledge Manager, Change Manager and Incident Manager. Dave is currently supporting NATOs U.S. Battlefield Information Collection and Exploitation System (US-BICES) program as a Battle Captain in the virtual Network Operations Security Center.

Dave has obtained a Master of Business Administration in Technology Management, a Bachelor of Science, in Corporate Training and Development, an Associates in Applied Science in Avionics Systems, and an Associates in Applied Science in Aircraft Maintenance. He also maintains the ITIL v4 (Release, Control and Validation & Operational Support and Analysis), Certified ScrumMaster, Certified Ethical Hacker, CompTIA's A+, Network+ and Security+ CE certifications.

Military Awards and Honors: Meritorious Service Medal w/ 2 Oak Leaf Clusters, Air Force Commendation Medal w/ 2 Oak Leaf Clusters, an Air Force Achievement Medal, and was the Headquarters Air Force Reserve Command Senior Noncommissioned Officer of the Year.

Questions & Answers

1. Describe your journey from the service to your first job?

■ I retired from the U.S. Air Force in September 2000, but it was not as "smooth" as it could have been. Truth be told, I made it more difficult than it needed to be. During your military career, you build three things that should help your post-military career: your skills, your geographic location, and your professional network (colleagues). I discarded all three by changing my profession, moving to a new state, and leaving behind my entire support network – professional and personal.

I spent the first six months of my retirement studying for certifications. After 20 years in the aircraft maintenance arena, minus four years as a Military Instructor, I decided to move into Information Technology (IT). After months of self-study, I obtained a few IT certs and started posting my resume online.

2. How did you find your first job? Describe the process.

■ To be honest, I don't know how my first employer found me. I can only assume they read one of the hundreds of resumes I posted and took pity on me, lol. After going to numerous job fairs, shaking dozens of hands, and posting countless online applications, I lost track.

My second job search is much more memorable. After my first employer abruptly announced they would be reducing their IT staff from 17 individuals to two, I made a quick trip to HR and found myself unemployed. After 20 years of job security, I was in shock. It was the middle of November, with Thanksgiving and Christmas right around the corner, I panicked! I had a wife and two kids at home, all counting on me for food, etc. I didn't have time to start the online application game again. I needed a job, and needed it quickly! With a diverse background: military, maintenance, teaching and IT, one would think you'd have your pick of jobs, right? But no. After two weeks of going business-to-business, hearing rejections like, "you're over qualified for this position," and "if I give you a job, you'll just leave when you find a better one," my frustration was at a maximum. Fortunately, I didn't quit. I hesitantly went to one more business; after a short conversation with the store manager, he called the owner, after a 5-minute phone call, I was hired, and perseverance paid off.

3. When did you start planning your transition? What actions/activities did you take?

Unfortunately, I started preparing to leave the military way too late. By changing careers, I didn't have the experience needed to just walk into most IT jobs. Also, I only had low-level IT certifications. Fortunately, I had a Bachelor's degree; this helped me stand out from the other applicants.

By moving to a new state, I lost all friends and professional contacts who could have assisted me in obtaining a job.

4. Did you pursue any advanced degrees and/or certifications? Did they help?

Prior to retiring, I did complete a Bachelor's degree in Corporate Training and Development. This, and my military training experience, enabled me to obtain an adjunct instructor position at a local college.

Unfortunately, a Bachelor's degree and/or a Master's degree are not as sought after in my primary career, but specialized IT certifications are. That said, if you have the opportunity to gain either, I recommend doing the work to obtain the higher education because nobody can take it away.

5. Why did you choose the work/career you are in?

As I progressed through my military career, and computers were becoming more available, I was offered my first "office" job. As the Flight Chief, responsible for all administrative actions for the technicians supporting the day-to-day maintenance of the aircraft, I was introduced to the desktop computer. From that point forward, I gravitated to learning more about computers. At all of my remaining duty assignments, I was "the computer guy."

6. Have you encountered any obstacles in advancing your career?
During my transition, only the lack of experience in my newly-selected career held me back, but now that I've been retired for 20 years, no.

7. What were the 2 hardest efforts about transitioning?
Civilian Work: In my experience, "civilian work" should be further defined. I prefer government environment vs. industry environment. If your transition consists of moving from a military career in Communications, to a post-military career as a government contractor as an IT technician, you are still working in the same atmosphere – the government environment. But, if your new career path leads you to work in industries such as insurance, manufacturing, banking or medical environments, you will truly be working with a different culture of people, a new environment. That said, the first seven years of my post-military career were spent in "industry" jobs.

- **Professionalism:** When working in most industry positions, I found a large difference in the amount of professionalism in the workforce. Do not expect the majority of the individuals you work with, or for, to share the same amount of professionalism as you, most will not.

- **Strategic vs. Tactical thinking:** in the military, we are taught to think. To think about what our actions produce, short-term (Tactical) and long-term (Strategic). Many individuals who hold leadership roles in industry lack strategic thinking skills. Seven years at four companies led me to this determination. Do not get frustrated when your leadership changes its collective mind one month into a four-month project.

8. What do you think are the top issues for Veterans transitioning into a career?
The primary issue I see is preparedness. When you retire, be ready! Is your

MOS, ASFC or rate utilized in the civilian industry? You may have been the best tank mechanic, or bomb loader for you entire career, but how will you utilize those skills in your post-military retirement years? Select your new career path and have actual experience in that profession before you get out. Have your education, be it certifications, or a degree. Be educated.

How prepared is your family? Your retirement and transition to a civilian career impacts them as well. Is your spouse working? If so, this could minimize your stress by easing financial burdens. Do you have children, if so, what are their ages? Are they leaving Kindergarten or High School Have you prepared either way for their college years? Ensure your family is ready for your transition as well.

9. Do you believe there is a stereotype attached to being a Veteran in pursuit of a job?

If there is a stereotype attached to being a military veteran, I think it's a positive perception. Everyone I've worked with reacted positively when they found out that I was in the military.

10. What question(s) would you have liked to have known before taking your first job?

- How common is down-sizing?
    - o This may be rare, but understanding the difference between military and civilian job security is a must. Being laid off was traumatic.

- What has a higher priority, teenier or good job performance?
    - o In the military, I tried to perform at the highest level I could; this paid off by being selected for multiple "special duty assignments." In the civilian sector, many companies overlook great work performance to reward individuals with more of the teenier. "Last in, first out!"

11. What are the most important lessons you can share on making a successful job transition from the military?

1. Start preparing before you think you should. Read and learn from those who transitioned before you.

2. Get as much education as you can! Get your Associate's, or Bachelor's, or even Master's degree before retiring. It will help more than you might realize.

3. Obtain as many certifications as you can. If your career focuses more on certifications than degrees, be well rounded.

12. If you could do it again, what would be the one thing you would do (better) or not do to help in your transition?

If I had to do it all again, I'd start preparing much sooner! I'd get additional IT certifications before retiring. To transition into a new career, I'd work part-time jobs, while still on active duty to gain the experience needed.

About the Author

Sandy works as an author, instructor, consultant, and a willing contributor of expertise when it comes to helping people, start-ups, and structured organizations transform and transition in order to reach and exceed their goals. Sandy is a life-long learner and has been a consultant in various forms of Project & Program Management for close to four decades. She currently owns and operates Monster Smarts, dedicated to offering career coaching as well as helping small to medium organizations work to assess and deliver prescriptive recommendations for improvement on profitability, processes, efficiency, and employee health. Her volunteer focus has been primarily with the Project Management Institute (PMI), where she has been a member for over 15 years serving at both the chapter and global levels. She graduated from the PMI Leadership Institute Master Class (LIMC) in 2011, and in 2012 was honored to be the LIMC Advisor for the Europe, Middle East and Africa (EMEA) LIMC. Sandy holds certifications in Portfolio Management, Program Management, Project Management, Organizational Transformation, and Lean Six Sigma Green Belt.

Sandy co-founded GR8Transitions4U with Jay Hicks, and together they are recognized throughout the U.S. as Military Transition advocates. To date they have written and published six books in the Military Transition series. With over 5000 books in circulation, the series is available to military members in transition around the world seeking a smooth transition, and the expanse is growing. Sandy and Jay were key influencers in the Project Management Institute adopting a National Military Liaison program specifically designed to help Veterans work to achieve a fulfilling career in Project Management. Both Sandy and Jay speak around the U.S. at conferences, chapter meetings, webinars, and training events.

Books in the TRANSITIONING MILITARY SERIES include:

- The Transitioning Military Project Manager – 1st and 2nd Editions
- The Transitioning Military Cybersecurity Professional
- The Transitioning Military IT Professional
- The Transitioning Military Logician
- The Combat Arms Professional

GR8Transitions4U.com